Fantasy, Fashion and Affection

Fantasy, Fashion and Affection
Editions of Robert Herrick's Poetry
For the Common Reader, 1810-1968

Jay A. Gertzman

Bowling Green State University Popular Press
Bowling Green, Ohio 43403

To My Parents

Copyright © 1986 by Bowling Green State University Popular Press
Library of Congress Catalogue Card No.: 86-70570
ISBN: 0-87972-349-1 Clothbound
    0-87972-350-5 Paperback

CONTENTS

Preface   1
Introduction   3
Chapter 1
    "A Genuine Old English Poet": Herrick, Bellestrists,
    and the Reading Public, 1796-1915   8
Chapter 2
    "For Scholars and Readers": Gilded Age, Victorian,
    and Edwardian Trade Editions   32
Chapter 3
    "Life's Sweet Without Its Sting": Recreations of
    Herrick's Time and Place, 1877-1910   55
Chapter 4
    Herrick and Art Nouveau: A Discreet Ramble Through a
    Fashionable Elysium   82
Chapter 5
    Private Presses: Daniel, Kelmscott, Elston, and the
    Aura of the Past   113
Chapter 6
    British Private Presses, 1927-1955:
    The Twentieth-Century Common Reader   133
Chapter 7
    Hesperides for Children: From Charles Robinson to
    Lynton Lamb   162
Chapter 8
    Portraits: The Comic, Wanton, Witty Gentleman-
    Poet-Priest   175
Appendix
    A Check-List of Reprints of Herrick's Works, 1810-1980   193
Index   237

Preface

This book could hardly have been begun, and certainly not completed, without the generosity of teachers and scholars who read chapters or parts of chapters and made comments. I wish to express sincere thanks to the following: Robert A. Donovan, S.U.N.Y. Albany; Dale B. J. Randall, Duke; Susan Otis Thompson, Columbia; Humphrey Tonkin, S.U.N.Y. Pottsdam; L. K. Uffelman, Mansfield Univ., and Carl Woodring, Columbia. Their comments were essential to whatever merits this book may possess; for any of its faults, I alone am responsible.

A special word of thanks is due to two booksellers. The diligent and skillful efforts of Lucile Coleman of North Miami, Florida in searching out volumes of Herrick for me were a revelation. She located more than one book for which not even the British Library, Harvard, or the Library of Congress record copies. From Mr. Adam Mills of Cottenham, Cambridge, I have received several rare early editions in beautiful condition and in contemporary bindings.

The staffs of the libraries mentioned above were very accommodating to me during my visits, as were those of the universities of Pennsylvania, Texas, Columbia, Cornell, and Mansfield (Pa.).

Finally, I gratefully acknowledge the permission granted by the editors of *American Book Collector, Studies in the Humanities,* and *Western Humanities Review* to publish herein those parts of Chapters 6, 3, and 8, respectively, which first appeared in those periodicals.

1

Introduction

"Who now reads Herrick?" asked Walt Whitman, in a poem by Alan Tate. Indeed, the seventeenth-century royalist vicar is considered by many a minor poet, of little account in our apocalyptic times. But I could answer this question with a list, from both Whitman's and Tate's centuries, of writers (Swinburne, De la Mare, James Branch Cabell, Rose Macauley, T.B. Swann, **Mark Van Doren**) and artists (E.A. Abbey, Reginald Savage, Albert Rutherston, Lynton Lamb, William Russell Flint), all of whom thought differently.

During the eighteenth century, Herrick was little known, although "To The Virgins" was very often printed and sung. At the turn of the nineteenth century, he benefitted from the renewed interest in Britain's past, and from the romanticizing of the high-minded Cavalier: benevolent, generous, compassionate. The period's moral idealism merged with admiration for a pre-industrial Arcadia of romantic castles, quaint inns, joyful rustics, and chivalrous aristocrats. In this costume-drama atmosphere, a benevolent, witty poet-parson had a minor but significant role. Secondary to this interest, however, was a suspicion bordering on hostility, because Herrick's sensibility was considered that of a "voluptuary" on the basis of a coarseness and sensuality in both his verses and physical features. Editors and publishers well knew how their readership had been schooled to believe that stability of family and society depended on raising one's sights above "fleshly" instincts. As is usual in such cases, the poet's supposed prurience may have helped stimulate curiosity, if not in respectable drawing rooms, then in the privacy of gentlemen's libraries.

Expurgated editions of *Hesperides* were common throughout the Victorian period. A sizeable middle-class audience for recreational reading was developing, especially in the hospitable drawing-room, and its tastes, however squeamish, were to be tolerated in direct proportion to its growth and buying power. As the century wore on, Herrick's star rose, especially in the "aesthetic" last decades. At this time, his perfect craftsmanship in the smallest parameters of lyric, his urbane wit, and his frank delight in "sweet and civil" verses endeared him to Swinburne, Gosse, Dobson, and Lang, and brought him attention not only as a gracious gentleman, but as a pagan bard.

Admiration for Herrick carried over to the private press movements of the twentieth century, as defiantly independent publishers endeavored to refine perception by bringing out volumes which recreated aspects of Renaissance craftsmanship (Cresset Press) and/or provided a *vade mecum* into a "Hellenistic" expansiveness (Fanfrolico, Golden Cockerel). Illustrations of beautiful women, often nude, were frequently found in *editions de luxe* of this period. Herrick, who liked his mistresses both clothed and naked, provided congenial verses for book artists.

A diverse band of readers influenced by the attitudes just summarized could hardly be expected to entertain uniformly perceptive insights regarding a Renaissance poet. Herrick's more sententious and sentimental verses were rifled for "incidental felicities." As critics worked out assumptions with which to approach the poetry, they sometimes confused the personality of the writer with that projected by a speaker in his poems: the intentional fallacy. Interest in Herrick's classical sources often became exercises in whether Horace, Catullus, or Martial was more congenial to the individual critic. One often finds impressions based on the tastes and values of men of letters, not on study of Renaissance genres, habits of mind, or techniques of composition. However this may be, it is also true that in a variety of cultural ambiences over the past two centuries Robert Herrick has won the attentions of a large number of literate general readers: Victorian ladies, curious children, emulators of upper-class taste, and romantic lovers and gentlemen-aesthetes contemptuous of the shibboleths of "respectability" and "decency." In the threefold cooperation of illustrators, men of letters, and publishers which brought this about, the work of the illustrators is in one sense preeminent. Its immediately arresting, emotional appeals touch (as does Herrick) readers' fundamental obsessions and fascinations. These include love and courtship, gallantry, rural serenity as reflected in sunshine days and spring flowers, dreams of sensual abandon, calm acceptance of mortality, and harmony with nature's rhythms and with one's family, peers, and dependents.

Illustrators sometimes fall victim to romantic excesses. Sentimentality is exploited in treatment of poems on flowers, children, and music. Jejune nostalgia for roistering Cavaliers and good-natured country parsons is indulged in. Herrick's mistresses are shown as fashionably languorous aesthetes. However, a high degree of originality and critical acuity is possible as lovers, rustics, country squires, statuesque beauties, and even introspective poets strike graceful poses, display archaic fashions in jewelry, architecture, and costume, and enjoy an uninhibited interaction, largely unavailable to readers, in the service of "love, liking, and delight." Thus my title: fashion, fantasy, and affection.

I admit that, for a book which undertakes an academic study of a poet's reputation, it is a gaudy title. However, my strongest impression of the editions I discuss is that their illustrators and designers manage to stimulate readers' social aspirations and personal desires. What middle-class people may wish to gain in social status, a modishly-illustrated and skillfully-printed volume, bound in leather or decorated cloth, may help provide. Even more interestingly, what one can not or dare not actually do, he or she can dream of in the safe confines of the imagination, as Herrick himself, in his

Devon parsonage, once rapturously envisioned Julia, Electra, or Dianeme. The poet himself becomes a cherished companion whose zest for life, and subtle manner of exercising it, a literate person can understand as in some degree like his or her own, and with whose secret frailties and frustrated ambitions he or she can sympathize. "Books," said Alexander Smith in *Dreamthorpe*, "are the true Elysian fields where the spirits of the dead converse, and into these fields a mortal can venture unappalled.... There is Pan's Pipe, there are the songs of Apollo."[1] For at least two generations before this was published (1863), and (possibly) until our own time, that books offered this experience was a consoling fact which profited many popular illustrators and publishers.

Quentin Bell calls book and magazine illustration "low art."[2] It engages attentions for short periods of time and is successful if it strikes one's fancy or forces a smile. It flourished, in the nineteenth century, as techniques of mechanical reproduction (steam-driven presses, process engraving, half-tone reproduction) made possible dissemination of printed matter to ever-larger numbers of readers, who themselves, by their unsophisticated reactions, distinguished the successful from the unsuccessful plate. For such an audience enjoyment coincides with emotional, immediate appeal. This is popular culture, and, measured by pragmatic standards, what is good is what arrests immediate attention and what sells. But the art of book illustration, in the nineteenth and twentieth century, cannot be easily stigmatized. In addition to what it reveals about the popular imagination, it borrows conventions from traditional painting and has more in common with it than with movies or photojournalism. Walter Benjamin's contrast of painting with film makes this clear, for, like painting, illustration "invites the spectator to contemplation; before it the spectator can abandon himself to his associations. Before the movie frame he cannot do so."[3] Further, it appeals (as sheer escape literature need not) to a genteel (or would-be genteel) audience for whom *belles-lettres* are important. It reflects, and often is directly based on, opinions of serious essayists and reviewers who write with respect for the tastes of a general audience. Illustration is located approximately in a middle position on any scale which would measure it as elite vs. popular (or "highbrow" vs. "lowbrow") art. This makes it especially valuable as evidence of the immediate appeal of a poet to readers, and of how artists who are conscious of their audience's basic interests can provide insights which stimulate appreciation for the literature they are contemplating. As Bell puts it, successful graphic artists "do arrive at a certain profundity of feeling by entering what we may call the marginal areas of art...and, protected as it were by an ostensibly modest purpose, [they] conceal their high intentions beneath a low disguise."[4]

Two "highbrow" characteristics of the books under discussion here are that they are intended to improve their owners' sensibilities not their purses, and to be contemplated at leisure, as prized (although in many cases inexpensive) possessions. Consider the Everyman Library's first printings: the Old Face type, the title-page openings modelled after the Kelmscott Press books, the imposing mottoes, the endpapers with Good Deeds surrounded by leaves and vines after William Morris, offering her services. Such books announce their importance by a provocative harmony of subject and printing style. J. M. Dent and Co. manages to suggest that its books, however mass-produced, and however stolid the middle-class virtues its mottoes and emblems symbolize, present *belles-lettres* with deference, and that the purchaser must approach the reading experience with careful thought and refined feeling. Everyman books, in the tradition of the Kelmscotts, produce what Benjamin described as an "aura": a unique significance with which a work of art is traditionally perceived as a cult object, revealing itself to fit readers with special preparation and interests.[5] I am aware that Benjamin felt the aura is destroyed by mechanical reproduction, which emphasizes the ordinariness of artifacts, and the possessor's casual use of them. But he was himself a book collector, and said that any collector "retains some traces of the fetishist and...by owning the work of art, shares in its ritual power."[6] Herrick's readers have been very often invited to do something similar, by commercial as well as by private-press book designers.

To take one example, the reviews of the Muses' Library edition of Herrick (1891) suggest that it was a book with an aura. *The Athenaeum* approves the "daintiness and elegance" of typeface, cover design, and format as appropriate, and opines that *Hesperides* "should be read in a hammock or pleasant garden, in a country inn or beside the sea...."[7] *The Speaker's* reviewer declares the same edition to be

...a delightful possession: the sort of book one handles affectionately, turning over its pages and feeling a certain pleasure merely in holding it, long after one has ceased to read. And, of course, Herrick himself shares the credit of this with his latest editor and publishers. There are poets whose pages you would feel some impropriety in caressing, no matter what the type or paper may be. What is Herrick's peculiar charm, and where does it lie?[8]

These reviews are far from scholarly appreciations, but they and others like them stand as evidence that by 1930 Herrick had attained the "Pillar of Fame" he aspired to. There were 45 trade editions from 1870 to 1915, and this figure includes neither the subsequent impressions of each edition, nor children's books or private press issues. In each of these latter two categories he has been represented by artists such as Charles Robinson, Ellen Raskin, and Lynton Lamb, and by editors such as William Morris (Kelmscott), Jack Lindsay (Fanfrolico), and Christopher Sandford (Golden Cockerel). Even within the past few decades, with the disappearance of these British private presses, selections from *Hesperides*, sensitively introduced and edited, have been published in paperbacks by Penguin (1961), Dell (1962), and Carcinet New Press (1980). These take their place in a line of Victorian and Edwardian cheap reprints edited by Palgrave, John Masefield, Alice Meynell, H. B.

Aldrich, and Herbert Horne, and in the parade of twentieth-century editions for general readers by the Medici Society (1922), Haldeman-Julius (in his "Little Blue Books," 1924), Ernest Benn ("The Augustan Books of Poetry," 1931), New Directions ("The Poet of the Month," 1942), and The Grey Walls Press (introduced by Jack Lindsay, 1948). This abiding interest can best be explained by analyzing, in the appropriate social and literary contexts, the techniques and rationale of artists and decorators in bringing together for their audiences illustration and what Francis Meynell called "allusive typography," which seeks "the idiom, in type and paper and ornament and arrangement, which will illustrate or illuminate the author, or his subject, or his time, or his taste, or his style."[9] This study is an attempt to specify the auras, or charismas, of *Hesperides* which have been generated from the "look of the book" over the past two centuries, and which make it and its author memorable.

Notes

[1]"Books and Gardens," *Dreamthorpe*, The World's Classics (London: Oxford U. Press, 1914), p. 221.

[2]*Victorian Artists* (London: Academy Editions, 1975), p. 41.

[3]"The Work of Art in the Age of Mechanical Reproduction," in Hannah Arendt, ed., *Illuminations*, trans. Harry Zohn (New York: Harcourt, Brace, and World, 1968), p. 240.

[4]Bell, p. 42.

[5]Benjamin, pp. 223-26.

[6]Benjamin, p. 246, n. 6.

[7]July 26, 1892, p. 124.

[8]January 16, 1892, p. 82.

[9]*English Printed Books*, 2nd ed. (London: Collins, 1948), p. 43.

Chapter 1

"A genuine *Old English* poet": Herrick, Belletrists, and the Reading Public, 1796-1915

> "The *Hesperides* of Herrick is truly a *garden grown wild,* where flowers and weeds are so mingled together, that it is difficult to cull the former without gathering some portion of the latter. The most delightful and most innocent poetry, may be found in the same page with conceits and impurities, equally at variance with good taste and with delicacy."
> —"Biographical Notice," *The Works of Robert Herrick,* ed. Thomas Maitland (1823)

Hesperides (1648) is an English garden of humor, fantasy, erotic verses, and gentle, elegant statements of friendship, amatory affection, bucolic contentment, and love of God and nature. Herrick's variety, sensuality, and wit account for his appeal since his "rediscovery" at the beginning of the nineteenth century. At his first flush of popularity, the scholar (as we know the fellow) was still comely, being in his swaddling clothes, the gap between scholarly and general readers, consequently, did not exist as it does today, and books and reading were a more significant part of the social fabric (as far as ornaments of table and bookcase, and conversation, were concerned). The general reader and his or her tastes were what critics, publishers, and later in the century, their book artists—the first two might be termed "men of letters"—had to work with when, aspiring to refine and even shape public taste, they went about presenting a "classic" English poet to a curious and receptive audience.

To pin down that elusive term "man of letters" is necessary, because it was upon his evaluations that Herrick's reputation rests. I mean, first of all, one who at least significantly increases his income by writing. This professional may be a scholar, creative writer, or journalist, and is motivated by a conviction that literature can play a role in the moral and aesthetic value system with which one builds an identity for oneself, and a public image. The man of letters' *raison d'etre* was the existence of a growing reading public ("general readers," including scholar-antiquarians, diligent merchants, professional men, politicians, and cultured gentlemen and ladies with time to read and converse). Such people were interested in finding a respectable place in their enlightened and progressive society, and curious about sources of edification and amusement for their families. For them, books and magazines were prime instruments of intellectual and social self-improvement.

8

Herrick's "Rediscovery," 1796-1839

Hesperides was first brought to the public's attention (after more than a century of neglect) by literary journalists writing for the most respected of the reviews and magazines. In the vanguard were periodicals very influential in shaping public taste and opinion (the dates of the articles on Herrick are in parenthesis): *Gentleman's Magazine* (1796), *Quarterly Review* (1810), *Retrospective Review* (1822), and *Blackwood's Edinburgh Magazine* (1839). This work was supplemented by that of a pair of physicians. Dr. John Nott's *Select Poems from the Hesperides* (1810) was the first edition of Herrick since the first, in 1648. And, in keeping with the spirit of magnanimous curiosity which animated gentlemen during their leisure hours, Dr. Nathan Drake wrote three essays "On the Life, Writings and Genius of Robert Herrick" in his *Literary Hours* (1804), a work "devoted to elegant literature during intervals of professional study," and undertaken as a restorative: "happiness in this life depends on our facility in acquiring a taste for innocent and easily procurable pleasures."[1] A seventeenth-century gentleman would have termed such pleasures "harmless mirth"; in its general outlines the aristocratic notion of ingenuous use of leisure was still alive in 1800. Moreover, it seems to have been a touchstone by which men and women who had recently acquired the time and money to buy reading matter for their drawing rooms and libraries could show sensitivity and taste.[2] As we review these early praises of *Hesperides,* we need to keep in mind that they are accompanied with gestures of well-bred eclecticism. They are the work of lawyers, physicians, divines (and professors and poets)[3] who, although they would respond to Carlyle's admonition to close their Byrons and open their Goethes, kept their Herricks close at hand for times when the amusing and curious were called for. Such writers present themselves as men of breadth of knowledge, antiquarian interests, and genteel respectability, with an impartiality which made them wary of signing their essays.

Nineteenth-century periodicals for whom these gentlemen wrote were instrumental in creating on both sides of the Atlantic a literate reading public. To whom did they appeal? Not, at first, to the freshly-literate skilled workers, with whom piety and self-improvement (or, for entertainment, lurid novels), were likely to be popular, and for whom Herrick's unabashed sensuality therefore would have been puzzling, but to gentry and middle-class readers. By mid-century, however, these periodicals and others (especially Dickens' *Household Words,* which carried an interesting and idiosyncratic article on Herrick in 1857) were reaching as well the upwardly-mobile shopkeepers and clerks who subscribed to Dickens' novels. Through the end of the first decade of the twentieth century, literary periodicals, some becoming, like the *Cornhill* and *Harper's,* more devoted than formerly to a relaxed, leisurely approach, provided a valuable forum for writers such as G. H. Lewes, Agnes Repplier, William Lyon Phelps, Henry Morley, Jerome K. Jerome, and Edmund Gosse.[4]

In the earlier part of the nineteenth century, the literary reviewers appealed to readers proud of England's heritage, curious about polite accomplishments such as those that men of letters had mastered, and committed to propriety and aristocratic tastes in *belles-lettres*. The following three examples make note of the sensibility aspired to by these readers.

The *Retrospective* commends its article on Herrick as bringing to public light the researches of scholar-antiquarians, so his poems will not "waste their sweets in the desert of the bibliographer's library."[5] Second, as Sir Walter Scott noted, "no genteel family can afford to be without the *Edinburgh Review*, because...it gives the only valuable literary criticisms that can be met with."[6] Finally, the *Quarterly's* reviewer, Barron Field (lawyer, literary scholar, and friend of Wordsworth, Hazlitt, and Lamb), travelling in Devon, interviewed some of the "vulgar and uneducated" natives of Dean Prior. He was rewarded with fascinating information about the impression the poet-parson had made upon their ancestors.[7] In keeping with the anti-democratic Toryism of the *Quarterly*, the reviewer implies contempt for his interviewees, especially their "budget of anecdotes" (which he disdains to record) regarding Herrick's ghost. On the other hand, the poet himself, despite his "prurience and obscenity," is tolerated as a "literary man" who, despite his trifling, was capable of "taste and feeling."

Modern scholars explain the revival of interest in Herrick by referring to the romantic sensibility and its reordering of the hierarchy of genres so as to place lyric at the top. Equally important, it seems to me, is the general concern about English culture and traditions which generated revival of interest in many Renaissance poets. One could not expect to find in Herrick Wordsworthian depths of mystical insight or Keatsian personal anguish— nor, indeed, from the kinds of critics who first brought Herrick to public notice, a clear appreciation for such qualities. What one does find praised are his variety of lyric themes and moods, his pastoral charm, and his personal character as a happy man.

As for the first criterion, Drake's essays note Herrick's range— "Amatory," "Anacreontic," "Horatian," "Moral," and "Descriptive."[8] Thomas Maitland, editor of the first reprinting of the entire canon (1823), notes "he is alternately gay and melancholy, witty and tender, didactic and descriptive."[9] Other writers commend his good humor, his occasional passionate intensity, his delicate vein of melancholy about time passing (the "moral-pathetic"[10]), his fanciful word-pictures, his playfulness, the aptness of his classical imitations, and, especially, the range and perfection of his metrical skills.[11] "The spirit of song dances in his veins and flutters around his lips—now bursting forth in the joyful and hearty voice of the epicurean; sometimes breathing forth strains as soft as the sigh of 'buried love'; and sometimes uttering feelings of the most delicate pensiveness."[12]

In the *Retrospective*, Herrick's verses on music, youth and love, flowers and springtime earn themselves credit for "pastoral naivete," and their author admiration for being "abandonne... [he] wholly gives himself to his present feelings" (p. 158). Drake finds a gay, childlike elan, honest "warmth of sentiment" and "pleasing melancholy" (pp. 48, 55, 58, 59, 85). Herrick's most-appreciated poems are cried up for a charm and sweetness associated (one would think) with the milkmaids and shepherds to be found, not in fields, but in the painted meadows of vase, canvas, and tapestry. These impressions are samples of an escapism which saw the past ("merrie England") as an enchanting romance, and which accounted for lucrative sales of illustrated books for drawing rooms of respectable ladies (we will return to both escapism and the drawing room later in this chapter). By mid-century, a "vogue" of Herrick appreciation had developed;[13] it was especially given to eulogies along these lines. The bluestocking author of *Recollections of a Literary Life*, in a passage which echoes Mrs. Browning, states that "these graceful and delicate lyrics...are what they pretend to be: airy petals of the cherry blossom, hinting of fruit, bees fluttering and musical, giving token of honey."[14] Taking some poems as emblems of an innocence lost to their own century, Herrick's early critics do not hesitate to apply the lines/life analogy. Barron Field, in a passage reproduced by many Victorian editors in their introductions, is the first to hail "young Herrick" as "the most joyous and gladsome of bards; singing, like the grasshopper, as if he would never grow old" (pp. 179-80).

To Herrick scholars today, the most valuable early comments regard his classicism, his metrical skill, and his use of sources. I have focussed here on the attractions which, in periodical articles and introductions to both *Selections* and *Complete Works*, rehabilitated Herrick's reputation for general readers of the early nineteenth century curious about the witty and recreative song lyrics of a Cavalier gentleman-poet, and about the variety and tenor of poetic feeling a cultured person should find in his verses. Herrick's commendations, however, come well attended by an almost-universal revulsion from "indecencies," especially evident in the epigrams. Dr. Drake makes no bones of reminding his readers that in the seventeenth century, poetry was not yet possessed of "an uniform chastity of style and thought"; that even Spenser and Milton mix brilliancy with "obscurity, vulgarity, obscenity, and colloquial barbarism."[15] And Dr. Nott, although disagreeing with Drake that only about one hundred of Herrick's secular poems could be selected "by the hand of taste," persistently alters lines in some of the 300 he publishes, "for very proper reasons."[16] See figure 1-1. Note in passing the care with which the typeface for both poem and footnotes was laid out, and complement that with the solicitousness with which the editor safeguards the propriety of his readers.

Encountering a Primitive Sensibility: Rationale for Selections
As highly as Herrick is praised during the nineteenth century, there is an ambivalence about even the most enthusiastic attitude. For example,

Swinburne, writing an essay (twice reprinted) in which Herrick's reputation reaches its absolute zenith ("the greatest song writer...ever born of English race") remarks the poet's "fantastic and brutal blemishes."[17] Herrick's references to his mistresses' breasts and thighs, and, in the epigrams, to almost every orifice of the human body, pathological states thereof, and excretions therefrom, were sure to annoy the squeamish. Not that there weren't complete editions. Maitland, defending his on the grounds of interest in the English past, makes a point of the book being for "libraries of the curious," not "ordinary readers of drawing-room poetry" (p. xxvi). Grosart (1876), whose scholarly intentions are clear from his 276-page "Memorial-Introduction," praises the many shorter editions which "carry Herrick whither we would scarcely choose to have the whole carried, for we would not choose to have our wives and children come on the sorrowful nastiness" [of some passages].[18] The Muses' Library edition (1891) grouped the epigrams in what the publisher Grant Richards laconically describes as a "separately printed appendix which had neither title on its wrapper, nor title-page, nor printer's nor publisher's name."[19] A glance at the poems appearing in editions meant for display in drawing-room and boudoir, such as Harper Brothers' folio gift-book (1882) or Routledge's *Flower Poems* (1906), makes clear that publishers have the sensibilities of their readers clearly in mind. The same is true of the cheap but attractively decorated reprints from Bohn's (1852) to Dent's, whose Everyman edition (1908) simply chained up offending passages in rows of elliptical dots. Not for gentle readers "The Vine," "Upon Julia's Breasts," or the poet's comments on such rheumy, flatulent parishioners as Peason, Umber, Smeaton, or Brock. Nor for one Lady Cecil, the 19 year-old dedicatee for Palgrave's *Chrysomela* (1877). This editor promised his publisher that he had made Herrick accessible to ladies' idle hours by eschewing "pieces in which the Muse unloosed her zone a little too freely for maiden grace."[20]

Concern about the effects of poetry upon readers of the "polite classes" was hardly limited to reprints of seventeenth-century poets. Their vulgarities, at least, might be excused on the basis of the primitive tastes of the age, and not attributed to their lack of social status, and their lack of moral and social respectability. To reinforce the connection between the pristine genteel virtues which men such as Herrick's rediscoverers recommended to socially-conscious readers, and class ideals, one could recall *Blackwood's* 1817 attacks on Leigh Hunt ("all the great poets of our country have been men of some rank in society...but Mr. Hunt cannot utter a note without betraying the Shibboleth of low birth and low habits"[21]), and the same "Maga's" obituary of Keats ("he wrote *indecently*, probably in the indulgence of his social propensities"[22]).

Contempt for Herrick's prurience, and extreme dissatisfaction regarding how, and to whom, his poems should be presented, runs from one end of the century to the other. There was no doubt that, he should be presented, although one wonders about Southey's response, made as an aside in an essay

XLIX.

LOVE PERFUMES ALL PARTS.

IF I kiss Anthea's breast,
There I smell the phœnix' nest ;
If her lip, the most sincere
Altar of incense I smell there ;
* Fingers, hands, and arms are all
Richly aromatical :
Goddess Isis can't transfer
Musks and ambers more from her ;
Nor can Juno sweeter be,
When she lies with Jove, than she.

* In this line it was thought better to deviate a little from the original.

Fig. 1-1a. "Legs" and "thighs" become "fingers" and "arms". Source: J[ohn] N[ott], ed., *Select Poems from the Hesperides* (Bristol, Eng.: J.M. Gutch, [1810], p. 36. See #1, Appendix.

THE VINE.

I DREAM'D this mortal part of mine
Was Metamorphoz'd to a Vine ;
Which crawling one and every way,
Enthrall'd my dainty Lucia.

me thought, her Long small Legs and thighs
I with my Tendrils did surprise;
Her Belly, Buttocks, and her waist
By my soft Nervelets were embraced

About her head I writhing hung,   }
And with rich clusters (hid among   }
The leaves) her temples I behung :   }
So that my Lucia seem'd to me
Young Bacchus ravisht by his tree.
My curles about her neck did craule,
And armes and hands they did enthrall :
So that she could not freely stir,
(All parts there made one prisoner).

But when i Crept with Leaves to hide
Those Parts which maids keep unespyed,
Such fleeting pleasures there I took
That with the Fancy I awoke;
And found (Ah! me) this flesh of mine
more like a Stock, than like a Vine

Fig. 1-1b. Erotic fantasies must not go below the waist. Source: *Herrick's Hesperides And Noble Numbers* (London: Dent, 1935). First impression of this edition was done in 1899. See #44, Appendix. (Holograph insertions, of course, are no earlier than 1935).

on minor poets: "Yet we have lately seen the whole of Herrick's poems republished [Maitland's edition, remaindered by Pickering in 1825], a coarse-minded and beastly writer, whose dunghill, when the few flowers that grow therein had been transplanted, ought never to have been disturbed."[23] *Household Words* alludes to this passage approvingly in an 1857 article calling for "that general object of our abhorrence, a revised or excerpted edition."[24] Other demurs to Maitland's contention that study of the manners and literature of a former age warrants free access to the poems are William Allingham ("at least let these literary coprolities [but not deodorized by time] rest as far as possible among the shadows of learned shelves"[25]), and reviewers in *Temple Bar* (1883) and *Edinburgh Review* (1904).

In both their praises of and their discretion regarding Herrick's poetry, English and American editors and critics were most concerned with making life comfortable for their squeamish readers, and for themselves, by giving the public what they thought it wanted. Both their motives and the tastes of the reading public can be clarified by reviewing the forces at work to make adherence to rigorous moral standards a prerequisite for publishers and editors.[26] By 1810 many newly-wealthy industrialists, bankers and lawyers had appeared. A bit later publishers and politicians who catered to nouveau-riche interests were rising. Previously unskilled laborers could increase their stature by becoming clerks, foremen, or skilled workers with machinery. These energetic folk, largely favorable to evangelical preaching about rectitude and sobriety as ways to achieve personal success and national strength (Englishmen contrasted themselves to the French, who became victims of revolution and its excesses), found themselves with the power to sway colleagues and public opinion, and thus manners and morals. Their leaders convinced them of the urgency of this. Thus Thomas Bowdler: "The only reform which can save us, if adopted in time, is a thorough reform of principles and practices." All classes felt the attraction of Evangelicism; some assimilation of the social conventions of the entrenched aristocracy with evangelical religious convictions was inevitable.

In England, the aristocracy itself could, if so inclined, stand back in amused detachment from the most fervid exercises of respectability, and thus provide some counterweight to the extremes of prudery. This was not so in America. A puritanical rectitude, given lip service only in the board and committee rooms, maintained a vital grip on home life and feminine deportment; nowhere other than in a proper American household was polite indifference to the "animal passions" more assiduously observed.[27] Here, where bulls were "gentlemen cows" and cocks were "hens' husbands,"[28] one can imagine the matriarchal contempt which Herrick's epigrams might call forth, if by chance they were encountered in copies of the first American printings (1856, 1875, 1879, *et. seq.*), had the books chanced to stray from Father's *sanctum sanctorum*, the library, to the drawing room.

To apply this to the Notts, Grosarts, and Harpers, we should recall

Bowdler's expurgations, and mention those of the busy Rev. James Plumptre, who, in the cause of making literature teach earnest moral lessons in a decent manner, not only deleted but with less restraint than Bowdler added words and lines to the poems and dramas he edited. Dr. Nott might substitute "fingers" and "arms" for "thighs" and "legs"; for his collection of songs (1805), Plumptre not only disallows "lie" in Shakespeare's "Under the Greenwood Tree/Who loves to lie with me," but replaces it with "work"! The men of letters who revived interest in Herrick were more liberal, at least, than this, and we should remember that earnest moralism, in a really enlightened sensibility, produced a deep humanistic respect for "the best that had been thought and said," and its dissemination to all citizens, who needed to be taught to see beyond the superficial use of art and literature as a badge of religious conviction and social respectability. The essayists on Herrick, their sensitivity to "Society" notwithstanding, did make, in the service of their "moral aesthetic," original and perceptive interpretations. Dr. Drake would be one example, and the Americans Thomas Bailey Aldrich and E. E. Hale are others. The remainder of this chapter will add to their number. However, to focus on how the legacy of Plumptre affected reading habits, here is Richard Aldington's reminiscence:

The English family can still be relied on to present a united front against any of its members indulging in the obscene pursuits of literature or art.... The great English middle-class mass...will only tolerate art and literature that are fifty years out of date, eviscerated, detesticulated, bowdlerized, humbuggered, slip-slopped....[29]

George Santayana's ridicule of the Gilded Age makes with less heat the same point. The poetical taste of genteel Boston and Philadelphia he stigmatized as "simple, sweet, humane,...grandmotherly in that sedate, spectacled wonder with which it gazed at this terrible world and said how beautiful and how interesting it all was."[30]

"A genuine Old English poet": Cavalier vitality and the gentleman-poet-priest

If *Hesperides* required excisions and ellipses, a few of those who recommended and/or undertook the tasks assured themselves that it was the poet's own character as well as the tastes of his times that needed the censuring. The antiquarian Thomas Corser, in his generous and valuable notes on Herrick ("a writer of exquisite taste and genius"), deplores the weakness, especially in a clergyman, of allowing libertine indelicacies (not to mention tortured conceits and pedantic obscurity) to sully even his best lyrics.[31] A reviewer for *Blackwood's* in 1839 goes further by asserting that Herrick's sensuality was idiosyncratically overheated and that he even lacked self-respect. Had he not written, "Herrick, thou art too coarse to love"? As well he might have: to praise a lady's cheek as a kind of iced potable ("claret and cream commingled") is proof of a vulgar mind ("a pretty mess!").[32] Had the reviewer glanced at Herrick's portrait as it was displayed as frontispiece for Nott's, Maitland's, or Pickering's editions, he would probably have strengthened his opinion.

William Marshall's original engraving for the 1648 *Hesperides* (see fig. 8-1) sets a profile of Herrick, which displays curly hair, an outsized Roman nose, double chin, a bull-like neck, against a background of dancing Muses, Cupids, trees and fields, Pegasus, and Helicon. The viewer is encouraged to make a subtle comparison between the man and his book: whatever one might expect of a man with such features, he has produced poetry of pastoral grace. But few earlier nineteenth-century publishers used Marshall's iconographical background. Instead, most presented the reader with a "head of the poet." With only the facial characteristics to guide them, designers of frontispieces missed the original's suggestive juxtaposition of nature and art, and the worlds of sense and imagination. Readers were left to remark "no favorable idea of his physiognomy"[33]: the "massive nose and jaw,"[34] the "broad bull throat, which loved to quaff the blushing wine-cup,"[35] and the "glassy eyes, that showed round them the red lines bego ten of strong portions of canary."[36] Walford, who published a *Complete Works* in 1859, recalled thirty years later how "sensuous and ugly in the extreme" were the features rendered in the frontispiece he used.[37] If several critics wish Herrick's offensive verses had been lost to posterity, some feel the same about Marshall's portrait.

It is no surprise to find a grudging distrust of the sensual or "merely" recreative; one of the Victorian trepidations concerning free libraries was that impressionable youth might founder therein on the shoals of the romantic novel or profane poetry.[38] Therefore one fully expects the ambivalence with which Herrick was regarded not only by the genteel lady in her drawing room, or the gentleman in his library, but also by a conservative Southey, a scholarly Grosart, a pre-Raphaelite Allingham, an aesthetic Swinburne, and a proper Bostonian such as E. E. Hale. Why then, did publishers such as Pickering, Harper's, Houghton-Mifflin, Macmillan, Osgood, and Dent do so much to put him before the public? Clearly, because *Hesperides* was likely to provide marvelous entertainment in literate, respectable households. It only required responsible editing, so as to be either sanitized for informal social groups, or (for library study) to be provided with annotations stressing seventeenth-century social customs and literary traditions. George Saintsbury states the matter with insight: "The sole blot of his verse, the dull and dirty epigram section, is rather an excrescence than a fault in grain; his deficiencies...are connected in a singular and intimate manner with his excellencies, and his charm is of the first and greatest."[39]

His portrait inspired revulsion, but many considered it a poor likeness. Ernest Rhys and Herbert Horne blamed Marshall,[40] while Grosart heaped derision on nineteenth-century engravers, each of whom drew the fire of a single perjorative: "preposterous," "untrue," "monstrous," "outrage." So the reader can appreciate, if he has a mind to, the differences Grosart sees between the vulgar and the sublime, Figure 1-2 reproduces the Pickering frontispiece, and Figure 1-3 the Grosart. Here is how the latter is commended:

...its aquiline nose, and twinkling eye under its arched and shaggy penthouse, and slight moustache, and short upper lip, and massive under-jaw, and "juicy" neck, with much of the voluptuous force of the best type among the Roman emperors, and affluent curls, interprets to us [Herrick's] book, and unmistakably gives us assurance of a Man, every inch of him. (pp. cclxix-cclxx)

No saint, but a commanding Cavalier presence, in whom intense *joie de vivre* is not the pleasing outside of a Satanic voluptuary. Rather, one may sense the robust worldliness of the best of the Sons of Ben.

When we consider nineteenth-century critics' evaluations of Herrick the man in the context of what they understood of his own society, we find intense curiosity about the grace and equanimity of pre-industrial England. In Herrick's case this is evident in biographical notices, copious annotations, travellers in search of relics, critical essays—and even poems—in such magazines as *Cornhill, Temple Bar, Blackwood's* and *Scribner's*. To be sure, there is some ridicule of his "trifling" in love poems, songs, pagan myths, and English folk customs while civil war raged.[41] Evangelicals could easily equate the manners of seventeenth-century gentry with Regency licentiousness. But more prominent is the fascination with how pleasantly he found it possible to live in the leisurely countryside. As an Edwardian roundelier put it in the *Cornhill:*

Carving thy cameos rare
Of country customs and our fathers' ways,
The hearth serene
And humble tenement,
And the slow round of rustic months and days...[42]

Social historians have written extensively about "Victorian escapism": a nostalgia for the past manifested in a perpetual desire, satisfied by a large number of illustrated books by such artists as E.A. Abbey, Hugh Thomson, the Brock brothers, and E.J. Sullivan, for illusions such as the snug farmhouse, the quaint inn, the romantic castle, the lusty fox hunter, the joyful rustic, and also, the parson, be he the hunting, drinking, bookish, or, ideally, the "show" (eloquent) variety[43] (we will see that Herrick eased his way comfortably into each of the last three avatars). Although the past could be looked to as an instructive remedy for present social problems, it often became, especially for one who read for relaxation, a way of submerging them in a fabric of cliches about the English countryside as a kind of Arcadia. There was certainly room for marshalling facts about old traditions. However, while utilitarians pointed to gaunt crofters, despairing beggars, and bullying gentry, those drawn for political and social reasons to the romantic view

Fig. 1-2 A coarse-featured lyric poet. Frontispiece ils. by W.H. Worthington. Source: *Hesperides or Works both Human and Divine*... (London: Pickering, 1846), Vol. 1 See #39.

Fig. 1-3 "The voluptuous force of the best type among the Roman emperors." Frontispiece ils. by W.J. Alais. Source: Alexander B. Grosart, ed., *The Complete Poems of Robert Herrick* (London: Chatto and Windus, 1876), Vol. 1. See #7.

highlighted picturesque furniture, architecture, and costume.

A *locus classicus* of idealization of the past, as Prof. Alice Chandler has shown,[44] was Disraeli's Young England movement, a romantic—but not escapist—reaction against liberalism in politics, rationalism in religion, and contempt for traditional class structure. Young England focussed on medieval times, but there were several ways in which its admiration for knights — errant explains its idealization of Cavaliers: a social order in which the benevolence of aristocrats precluded the lower classes sinking into, idleness, poverty, and despair, and in which the former's magnanimity cast shame on the arrogance of their Roundhead opposites. In the large number of popular historical paintings of the mid-century, one finds the period of the Civil Wars treated more than any other. By no means did all such treatments idealize the nobility and gentry as benevolent, generous, and compassionate, and disdain those instrumental in bringing democracy to England. But it is the Young England ideology of history that I want to stress here. For it, irresistible attractions (identifiable with the seventeenth century as well as the fourteenth) were the fresh air, game, and produce of the countryside (as opposed to the choking dust of the factories), the great hall in which patriarchal kindness provided a "groaning board" of harvest fruits, game, and beer (not the meager handout of the workhouse)[45], and the Cavalier engaged in disinterested defense of English tradition (not a censorious contempt for whatever did not appeal solemnly respectable). Figure 1-4 reproduces one version of "merrie" England's communal harmony. suggested by a few lines from Herrick's "A New Year's Gift To Sir Simeon Steward."

40   FAVORITE POEMS.

Sit crowned with rosebuds, and carouse,
Till *Liber Pater* twirls the house
About your ears, and lay upon
The year, your cares, that's fled and gone:
And let the russet swains the plough
And harrow hang up resting now ;
And to the bagpipe all address,
Till sleep takes place of weariness.
And thus throughout, with Christmas plays,
Frolic the full twelve holy-days.

OBERON'S FEAST.

HAPCOT! *to thee the Fairy State*
I with discretion dedicate :
Because thou prizest things that are
Curious and unfamiliar.
Take first the feast ; these dishes gone,
We'll see the Fairy-court anon.

A little mushroom-table spread,
After short prayers, they set on bread,
A moon-parched grain of purest wheat,
With some small glittering grit, to eat

" And thus throughout with Christmas plays
Frolic the full twelve holy-days."

Fig. 1-4 In procession to the Old English "groaning board." Source: *Favorite Poems of Robert Herrick.* The Vest Pocket Series (Boston: Osgood, 1877), p. 41. Ils. for "A New-Year's Gift to Sir Simeon Steward." See #40.

That the volume in which this drawing appears, the first illustrated edition of Herrick, was published in America (as was the second) is a measure of the Gilded Age's interest in the myth of the English past as a genteel pleasant place. Let me point out, however, that despite the Anglophilia of Irving's *Bracebridge Hall*, many creative and independent advocates of a national literature found no need to glamorize another country's history or to retreat into a romantic illusion of nature when in fact the "American spirit" was boldly exploring it. Those who did turn to the past could more imaginatively write about the Indian or the frontiersman than the knight-errant or Cavalier. In fact, before Young England there was Young America, a whiggish group which fought the literary establishment in New York and Boston.[46] For my interest in the congruence of American with British tastes in seventeenth-century lyric poetry, history, and biography, I put stress on the "genteel tradition" as practiced after the Civil War by Aldrich, Boker, Stedman, Stoddard, and Gilder, and on the audience they commanded.

Now we return to England, to note the salutary effect the romanticization of the past may have had on the taste and manners, as well as the morals, of the growing middle classes. Upward mobility may foster complacent self-righteousness. Or, it could encourage personal aggrandisement through vulgar display and syncophantic aping of the *bon ton* (as had happened in Regency times). Young England, on the other hand, held up for emulation an aristocratic equanimity, and a concept of good-natured service. In England and America, these virtues of time-honored gentlemanly behavior were, to those who could afford to affect them, important in maintaining a sense of decency, purpose, and refinement in the midst of social change. Part of this was an ingenuous use of leisure: the enjoyment of art and *belles-lettres*. In this spirit readers grew to love the Cavaliers and Roundheads of Scott's *Legend of Montrose* and *Peveril of the Peake*, and later to develop strong interests in Ruskin's essays on medieval social bonding, and Charles Eastlake's neo-medieval architecture and interior designs.[47]

Young England makes use of romanticism's emphasis on the emotions, and allows for a relaxed, even dandified sensibility. Disraeli's writings encourage a tolerant, humanistic attitude in which fancy as well as intellect is important. Something of this sort, in fact, seems to have made its way into the social and intellectual life of the period even before Disraeli. It was associated with the romantic attachment to the English past. The *Retrospective* was especially noteworthy in reprinting obscure texts of Renaissance writers in generous samples, together with enthusiastic appreciations.[48] Mr. John Gross describes the "literary revivalism" of the *London Magazine* in the 1820s: its "antiquarian anecdotes," the "Jacobethan echoes" woven into its articles, its poems on "costume drama themes" (the ballad quoted above is a descendant of those), and its encouragement of "bibliolatry."[49]

People imagined that in the pre-industrial past one could more freely indulge his or her private idiosyncracies, and could relish an order and closeness to nature which vanished with factories and railways. Thus an early nineteenth-century American architect commends the Gothic villa for the "nooks about it, where one would love to linger; windows, where one can enjoy the quiet landscape at his leisure...and the quiet, domestic feeling of the family circle. Those who love shadow, and the sentiment of antiquity and repose, will find in it the most pleasure."[50] Here we find another congruence (to supplement Scott's novels and Yeames' paintings) between Victorian domesticity and the "romance of the past." Let us consider one other: the notion of the ideal woman. This will bring us back to Herrick, for the attractions of his kind of lyric, especially as represented in drawing-room books, were recommended (as we have seen in the case of Palgrave's *Chrysomela*) to genteel ladies in their leisured hours. The ideal woman's moral inviolability, selfless dedication to domestic duties, and feeling for the charm of interior decor, garden, and recreative song and verse tie in neatly with notions of what female roles were in an idyllic, chivalric past. Equally, such concepts of femininity isolate the passive female from the breadwinner's workday world, leaving her "free" to tend the garden realms of imagination and poetic feeling.[51] Mrs. Sarah Ellis, writer of several courtesy books for ladies, describes for her audience the magnanimous "Spirit of Poesy, that weaves a garland of the flowers which imagination has culled; and from the fervency of its own passion, to impart as well as receive enjoyment, casts this garland at the feet of the sordid and busy multitude."[52] She goes on to say that woman herself, who lives passively, with "feeling," rather than "action," is the most poetic subject, "with her beauty, and grace, and gentleness, and fullness of feeling, and depth of affection...."[53] For how these strands of romantic escapism come together, see Figures 1-5 and 1-6, from a collection of *Elizabethan Songs in Honour of Love and Beauty* (1894). The frontispiece (Figure 1-5) and an illustration for Herrick's "To Sappho" (Figure 1-6) show precise antiquarian detail in recreating "Jacobethan" furniture and male costume (hairstyle is contemporary). In this setting the lover, in a tableau of chivalric gallantry, approaches his lady with deep feeling, obligation, and rectitude. The Elizabethan Sappho (the same girl courted in the frontispiece) sings for the reader and her lover with warmth and ingenuous affection (so oblivious is she and the artist to Herrick's virile pun regarding a desire to "die away upon [her] lute"). The drawings are playful and domestic as well as romantic; a Victorian lady and gentleman are delicately invited to put themselves in the place of the couple who are used to illustrate the poems. This is the genteel and cleanly pleasure to which the wainscotting and mullioned windows of a Gothic villa invite the English or American family. The ethos of the drawing recalls Mrs. Ellis' definition of poetry as "whatever is so far removed from vulgarity, as to excite ideas of sublimity, beauty, or tenderness."

Editors and critics stress characteristics of Herrick, the man and the poet, which would attract those receptive to the nexus of romantic ideals

Fig. 1-5 Chivalric gallantry and rectitude in "merrie" England. Frontispiece ils. by Edmund Garrett. Source: *Elizabethan Songs in Honour of Love and Beauty* (Boston: Little, Brown, 1894).

Fig. 1-6 Jacobethan beauty, costume and furniture. Illustration by Edmund Garrett for Herrick's "To Sappho." Source: *Elizabethan Songs in Honour of Love and Beauty* (Boston: Little, Brown, 1894), opposite p. 138.

incorporated in the values of Young England, historical painting, neo-gothic architecture, and the genteel drawing room. His first editors recommend his lyric descriptions of flowers and faerie, rustic customs and folklore: "England as left by Elizabeth," as Palgrave put it. He is a drinking, a bookish, a histrionic parson, and a gentleman of the old school: loyal to king and friends, a man of habitually easy tolerances but on occasion badtempered, and possessed of a sense of limitation which gives him time idly to appreciate beauty and to indulge his whimsical, melancholy and satirical moods.[54] A reader gets to know him more intimately than is possible with any other lyric poet of the age. *Household Words* describes a "mad wag" of a roistering parson, flushed, his clothes rumpled, with clerical collar askew and slopped with wine, "just as one may still see him drinking and singing to this moment—anyone who cares to turn over tenderly, the leaves of that garden of sweets, his song-book, called the *Hesperides*."[55] This verbal portrait may have been thought "monstrous" by Rev. Grosart, but in spirit it is not far from the latter's own description of the frontispiece he commissioned for his edition: a virile, hearty, jovial man of "voluptuous force," profane, but genial, humble, and spontaneous. One cannot find heroic or tragic themes in his poetry (nor, in selected excerpts, anything prurient) but rather the "rarest appreciation of what is delicate and pure and faultless. . . . They seem to shed light, these poems, like delicate flowers at evening."[56] By general consensus,[57] he usually got along well with his parishioners, for he was not a snob (witness his long relationship with his maid Prue) or hypocrite ("of sound heart and naive simplicity") and was fascinated with their rustic traditions and ceremonies. Had he been a voluptuary, nineteenth-century admirers ask, would the natives have remembered, 120 years after his death, so much about his idiosyncrasies, as Barron Field recorded (his pet pig, his vow never to return after being "ousted" for royalism), and would they have memorized so many of his verses?[58] Another source of Herrick's contentment would have been the local royalist gentry, for whom he proved a boon companion. "It is easy to conceive with how greatly increased a relish they turned over the folios of Drayton or 'rare Ben,' that lay in their hall windows, after listening to Herrick's stories of his London life. . . ."[59]

Herrick the Urbane Craftsman: Aesthetic and Edwardian Literary Taste
    The largest number of reprints of *Hesperides* date from 1870 to 1915, with landmark editions stretching from Harper Brothers' illustrated *Selections* (1882) through F.W. Moorman's definitive *Complete Works* (1915). We have selections for children ("The Children's Poets," illustrated by Charles Robinson [1915]), lovers ("The Lovers' Library" [1903]), gardeners (*Flower Poems* [1905]), lovers of calligraphy ("with Designs by T. R. R Ryder" [1913]), musicians (*A Country Garland of Ten Songs Gathered from the Hesperides* [1897]), travellers ("The Vest Pocket Series" [1877]), and collectors of calendars (*The Herrick Calendar for 1908*). Fascination with a

rustic gentleman-poet from a simpler, more gallant age had something to do with this; several of the passages discussed in the previous section date from the late Victorian and Edwardian periods, as does the ballad stanza about Herrick's rustic muse. However, the moral idealism and social cohesion that Young England, historical novels, and genteel ladies associated with Cavaliers account only in part for Herrick's nineteenth-century reputation. The magnanimity which was thought to have made possible a pre-industrial English society of edenic contentment and organic unity came to share attention with another type of aristocratic behavior, which, although just as amenable to drawing-room conversation and romance of the past, embodied a cool detachment from social responsibilities, and boasted a single-minded immersion in rarified beauty which only a refined temperament could grasp. There came to be as much description of Herrick the detached aesthete as of Herrick the jovial Cavalier. This occurred as part of the changes attendant upon the *fin de siecle* retreat from high seriousness, a change which encouraged what John Gross described as a "new race of critics...book-lovers, bookmen, vignettists, gossipers in libraries, adventurers among masterpieces...." Gross goes on to discuss "the large, vague, but very real question of the whole Late Victorian mood.... The commonest reaction was withdrawal, a retreat into nostalgia, exoticism, fine writing, *belles-lettres*."[60]

In many ways the aesthetic notions drew on and merged with those which idealized the Cavalier. Both attitudes, on both sides of the Atlantic, proved engaging to affluent folk whose sense of well-being benefited from a genteel screen separating them from the religious, political, and social convulsions of the day. The image of the detached aesthete is no more responsible than that of the gentleman-priest for Herrick's heyday of popularity. In fact, one finds the same critic praising the poet as both. Herrick's late nineteenth-century vogue had more to do with publishing practices, growth of the reading public, and booksellers' cleverness at exploiting the personal (including the social) ambitions of the book-purchaser than with late-century changes in literary and social values *per se*. Coincidently, as doctrinal factionalism relaxed and social barriers became further blurred, mechanical innovations to produce more cheap and more illustrated books to accommodate the growing reading public became irresistible to publishers. However, as the climate of opinion helps determine what people read, we need to deal with what men of letters influenced by literary tastes of the eighties and nineties found in Herrick that was congenial.

Before we do, one proviso is necessary. It is true that for a Victorian exercised about church and party ideology, and for Americans proud of their sober rectitude, whether one admired the seventeenth-century Cavalier or the Puritan had much to do with his or her stance on political and social issues.[61] For such people large differences should appear between an aristocratic temperament which makes service to one's dependents and peers integral to his own personal enjoyment and one which disdains social obligations to develop artistic sensibilities in the exclusive company of like-minded companions. However, such distinctions are more relevant to those who bring ideological assumptions to their reading than the audience we are discussing, which, after all, was looking for genteel amusement. In addition, there are a great many works more likely to stimulate philosophical assumptions than is Herrick's poetry. As for the expectations with which a general reader opened *Hesperides*, a Cavalier's aristocratic magnanimity in the face of Puritan attacks on king and country might be very much like a moralist's aloofness from acquisitive sensual obsessions. Both postures would be somewhat interesting to people for whom familiarity with gentility, and even its affectation, were desirable.

With this *caveat*, let us consider those minor poets of the 1870s and 80s, the Parnassians or Roundeliers. This was a group which, from the late 60s through the 80s, brought the French experiments in lyric craftsmanship to England.[62] Many of these poets wrote essays on Herrick (Swinburne, Gosse, Lang, Dobson). As we have seen, they were intrigued by the occasions he found fitting for poetry, his genial attachment to the sensual and the profane, his way of making such lyrics "cleanly," his social, political, and artistic priorities, and his mastery of prosody and diction. Their own work was similar, occasionally in content and often in form. Their roundels and ballades appeared in many periodicals and some elegant volumes of poetry with wide margins, old style typeface, handmade paper, and art nouveau decorations. The undergraduate Oscar Wilde remarked the "exquisite intricacy and musical repetitions of the ballade" and "the proper temper in which a triolet should be written."[63] As prominent as the metrical precision was the mood of langorous refinement, "pure art devoid of moral concerns."[64] The lack of interest in either social progress or social problems was studied, not casual—therein lies a large difference from the harmonious, carefree existence of rustic gentry and genial peasants which romantics ascribed to "merrie" England. Interestingly, it was the Roundeliers who first looked wistfully to the eighteenth century as a time of graceful elegance. Young England and the Oxford Movement were too aware of the peasants' poverty, the nobles' licentiousness, and the clergy's ineffectuality to do so.[65] It is not surprising that whiggish aristocrats looked with favor upon the work of these aesthetes, as a rejection of Philistine tastes.[66] If inconsequential (or because it was so), it also received encouragement from periodicals which, with their more pressing political and social concerns, found such escapist literature easy to put in its proper place as much less significant than issues of the day.[67] An example from the United States is *Harper's Christmas*, 1882 (simultaneously published in England): a book of drawings and stories compiled by "The Tile Club," a group of artists inspired to contribute to the new "decorative vitality." There were stories and poems by Edmund Stedman, T. B. Aldrich, Joel Chandler Harris, and G. W. Curtis; illustrations were by Albert Parsons, Elihu Vedder, and E. A. Abbey, among others. The latter's illustrated *Herrick,* with a preface by his friend Austin Dobson, had appeared earlier the same year.[68]

Ifor Evans' appreciation of the Roundeliers[69] shows how they could have seen Herrick as a kindred spirit. Austin Dobson's best poems have, beside virtuosity, a wistful pathos and playful elegance. He applies *carpe diem* to descriptions of eighteenth-century places and people. Andrew Lang has a vein of pleasant melancholy, and his imagery is suffused with perfumed odors, roses, languid sunsets, and faerie. Gosse's romantic nostalgia is often delicately stated. We have seen similar criteria applied to Herrick's poetry quite often, and by these very writers. *Hesperides,* with its jewel-like tiny perfections of imagery and versification, would naturally attract the authors of *Proverbs in Porcelain* (Dobson) and *Ballades in Blue China* (Lang). However, while Herrick used *carpe diem* to celebrate earthly pleasures, in the Roundeliers, this *topos* became what Jerome Buckley says it was in Fitzgerald's version of the *Rubaiyat* (the 1890s most popular poem)—a way of "escaping the regrets, fears, confusions of a difficult age."[70] Poetry, said the editor of the *Atlantic* in 1895, "should create nothing but what is beautiful." But the moral tenor of American society was less adaptable to sensual indulgence than was England's, and the theoretical justification for poetry remained didactic.[71]

The Roundeliers' vogue was short-lived, but in England the aesthetic fashion of escapism was not. Shortly before World War I another group of genteel poets flourished, the "Georgian" school. Rupert Brooke, who confessed his poems of 1911 risked deflecting experience "to favour and to prettiness,"[72] is the best known. They celebrated

the rural England of Shakespeare, Milton, Wordsworth and Hopkins . . . where passion perspires roses, and the abandoned heart slowly freezes into the complacency of ice cream, where it is almost always either spring or autumn, or exactly midsummer, . . . where sorrow dies at sunset and even despair is crowned with new-mown hay.[73]

How many nineteenth-century critics felt this way about *Hesperides?* Fanciful illusions, urbane wit, craftsmanship in narrow limits, contentment with small resources, and delight in the bright and graceful surfaces of things: these were century-long obsessions.

Aestheticism may have begun as a contemptuous response to insistent bourgeois sensibilities, but its enthusiasms caught on widely. The gentlemanly values it espoused, popularized by tolerant periodicals and clever publishers, were very amenable to drawing rooms at a time when social position was in flux and notions of polite accomplishments were important. As *Punch,* and Gilbert and Sullivan, delineated, throughout "passionate Brompton" and "intense Kensington" (and Boston, Philadelphia, and San Francisco) one found attachment to vague romantic sensations regarding flower arrangement, perfumes, and porcelain. Also current were the feeling that beauty was ethereal and required a devotion antipathetic to mundane experiences (such as the formerly-much-approved social work for women), and an approved feminine dress and posture: flowing medieval or severely classical lines; an aloof, heavy-lidded look.[74] For this audience, to wander in *Hesperides* was an occasional ramble (but always a polite one, with one eye on the frontiers of prurience and indelicacy often marked by *Selections*) in a recreative garden of pagan antiquity. Figure 1-7 reproduces a title page making such an invitation. Herrick's incarnation as jovial Cavalier was attractive, but even more relevant was Swinburne's critique: his perfection in the smallest parameters of secular lyric. He consciously surrounds himself with luxurious and delicate artifacts.[75] For those refined enough not to be bored by a poet dedicated simply to saying more perfectly what has already been said,[76] he creates a pre-lapsarian world of sunlight and spring flowers, classical maidens, faerie, and whatever other delights would suit the mercurial temper of a "respectable British Bacchus."[77] Perhaps the emphasis on Herrick as pagan bard was a logical extension of aesthetic detachment from the kind of earnestness which read "pagan" as "heathen," and from the new scientism, which disdained wit and fancy for the perusal of empirical data.[78] Gosse declares Herrick's verses to be "permeated with strong neo-pagan emotion":

...the sun shines on a world re-arisen-to the duty of pleasure; Bacchus rides through the valleys,...loose-draped nymphs, playing on the lyre, bound about the forehead with vervain and the cool stalks of parsley, fill the silent woods with their melodies and dances; this poet sings of a land where life is only a dream of sweet delights of the bodily senses.[79]

As Gosse sees them, Herrick's "sweet and civil" verses are indeed devoted to pleasure. So, are the illustrations of and designs for the books in which the poems are incorporated. Pictures and decorations set the stage for an escape from the dullness of one's daily round, from anxieties and depressions—the kind of retreat which only the life of the mind allows, into reverie and imagination. The promise of this escape is very important in understanding Herrick's appeal to the nineteenth- and twentieth-century reading public; discreet invitations to it were certainly much in the mind of those who wanted to sell editions of his poetry. Two revealing symbols of it are the frontispiece to Bohn's edition (see Figure 2-6a) entitled "The Pleasure Tired," and Abbey's "The Night Piece, To Julia" (see Figure 3-4). Both show languorous, self-absorbed women who preside over casements beyond which are late-night breezes, waning stars, soft music, and faerie: the kind of scene which may well dissolve, when dawn breaks, into the one Gosse describes. Its pleasures entice readers with the suggestion that the poetry, pictures, and decorations the book contains will fulfill half-articulated fantasies, soothe frustrated egos, and demonstrate the graceful postures and soft words which assure that a person who feels deeply will be feelingly rewarded. That publishers knew of the relentless human need for such pleasure is clear from

Fig. 1-7 An aesthetic garden of pagan antiquity. Source: Ernest Rhys, ed., *The Lyric Poems of Robert Herrick,* The Lyric Poets (London: Dent, 1897), title page. See #22.

the way they worked to incorporate that need into the expectations with which the general reader was taught to approach Herrick. His idiosyncratic treatment of youth, love, nature, time passing, and faerie was interpreted so as to induce tenderness, pathos, compassion, a relaxed cheerfulness, admiration for child-like innocence, and wistful idyllicism. To conclude by putting all this in proper perspective, the implications of these publishers' success are most profoundly suggested—life and art being what they are—not by flesh-and-blood purchasers of the volumes themselves, nor by the men of letters who introduced them, nor by their illustrators, but by the romantic fantasies of Emma Bovary, with whose career her creator, it is said, could deeply identify.

Notes

¹Nathan Drake, *Literary Hours,* 2nd ed. (London: Cadell and Davies, 1800), I, iii.

[2]Leo Lowenthal and Ina Lawson, "The Debate on Cultural Standards in Nineteenth-Century England," *Social Research*, 30 (1963), 426.

[3]R.G. Cox, "The Reviews and Magazines," in *From Dickens to Hardy*, ed. Boris Ford, vol. 6 in *A Guide to English Literature* (London: Cassell, 1963), pp. 190-98.

[4]Cox, "Reviews and Magazines," p. 202; R. K. Webb, "The Victorian Reading Public," in Ford, ed., p. 206; Malcolm Elwin, *Victorian Wallflowers: A Panoramic Survey of the Popular Literary Journals* (1934, rpt. Port Washington, N.Y.: Kennikat Press, 1966), pp. 19-21, 203-07, 310-12; John Gross, *The Rise and Fall of the Man of Letters* (New York: Collier Books, 1970), chapters 1, 3-5.

[5]"Article VII. Hesperides: or the Works...." *The Retrospective Review*, 5, pt. 1 (1822), 157.

[6] Quoted in Ian Jack, *English Literature 1815-1832*, Oxford History of English Literature, vol. 10 (Oxford: Clarendon Press, 1963), p. 12.

[7][Barron Field], "Article XII, Select Poems from Herrick, Carew & et." *The Quarterly Review*, 4 (1810), pp. 171-72. For authorship of this article, see "Herrick and Southey," *Notes and Quaries*, 1st Series, 10 (1854), 27.

[8]Drake, *Literary Hours*, 3rd ed. (London: Cadell and Davies, 1804), p. 49.

[9]Thomas Maitland (Lord Dundrennan), ed., *The Works of Robert Herrick* (Edinburgh: W. and C. Tait, 1823), I, xxvii.

[10]"Dii Minorum Gentium, No. 1: Carew and Herrick," *Blackwood's Edinburgh Magazine*, June 1839, p. 793.

[11]Drake, 3rd ed. (1804), pp. 53-55; J[ohn] N[ott], *Select Poems From The Hesperides* (Bristol, Eng.: J. M. Gutch [1810]), pp. 27, 42, 117, 175; "Article XII," *Quarterly*, p. 171; "Article VII," *Retrospective*, pp. 157-58; "Dii Minorum Gentium," *Blackwood's Edinburgh Magazine*, p. 791.

[12]"Article VII," *Retrospective*, p. 158.

[13]Floris Delattre, *Robert Herrick: Contribution a l'Etude de la Poesie Lyrique en Angleterre au Dix-septieme Siecle* (Paris: Alcan, 1910), p. 496.

[14]Quoted in Delattre, p. 497. See *The Greek Christian Poets and the English Poets*: "...sucking where the bee sucks, from the rose heart of nature." Mrs. Browning's piece was first published in 1842.

[15]Drake, 2nd ed. (1800), p. 156.

[16]N[ott], "Advertisement," p. iv.

[17]"Preface" to Alfred Pollard, ed., *Robert Herrick The Hesperides and Noble Numbers*, The Muses' Library (London: Lawrence and Bullen, 1891), I, xi, xii.

[18]Alexander B. Grosart, ed., *The Complete Poems of Robert Herrick*, The Early English Poets (London, Chatto and Windus, 1876), I, xiii.

[19]Grant Richards, *Author Hunting By An Old Literary Sportsman* (London: Hamish Hamilton, 1934), p. 82.

[20]Simon Nowell-Smith, ed., *Letters to Macmillan* (London: Macmillan, 1967), p. 108.

[21]Quoted in Jack, p. 19.

[22]Quoted in Jack, p. 21.

[23]*The Lives and Works of the Uneducated Poets*, ed. Childers, pp. 85-86, quoted in Paul W. Whitney, "Robert Southey's Views on English Literature," Dissertation, University of Pennsylvania 1960, pp. 189-90.

[24]"Herrick's Julia," *Household Words*, Oct. 3, 1857, pp. 322-26. By William C. M. Kent; reprinted in his *Footprints in the Road* (London: Chapman and Hall, 1864). See Anne Lohrli, *Household Words* (Toronto: U. of Toronto Press, 1973), p. 331.

[25]William Allingham, "Rambles by Patricius Walker," in *Varieties in Prose* (London: Longman's Green, 1893), I, 135. The "Rambles" first appeared in 1873.

[26]The views of social history in the next two paragraphs are taken from the following sources: William S. Knickerbocker, "The Idea of Culture," in Joseph Baker, ed., *The Reinterpretation of Victorian Literature* (Princeton: Princeton University Press, 1950), pp. 104-29; Lowenthal and Lawson, "Debate on Cultural Standards," pp. 425-33; Gertrude Himmelfarb, *Victorian Minds* (New York: Knopf, 1968), ch. 10; Maurice J. Quinlan, *Victorian Prelude, A History of English Manners, 1700-1830*, Columbia University Studies in English and Comparative Literature, no. 155 (New York: Columbia University Press, 1941), pp. 104-07, 180-97, 229-39.

[27]Eric J. Dingwall, *The American Woman* (N.Y.: Rinehart, 1957), pp. 81-87

[28]Dingwall, p. 87

30D.L. WIlson, ed., *The Genteel Tradition* (Cambridge: Harvard University Press, 1967), p. 73.

31*Collectanea Anglo-Poetica...A Bibliographical and Descriptive Catalogue*, Part VII, Publications of the Chetham Society (Manchester: Chetham Society, 1877), pp. 200-01. See also H. J. Nicholl, *Landmarks of English Literature*, 2nd ed. (1885; rpt. N.Y.: Haskell House, 1973), p. 111.

32"Dii Minorum Gentium," *Blackwood's Edinburgh Magazine*, p. 791. For a discussion of nineteenth-century expurgations of Herrick, see Noel Perrin, *Dr. Bowdler's Legacy: A History of Expurgated Books...*(New York: Atheneum, 1969), pp. 199-202.

33E. Walford, ed., *The Poetical Works of Robert Herrick...*(London: Reeves and Turner, 1859), p. xiii.

34E[dmund] G[osse], "Robert Herrick," *Cornhill Magazine*, August 1875, p. 179.

35Charles Dudley Warner, ed., *Library of the World's Best Literature Ancient and Modern* (New York: Hall, 1902), 13, 7307.

36Donald Mithcell, *English Lands, Letters and Kings* (New York: Scribner's 1890), II, 124.

37*Notes and Queries*, 8th Series, 6 (1894), 359.

38Richard D. Altick, *The English Common Reader, A Social History of the Mass Reading Public, 1800-1900* (Chicago: University of Chicago Press, 1963), pp. 197-98, 231.

39George Saintsbury, ed., *The Poetical Works of Robert Herrick*, The Aldine Edition of the British Poets (London: George Bell and Sons, 1908), I, iii-iii (first published in 1893). See also Henry Morley, ed., *Hesperides...*Morley's Universal Library (London: Routledge, 1884), p. 7.

40Herbert Horne, ed., *Hesperides: Poems by Robert Herrick*, The Canterbury Poets (London: Walter Scott, 1887), pp. xxi, 301.

41Laurie Magnus, "Robert Herrick," *Bookman* (London), May 1910, pp. 89-90; Walter de le Mare, "Robert Herrici," *Bookman* (London), May 1908, p. 52.

42T. Bruce Dilks, "To Herrick," *The Living Age*, May 13, 1911, p. 386.

43Roy Strong, *Recreating the Past, British History and the Victorian Painter* (New York: Thames and Hudson, 1978), pp. 36-40.

44Alice Chandler, *A Dream of Order: The Medieval Ideal in Nineteenth-Century English Literature* (Lincoln: University of Nebraska Press, 1970), ch. 5.

45J. W. Burrow, "The Sense of the Past," in *The Victorians*, ed. Laurence Lerner (London: Metheun, 1978), pp. 128, 130.

46R. Gordon Kelly, *Mother Was A Lady. Self and Society in Selected American Children's Periodicals 1865-1890* (Westport, Conn.: Greenwood Press, 1974), pp. 61-67; John Steegman, *Victorian Taste* (1950; rpt. Cambridge, Mass.: MIT Press, 1971), pp. 92-93; Chandler, pp. 190-95.

47G.D. Klingopulos, "Notes on the Victorian Scene," in Ford, ed., *From Dickens to Hardy*, p. 18; Burrows, pp. 120-38.

48Oliver Elton, *A Survey of English Literature, 1780-1830* (London: Macmillan, 1912), I, 119.

49Gross, p. 14.

50Andrew Jackson Downing, quoted in Roger Gilman, "The Romantic Interior," in George Boas, ed., *Romanticism in America* (New York: Russell and Russell, 1961), pp. 111-12.

51Ralph P. Boas, "The Romantic Lady," in G. Boas, ed., *Romanticism in America*, pp. 64-66; Strong, pp. 152-53; Ola E. Winslow, "Books for the Lady Reader, 1820-1860," in G. Boas, pp. 90-109; Carol Dyhouse, "The Role of Women: From Self-Sacrifice to Self-Awareness," in Lerner, pp. 174-76.

52Sara Stickney (Mrs. William Ellis), *The Poetry of Life* (New York: E. Walker, 1850), pp. 5-6 (bound as part of Ellis, *Guide to Social Happiness*).

53Sarah Ellis, *The Daughters of England* (New York: E. Walker, 1848), pp. 43-44 (bound as part of Ellis, *Family Monitor and Domestic Guide*).

54Morley, ed., *Hesperides*, pp. 5-8.

55"Herrick's Julia," *Household Words*, pp. 322-23. See a similar discussion by Ernest Rhys in the introduction to Horne, ed., *Hesperides*, p. xxi, and Allingham, *Varieties in Prose*, I, 131-32.

56Gosse, "Robert Herrick," p. 52. See also E. L. Darton, ed., *Robert Herrick, The Children's Poets* (London: Wells, Gardner, Darton, and Co., [1915]), p. 99.

57See especially Richard J. King, "Robert Herrick and His Vicarage," in *Sketches and Studies: Descriptive and Historical* (London: John Murray, 1874), pp. 372-73; H. C. Beeching,

"The Poetry of Herrick," *National and English Review*, 40 (1903), 788-99; "Robert Herrick," *Temple Bar*, May, 1883, p. 124.

58Walford, ed., p. x.

59King, p. 367.

60Gross, pp. 131-32.

61J. W. Burrow, p. 123.

62See the two articles by James K. Robinson: "Austin Dobson and the Roundeliers," *Modern Language Quarterly*, 14 (1953), 31-42; "A Neglected Phase of the Aesthetic Movement: English Parnassianism," *PMLA* 68 (1953), 733-84.

63Quoted in Robinson, "Dobson and the Roundeliers," p. 38.

64Jerome Buckley, *The Triumph of Time: A Study of the Victorian Concepts of Time, History, Progress, and Decadence* (Cambridge, Mass.: Belknap Press, 1966), p. 143.

65J.W. Burrow, pp. 129-30.

66Jerome Buckley, *The Victorian Temper* (Cambridge, Mass.: Harvard University Press, 1969), 217; Cox, "Reviews and Magazines," pp. 199-200.

67R. G. Cox, "Victorian Criticism of Poetry: The Minority Tradition," *Scrutiny*, 18 (1951), 15-17; Robinson, "Dobson and the Roundeliers," p. 38.

68E. V. Lucas, *E. A. Abbey, Royal Academician* (New York: Scribner's 1921), I, 51, 116.

69Ifor Evans, *English Poetry in the Later Nineteenth Century*, 2nd ed. (New York: Barnes and Noble, 1966), pp. 288-98.

70Buckley, *Triumph of Time*, p. 127.

71John Tomsich, *A Genteel Endeavor: American Culture and Politics in the Gilded Age* (Stanford: Stanford University Press, 1971), pp. 145, 148. The quotation is by T. B. Aldrich, in a letter to Francis Bartlett, Aug. 5, 1895.

72Brooke's letters, pp. 315-16, quoted in Samuel Hymes, *Edwardian Occasions, Essays on English Writing in the Early Twentieth Century* (New York: Oxford University Press, 1972), p. 147.

73George Dangerfield, *The Strange Death of Liberal England* (1935; rpt. New York: Capricorn Books, 1961), p. 433.

74William Gaunt, *The Aesthetic Adventure* (London: J. Cape, 1946), p. 62.

75John Masefield, ed., "Biographical Introduction," *The Poems of Robert Herrick*, "The Chapbooks" (London: Grant Richards, 1906), p. xiv.

76[C.F. Warre], "Robert Herrick," *The Edinburgh Review*, 199 (1904), pp. 113-15.

77Herrick's *Women, Love, and Flowers*, The Bibelots (London: Gay and Bird, 1899), p. vii.

78Raymond Chapman, "Books and Readers," *The Victorian Debate* (New York: Basic Books, 1968), p. 62.

79Gosse, "Robert Herrick," p. 183.

Chapter 2

"For Scholars and Readers": Gilded Age, Victorian, and Edwardian Trade Editions

There is a perfect rage today for reprinting, and we suppose re-purchasing
(more problematically for re-purusing) the poets of the seventeenth century.
Among the ranks of the reprinted Herrick is easily first favourite.
—Thomas Seccombe and W. Robertson Nicoll, *The Bookman
Illustrated History of English Literature* (1907)

For sociologists, literary critics, historians, and graphic artists, the story
of nineteenth-century publishing is fascinating, because this period saw the
growth of a large, increasing literate segment of the population and the
accommodation of its practical and psychological needs by the print media.
At the beginning of the century most established publishers catered to a fairly
homogenious audience drawn from the upper ranks of society. By century's
end, the "reading habit" had spread from gentry and professional men to
industrial managers, shopkeepers and skilled workers, and from libraries to
drawing rooms, "cosy corners," boudoirs, living rooms and servants'
quarters. Publishers started as gentleman-scholars and became, as the
existence of a mass market loomed, not less genteel or resourceful, but more
persistent businessmen. As the epigraph to this chapter suggests, editions of
Herrick are a significant aspect of that part of the nineteenth-century book
trade which has to do with literary texts. The formats of these editions, and
the contexts in which they appeared, are a microcosm which mirrors the
interests of the general reader in lyric poetry. Some of these are social and
recreational as well as aesthetic. What is important is that they were a reality.
They reflect the perspectives of a sizeable audience on Herrick's poetry, and
the sensibility which made him a "first favourite."

Nineteenth-century publishers, English and American, were scrupulous
men, and conscious of their function as guardians of knowledge. Daniel
Macmillan fortified himself for his pleasant labors with the conviction that
"we booksellers...[are] aiding our great Taskmaster to reduce the world into
order and beauty and harmony."[1] Charles Knight's *Passages From a Working
Life* offers ample evidence of his imaginative and salutary schemes to set the
fruits of literacy before the English masses.[2] Henry Holt, whose Leisure
Moment Series presented American readers with attractive 35-cent editions of
the best in world literature, and who thought of writers as friends not clients,
was appalled at the coming of the literary agent.[3] Charles Scribner could not
bring himself to describe publishing as a "business"; it was rather a "career"
(modesty prevented him from using the word "profession"[4]). The most

influential men in the nineteenth-century book trade were either men of letters themselves or their energetic, enthusiastic supporters.

In addition, they made money by recognizing popular taste and fashions, and the ways in which purchasing books were signs of social status. The balance in which the gentleman and the businessman were measured was a delicate one. Early in the century, there was much resistance, in the established houses, to lowering prices of books so that the masses could buy them. While some actually might have feared the power of the press in the hands of polemicists who would exploit newly-literate masses, in fact the market among the fashionable for high-priced books limited interest among most publishers for improving the lot of the common man.[5] Later in the century, so many books were issued on themes that proved popular that the sales-life of any one volume was very short;[6] it could be prolonged by favorable reviews in the magazines which the largest houses (Scribner's, Harper, Century, Macmillan, Longman) established to publicize their own books.[7] Professor Dudek describes the surfeit of gothic and "silver-fork" novels of high society, which outsold more original work as the gap between popular and "serious" work grew,[8] and with it a concept of the "highbrow" and his or her alienation from the general reader. One might conclude that by Thackeray's time there was an either/or dichotomy between commercialization for the popular entertainment market and disinterested promulgation of elite art: "once the 'profession of letters' becomes a business tied up with journalism and the book trade, it is like any other job...."

Neither a compelling natural impulse nor anything to communicate is necessary. An easy pen, a practical adaptability, hard work, is all that anyone needs to become a 'professional writer.' Almost anyone with average ability can break into 'the game.' Under such circumstances books are produced in astronomical quantities—like newspapers and periodicals—having no pretense as literature.[9]

However, in the late nineteenth century serious critics wrote for the established, eclectic literary journals. This was before the New Journalism, with its gossipy "tid bits" and sensational crime reporting, forced the demise of these reviews. It was only after this had occurred that those who loved literature found that serious interest in its study existed only in academia. Congregating therein, they learned to disdain as amateurish tastes which, untrained by new critical postulates, would mix literary analysis with incidental felicities of religion and morality. But as late as the reigns of Edward VII and Teddy Roosevelt, magazines such as *Atlantic Monthly* and *Bookman*, writers such as Thomas Bailey Aldrich and George Saintsbury, and publishers such as Dent and Harper appealed to a broad literate group of gentry and middle-class readers capable of deriving from their patronage intelligent appreciations which satisfied both conventional standards of artistic refinement and—more importantly—private needs for fantasies about perfumed air, a lover's smile, and the serenity of a quiet arbor.

Nineteenth-century publishers not only followed, but also solidified traditional standards of propriety in their attempts to make reading a family and national institution. In America, they clearly hindered the efforts of experimental writers from Whitman to Malcolm Cowley. In England, this kind of cliquish repressiveness was felt later, in the bitterness of Eliot, Pound, Wyndham Lewis, and D.H. Lawrence toward the literary establishment. However mixed publishers' motives, and however smug and superficial some of the results, the attempt produced an attractive variety of books meant to fulfill recreational and instructional functions in the lives of readers for whom *belles-lettres* were, for various reasons, important. Their standards were raised, and their reading habits encouraged, by such series as the Golden Treasury reprints, The Aldine (and the Temple) Classics, Everyman (and the Muses') Library, and by handsomely illustrated gift books for drawing room show, a beloved's boudoir, or a gentleman's library.

If the nineteenth-century book trade was a vital force in bringing literature to the British and American middle classes, two reasons were the lowering of book prices throughout the century, and the sensitivity of publishers to certain motives for reading (or, at least, for the possession of books) in English and American society. The number of books issued rose in inverse proportion to the decline in prices.[10] Charles Knight's autobiography states that the average price of a book fell about five shillings from 1828 to 1853 (from 12s 1d to 7s 2½d); one should keep in mind that in the Regency period books were expensive. But even in the mid-twenties in Britain Chambers, Knight, Murray, and Constable were inaugurating the cheaper, smaller volumes, to be soon joined by Pickering and Bohn. The decline in prices was a gradual, astutely managed one: By century's end, the small-format libraries were at a shilling a volume. In America, the fifteen years before the 1891 international copyright agreement were the heyday of cheap reprints, and 50¢ could buy a book of history or poetry. Of course, these reprints represented the lowest-priced works. Holiday gift-books varied in price enormously. In England, E. A. Abbey's illustrated Herrick, in cloth-bound folio, sold for 42s in 1882 ($7.50 in the U.S.). On the other hand, Maitland's two-volume edition of Herrick was 21s in 1823, while Lawrence and Bullens', in 1891, cost only 10s.

The century-long increase in volumes published and the decline in prices reflected rising literary rates, salaries, and amounts of free time. By 1890 a "mass market" for books and magazines had become a reality.[11] This of course meant the ascendancy of the new fashions and tastes which had incubated during Regency times. The use of expensive books as furniture, for example, is nowhere better foreshadowed than by Southey's observations about certain instructions to booksellers; one tailor's consisted only of "the dimensions of his shelves," and one merchant's of a request for "Shakespeare and Milton and Pope, and if any of those fellows should publish anything new to let him have it immediately."[12] Michael Sadlier tells us this period saw the creation of the "outer-suburban standard of gentility which has since become inherent in British culture."[13]

In America, men such as the poet-novelist T. B. Aldrich (editor of the *Atlantic Monthly*), the critic E. C. Stedman, and the editor George Curtis (*Harper's Weekly*) had by late in the century captured a large, and largely feminine, middle-class audience for whom respectable social standing could be equated with sensitivity to stories and poems about romantic adventures in exotic climes, pure-hearted and long-suffering heroines, idyllic pastoral scenes, and deeds of compassionate generosity. In George Santayana's view this "genteel" ethos spawned a bloodless and trivial notion of art and literature; for Malcom Cowley, like Richard Aldington looking back in anger, the genteel tradition dictated that "every cultural object that entered the home was supposed to express the highest ideals and aspirations. Every book or magazine intended to appear on the center table in the parlor was kept as innocent as milk. American women of all ages, especially the unmarried ones, had suddenly become more than earthly creatures...."[14] The perfect symbols of their guardianship of parlor and boudoir were the gold-tooled bindings, gilt-edged pages, and engraved illustrations of the expurgated literature and *au courant* conduct books they displayed for their family and guests.

A book, therefore, whether a copy of Mrs. Sigourney's poems, or Milton's or Byron's, had a certain "aura," originating in its traditional associations with gentility and high culture. In that it was devoted to the arts of genteel leisure, and meant for display, it served as an example of what Thorstein Veblen termed "conspicuous leisure."[15] If expensive, such books were evidence of conspicuous consumption. Since meant for ladies—the guardians of drawing room culture—they exemplified "vicarious consumption," in that the *paterfamilias* displayed his wealth by allocating to his wife its translation into symbols of social stature, the proof of genteel refinement. In all this, there was an equation between dignity and repose:[16] the gentleman had risen far enough above the common herd to allow his wife and daughters to entertain him and themselves with activities which refreshed the mind and spirit and did not serve pragmatic purposes. The delights simply of possessing good books were advertised by the binding, gilt-edged pages, illustrations guarded by tissue leaves, and decorous typeface set down in a generous field of white space. Beyond all these was an even more ethereal pleasure—the poems themselves.

Outside as well as inside the parlor, motives for reading involved a variety of leisure-time activities. Over fifty "libraries" of cheaply and compactly printed classical literature encouraged literary societies, Chatauqua clubs, and what Frank Luther Mott called the short-lived "literary ardors"[17] of the American eighteen-nineties. It should be noted, however, that a final well-exploited opportunity for publishers accompanied a purely instructional need: the emergence of English literature as a compulsory subject in schools meant a demand for standard texts and guidebooks.[18]

The numerous trade editions of *Hesperides* published from 1810 to 1920 tell a curious and genial story about publishers' motives and readers' tastes. For descriptive purposes, I have divided these books into five categories (See Appendix, I). First are editions for the gentleman's study, usually complete works. Second are gift books, meant for display on tables or nooks in drawing rooms and boudoirs. These include "bibelots." The word denotes a small curio or ornament, a conversation-piece for table or cabinet. I use it to designate a third group of twenty-four volumes meant as lovers' gifts (see Appendix I. C. 22-36). The fourth (and largest) group consists of cheap reprints, and the fifth of school texts. In all five groups, the reader will find far more English than American editions. This is not only because Herrick was an English poet but because many English works were published simultaneously in America by arrangement. That the first American reprints (see Appendix, #3) "follow" Pickering's 1846 volumes in style and editing procedures is some indication that American attitudes toward Herrick and what he had to offer the genteel reader paralleled the English.

In the subsequent chapters, and in the remainder of this one, the numbers given in parenthesis after titles of editions of Herrick refer to their entries in the Appendix checklist.

Library Editions

A nineteenth-century library can of course be a private sanctuary as we know it to have been for country gentry like Mr. Bennett in *Pride and Prejudice,* and as it still was well over a century later for Charles Ryder's father in *Brideshead Revisited.* Such a room had tables as well as bookcases in and on which were displayed a man's newspapers, "collectibles," and attractively bound books for "private study": reference sets, the classics, modern fiction.[19] See Figure 2-1. As the century wore on, only the wealthiest could afford to retain such rooms. Writing in 1881, Andrew Lang regretted that libraries, once spacious, are "now shrunk to a bookcase."[20] In late Edwardian Times, Elsie De Wolf considers, in her chapter on living rooms, that otherwise inessential space may become "a library eight by ten feet, with shelves all the way around and up and down, and two comfortable chairs, and one or two windows.... If the room is to be used for reading, smallness doesn't matter, you see."[21]

By the late nineteenth century many "libraries," instead of shrinking, had ceased to become retreats at all and had taken on the functions of family rooms for relaxed conversation and entertainment of visitors. While keeping its name, the library became indistinguishable from drawing, or "living" rooms.[22] In this sense an 1890s library was a necessity in genteel houses.[23] This presented a problem. Many of the books produced before mid-century were not as well suited to the discrete atmosphere of drawing rooms as they were to the masculine speculative climate of "libraries of the curious," as the editor of

Fig. 2-1 An Edwardian Library, with Boudoir in Background. Source: Nicholas Cooper, ed., *The Opulent Eye, Late Victorian and Edwardian Taste in Interior Design* (London: Archiectural Press, 1976), p. 194. By courtesy of the Royal Commission on Historical Monuments (England).

the first reprint of Herrick's complete works put it in 1823, while introducing an edition which carried, verso the title page of Vol. II, a seventeenth-century squib about the poet's superiority to "sowr-ass" Horace. The contrast is noteworthy, because it recurs in comments regarding the rationale for certain kinds of books and their designs. Thus, a reviewer of Hazlitt's 1869 edition suggests that publishers of Herrick should take a new direction. Complete editions were plentiful, but there were not as yet selections for polite company.[24]

Of course, library editions themselves could be designed for more than one kind of room, and for more than one kind of reader. This in fact seems to have become necessary as prestige value shifted, with the ascendancy of middle class literary tastes, living arrangements, and displays of conspicuous leisure, from the library to the drawing room table and shelves. Commercial publishers' response to the process shows their shrewd sense of where a book might be used and who its readers might be. From the 1870s onward, however, their complete editions generated confusion among reviewers regarding the purpose of a volume and the nature of its audience. Thus Edmund Gosse suggests that Grosart's encyclopedic "Memorial-Introduction" be placed by itself in Volume I of his edition of Herrick (see #7) for "the student" so that it "in no way interfere with the pleasant reading of the text." For the general reader, "it is certainly annoying to be buttonholed in the vestibule of a classic."[25] A reviewer of The Muses' Library edition (see #8, 9) questioned the rationale of the scholarly notes for "the intelligent amateur or *dilettante*," who reads "the 'Hesperides' and its classical parallels...as they should be read, in a hammock or pleasant garden." And again, "if the edition appeals to scholars, why should it be tricked out in daintiness and elegance?"[26] Even the practice of modernizing spelling for general readers was noted—and regretted as a miscalculation: "...the ancient form, and peculiar cut even of the types, seems to benefit the character of the poet...."[27]

It was clearer before the appearance of scholarly apparatus which a Grosart, Pollard, or Hazlitt brought to their editorial tasks that the ideal purchaser of a library edition was a gentleman with some leisure to spend on learning about English history or literature and desirous of a well-printed, privately bound ornament. By the 1870s, the situation was complicated not only by more elaborate scholarly techniques but also by the fact that libraries and drawing rooms were combining functions, thus widening and diversifying the audience. The Muses' Library edition, for example, is suitable for both locations. The striking gold stamping on the front covers made the volumes as inviting for lying flat on a table (where visitors would be drawn to admire them) as the equally elaborate stamping on their spines made them welcome additions to bookcases. See Figure 2-2b. One might even conjecture that the "detachable appendix" in which the epigrams were printed could be secreted in the gentleman's study, so, as Grosart puts it, their "sorrowful nastiness" would not offend the rest of the family.

Many library editions were designed for their gentlemen-perusers after either of two models of William Pickering. This London bookseller-publisher was a pioneer, as his bibliographer Geoffrey Keynes records, in the revival of fine printing. He was also a founder of the cheap-reprint movement (being the first to use cloth, thus precluding the expense of rebinding). He and his printer Whittingham the Younger at the Chiswick Press admired the disciplined elegance of the House of Aldus in 16th-century Florence; William Morris and Charles Ricketts owe them much.[28] Hoping that his Aldine Poets series would become the cornerstone of a "Library of the People," Pickering required that "these productions of genius, which exercise so powerful an influence over the heart, should be printed in the same beautiful manner" as had been his series of prose writers.[29] His 1846 Herrick (not an Aldine,

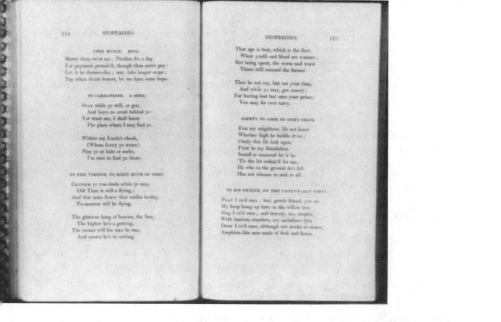

Fig. 2-2a Mise-en-page. *Works (Edinburgh: W. and C. Tait, 1823). (, 114-15. See #2 (Appendix).* (Appendix).

Fig. 2-2b Spine and Front Cover design. *Herrick The Hesperides and Noble Numbers,* ed. A. Pollard. The Muses Library (London: Lawrence and Bullen, 1891). See #8.

considered a cheap reprint; see #39) has a brilliant sense of period style: old face (Caslon) type, original spelling and long s (tied to a following h or t), running titles in caps, italicized poem-titles and proper names, and bold-face two-line initials to begin each poem. The asymmetrical arrangement of text on each page allows for a generous amount of white space. An occasional woodcut, as strongly black and legible as the text, sets off the poems from the front and end matter in each volume. This edition makes an interesting complement to the volumes which Pickering remaindered from a Scottish edition (#2; see Figure 2-2a). This 1825 reprint (#2a) made similar use of white space but was done in modern face, ubiquitous for poetry in the early 19th century.

Most subsequent library editions, perhaps because their printers were without Pickering's antiquarian enthusiasms and Whittingham's resources and sense of period style, used a format similar to that of the 1825 Pickering "Wreath" edition, which was similar to that used for his Aldine Poets series. This is true of the two Reeves and Turner editions (#4 and 6), the Little, Brown (#3, 3a), and its subsequent impressions by Osgood (#3b) and Houghton-Mifflin (#3c-h). These American "British Poets" series, it should be noted, intended that their volumes imitate in content and design Pickering's Aldines. No closer to the Caslon Revival format is that of Bell and Sons (#10); this firm bought the rights to the Aldine series after Pickering's retirement. Only J.R. Smith's Library of Old Authors Herrick (#5) and the Chatto and Windus entry in the Early English Poets series (#7) approximate the 1846 Pickering, the latter volumes especially, with their generous use of white space in margins and leads, their ruled running titles and footnotes elegantly arranged on the page, their occasional woodcut headpieces and initials, and their simple dark blue cloth bindings with paper labels printed in red.

"Selections" for Drawing-Room Tables and Shelves, and Bibelots for Lovers
In the drawing-room, books could have been most prominently displayed around the edges of broad tables. See Figure 2-3a (which shows an Italian, not an English, interior); one views people interacting with each other (the young couple, the discreet chaperone), the arrangements of tables and chairs, and the pleasant wall and table decorations. The painting on the left wall (only partially visible) is of the young lady as a child, with her pet dog. The table in the foreground is covered with books, the one in the center being open. In English and American rooms of this kind, books could also be found in inglenooks, or "cozy corners formed by settees at right angles or near a window."[30] Treated as furniture, their bindings might pick up some of the bright colors in which the walls and floors were decorated. Part of the Muses' Library edition's adaptability to the parlor has to do with its elaborately gold-stamped blue binding. If a publisher wished a volume designed for display, he had a venerable group of samples to draw from, the designs of which made

Fig. 2-3a An Opulent Drawing Room, c. 1865. Source: Mario Praz, *An Illustrated History of Furnishing* (New York: Braziller, 1964), p. 365. Plate 372.

Fig. 2-3b A Living Room, c. 1876, with a Merrie England motif: sculpture in Baroque style, bronze figures in Elizabethan costume. Source: Harold L. Peterson, *Americans at Home* (New York: Scribner's, 1971), Plate 175. By courtesy of the Bowers Museum, Santa Ana, California.

them attractive gift-offerings to the matriarch of the drawing room, the genteel female.

The Album or Keepsake was as much a part of a lady's accomplishments as her singing or conversational skills, and was very popular in both England and America from the 1820s to the '60s. It was often an annual, and its verses and stories were amply illustrated. It was sure to feature fashionably dressed and coiffeured "Kates" and "Ellas" (whose beauty merited one lyric apiece), tubercular expiring maidens, sloe-eyed brunettes of middle-eastern origin, sleeping babies, statuesque ladies gazing beyond casements, or (in white morning frocks) rescuing goldfish from housecats.[31] Throughout, the literature and graphics of these "bowers of magnanimity and delicacy"[32] extolled the domestic sensibility of Mrs. Sarah Ellis' ideal woman. She was trained to appreciate, during her "vacant hours," the sublimity of brooks and streams, and poems which delineate their charm with delicate, elegiac phrasing. Albums provided her with wholesome moralistic and romantic sentiments; with proper daydreams of the kind of gentleman who, for all his resource, could humble himself before amiable females; and with the cast of mind and tricks of deportment which would attract such a man. As for poetry included in Keepsakes, Thackeray's description is apt: "a song upon the opposite page about water-lilly, chilly, stilly, shivering beside a streamlet, plighted, blighted, love benighted, falsehood sharper than a gimlet, recollection, cut connextion...."[33] (see Figure 3-8, an illustration for Herrick's "To the Willow Tree"). But these books accomplished their end, bringing *belles-lettres* under the gaze (if not into the thoughts) of a large number of readers. Their eye-catching virtues included richly-inlaid bindings, or those of satin or silk. Their poems and stories were not only useful as an occasion for flirting and courtship, or as a diversion when dinner was late. *The Drawing-Room Table Book* introduces itself by detailing its most agreeable family-circle function as "an acceptable Present, at a period of the year wnen families meet in social intercourse...."[34] As the *Athenaeum* reviewer recognized in 1844, "Reading with us is our pleasure, our relief, and we must have such literature as will afford us this relief with a pleasureable excitement, without any great expense of thought...."[35]

The publishers' advertisements bound in *The Drawing-Room Table Book* are good examples of the successors of the Annual: travel books, illustrated poetry, children's books, histories. The magazines, especially their Christmas numbers, were another descendant, with their articles on travel, new fashions in dress and furnishings, and illustrated stories and verses. Drawings and photographs of beautiful debutantes abounded. There were also the more specialized illustrated books, which gave some of the best graphic artists their opportunities: Moxon's Tennyson, with wood-engravings by Rossetti, Linton, and Hunt; Birket Foster's *Pictures of English Landscape*; Dore's *Paradise Lost*, Pinwell's *Poems by Jean Ingelow;* Millais' *Parables of Our Lord;* and colorplate editions of *Poems of Goldsmith,*

Robinson Crusoe, The Prisoner of Chillon. and Common Wayside Flowers.[36]

By the 1880s the vogue of Queene Anne elegance, of Dobson, Lang, and the Roundeliers, had begun, as evidenced by Hugh Thomson's witty illustrations evoking the country domesticity of *Cranford*. It was also the start of the career of E. A. Abbey, whose first characteristic work was the *Selections from Herrick* (see #12, Figure 2-4a and Chapter 3). Eleven illustrated editions of *Hesperides* followed over the next twenty-eight years. See Figure 2-4 for some bindings and a title page, which make conventional and fashionable appeals to youthful purity and beauty, springtime delights, and the romance of the past. *A Country Garland of Ten Songs...*(#15) features an art nouveau format: illustrated endpapers with naked male figures intertwined with tree-branches and vines toward which birds flutter; cover and title-page are decorated with sinuous vines and flowers. *Flower Poems* (#17; Figure 2-4b) reproduces the illustration for "To Flowers" gold-stamped on the front cover. Three maidens water with their tears the plants which "flourish" on the poet's grave. The publisher notes (p. 7) that the anthology contains all of Herrick's poems "deal[ing] specifically with FLOWERS, excepting only one unimportant example which the compiler thought not suited to modern taste." The title-page of the "Golden Poets" volume (#18) includes a detailed engraving of the Old Parsonage and church at Dean Prior (Figure 2-4c); my personal copy contains a calligraphic gift-note (dated 1907) to the book's first owner: "Some pages of old Herrick. Something to 'stroll among the alleys' with."

The publishers of *Herrick's Women, Love and Flowers* (#23; Gay and Bird, 1902) made it part of their "The Bibelots" series of pocket-sized volumes. The term is appropriate; as we have seen, books were often considered small, ornamental conversation pieces for table or cabinet. This Herrick volume, and several others like it, seem to be designed as intimate and inexpensive courting gifts, perhaps more likely to be kept in boudoirs than drawing-rooms. They are only partially distinguishable from other books such as Harper Brothers' *Selections*, the Caxton Series Herrick (#16), Palgrave's *Chrysomela* (#41) and other "cheap reprints" to be considered in the following section. I have given them a separate heading in the Appendix, since they emphasize almost exclusively amatory themes. The "Bibelot" Herrick (see Figure 2-5a) organizes its contents into topics such as "Maids, Love, Kisses, Cupid, and Venus"; "To Julia"; "To Electra, Oenone, Prue, and Others." Its decorations include a heavily-lidded female smiling into a mirror, and Venus on a scallop shell. The "Laurel Wreath" edition (#31) prints "Let me ever dwell in thy remembrance" on the half-title leaf, and its decorations include flowers, globes, and a flaming heart entangled in leaf-bearing vines. The "Omar Series" (#29) entry begins with the joys and ends with the sorrows of love. John Lane's "Lover's Library" series[37] (#25; see Figure 2-5b), with stylized flowers decorating borders, endpapers, gold-stamped binding (in either green or violet cloth), and green-tinted letterpress,

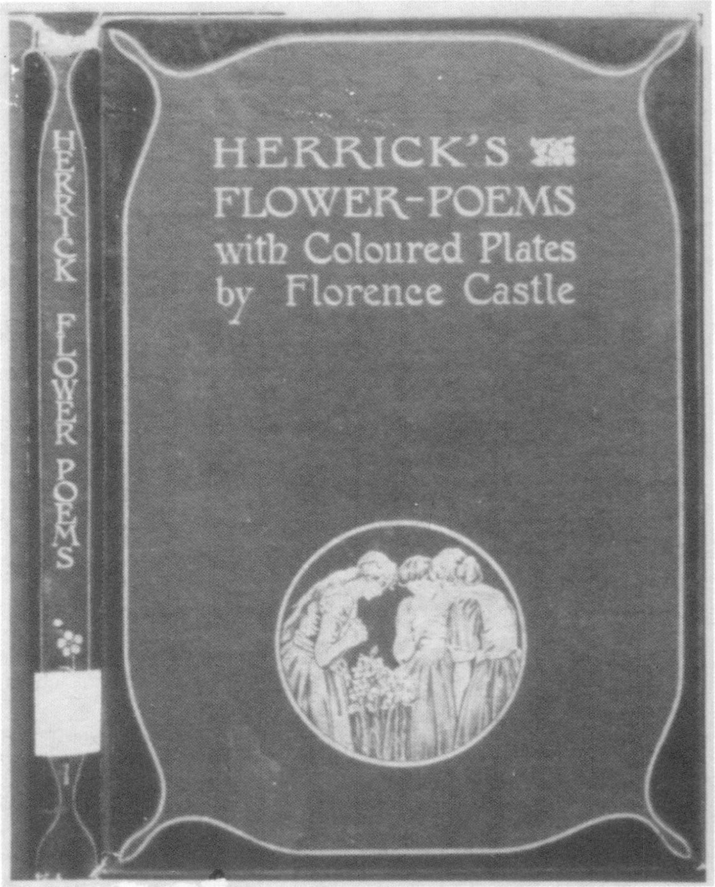

Fig. 2-4b Front Cover Design, *Flower Poems*, ils. by Florence Castle. The Photogravure and Colour Series (London: Routledge, [1905]). See #17.

2-4a Front Cover Design, *Selections...with Drawings by Edwin A. Abbey* (New York: Harper's, 1882). See #12.

Fig. 2-4c Title Page, *Poems of Herrick*, ed. H.C. Beeching. The Golden Poets (Edinburgh: T.C. and E.C. Jack; London: Caxton, [1907]). See # 18.

is high art nouveau. Firms such as Collins, Siegle and Hill, and Gay and Bird marketed such books as "elegant," "dainty" presents, easily mailable to friends and lovers as books-*cum*-greeting cards. See #26, 29, 30, 31. Collins' Clear-Type Press seems to have been the most active promotor of this kind of bibelot. Its Herricks (see #33, 34) may have been part of as many as six distinct series of "acceptable presents" offered from 1910 through the 1920s: "The culture of the age [1911] very rightly insists on a dainty format for the poets...."

Figure 2-3b shows a flower-bedecked living room in a California physician's home in 1876. The bronzed figures (left foreground) are in Renaissance dress; the sculptural group is done in baroque style. The fireplace (not shown) is decorated with an Elizabethan minstrel in tiles, and a reclining nude. The works of a genuine old English poet belong here—in selections. We must recall that "Ariel has sucked not only of the honey-dew of Paradise, but from any nearest flower, however poisonous, and hence the reason that Herrick has now only a partial fame.... Who will introduce [him] into a wider circle and enable him to share the popularity which is freely given to many a feebler poet, and less true a man?"[38] The answer: Harper's, Routledge, Macmillan, Collins, Newnes; Austin Dobson, H. C. Beeching, Paul Woodroffe, Reginald Savage.

Cheap Reprints

Cheap reprints, as gift books and library editions, have their specific locations and uses, as the following review of Osgood's "Vest Pocket series" suggests:

It will render a signal service to letters by lightly bringing to many vacant minds the intellectual occupation they would never seek. It is in compact and available shape a sort of introductory library to the best English literature—a collection to be kept at work-tables and window seats, where all the household may readily find and use it at any odd half-hour.[39]

The emphasis here is not on prestigious social intercourse but rather on instructional and entertainment value to individuals. One is tempted to say— but simplistic dichotomies should be avoided—that these books served serious purposes for real readers, and were not mere adornments for tables and shelves, or for the idly curious who liked to look at pictures or handle fine leather and silk. To say so would be to take a naive view of how imagination and thought are stimulated, and to deny the capacity of graphic artists to complement texts and jog curiosities. In fact, many of the small-format editions were attractively and originally decorated. Another easy conclusion must be kept in abeyance. Was the real *raison d'etre* of the small-format reprint of *belles-lettres* to educate the masses? Why is the reviewer quoted above vaguely contemptuous of readers the Osgood series serves, and of their "vacant" unfocussed minds (and did the homes of the uneducated classes have window-seats)? Just who were the readers enriched by world literature in

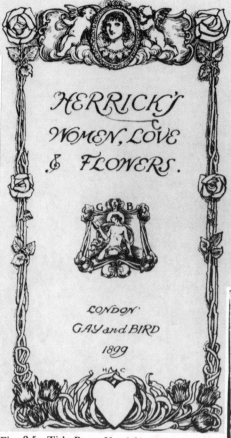

Fig. 2-5a Title Page, *Herrick's Women, Love, and Flowers* (London: Gay and Bird, 1899). See #23.

Fig. 2-5b Front Cover Design, *Love Poems of Herrick*, The Lover's Library (London: John Lane, 1903). See #25.

HESPERIDES;

OR.

WORKS BOTH HUMAN AND DIVINE,

OF

ROBERT HERRICK.

LONDON:
H. G. BOHN, YORK STREET, COVENT GARDEN.
1852.

Fig. 2-6a Title Page and Frontispiece, *Hesperides*...
Bohn's Mineature Classics (London: Bohn, 1852). See
#38a.

Chrysomela

A SELECTION FROM THE LYRICAL POEMS OF

ROBERT HERRICK

ARRANGED WITH NOTES BY

FRANCIS TURNER PALGRAVE
LATE FELLOW OF EXETER COLLEGE, OXFORD

Hic nullus labor est, ruborque nullus:
Hoc iuvit, iuvat, et diu iuvabit

London
MACMILLAN AND CO.
1884

Fig. 2-6b Title Page, *Chrysomela*..., Ed. F.T. Palgrave. The
Golden Treasury Series (London: Macmillan, 1884). See #41c.

cheap editions, which flourished during the late Victorian and Edwardian periods, the time of Herrick's peak of popularity?

It would be pleasant to report that cheap publications greatly refined the tastes of the British and American masses, as the reviewer of the Vest Pocket Series had hoped. But it was the middle rather than the lower classes for whom leisure time was increasingly available and whose tastes were refined enough for even the cheap good books. The laboring classes, not as yet susceptible to conspicuous consumption, continued to read chapbook reports of daring criminals, yellow backs and penny dreadfuls, not the classics.[40] To whom did *belles-lettres* appeal? When the prosperity and complacent respectability of the late nineteenth-century gave impetus to drawing-room, library, and boudoir reading, it was the middle classes who purchased The Leisure Moment Series, The Seaside Library, The Temple Classics, The Canterbury Poets, and Bohn's Miniature Classics (see Figure 2-6a). The attractiveness of such work was in part a response by good businessmen to the gothic novels and hackwork romances which lesser companies were turning out, with their flimsy covers, worn type, and substandard paper.[41] Profits were easier to come by because a Chaucer, a Milton, or a Herrick presented no problems of copyright. Thus, more capital could be put into fashionable book design, and this was a business necessity as well as an aesthetic pleasure. A small-format work with fine typography, headpieces, tailpieces, and fashionably sinuous natural forms of languid classical figures adorning end-papers, title-page, and case binding legitimized the work for consumption by large numbers of middle-class readers. Such a reaction against cheap potboiler throwaways was admirable. It shows that the practice of conspicuous leisure can be the basis for improved taste. *Publisher's Weekly*, in 1880, condemned the "bazaar spirit" of the day: "if literature and art are to be treated as common merchandise [some cheap remainders were being given away as premiums with purchases of soap] it will make commonplace the manners of our people.... Lower the tone of the individual audience and you lessen the dignity of the national character."[42]

Two bookmen especially dedicated to raising this tone were J.M. Dent and Walter Scott. The twelve departments of Dent's Everyman Library series, and his plans to issue fifty volumes at a time, show the scope of his enterprise. "If one began with one creative book [he] would want another and another till the great public had the world literature within his grasp."[43] The design of the Everymans served the attendant purpose of bringing William Morris' innovations in book design to the general reader (see Figure 2-6c for the title page opening of the Everyman Herrick of 1908). One of Walter Scott's earliest ventures was the Canterbury Poets. The advertisement in the Shelley (the second volume published, in 1884) is an accurate statement of the virtues of the series: "...well-printed on Toned paper, with Red-Line Border on each Page, strongly bound in Cloth, with Artistic Design on cover.... The desirabilities of clear and readable type, excellence in quality of paper,

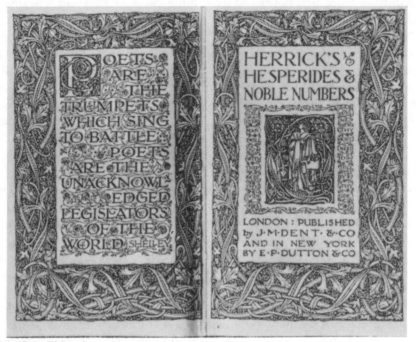

Fig. 2-6c Title mise-en-page, *Herrick's Hesperides and Noble Numbers*, ed. Ernest Rhys. (Everyman's Library, London: Dent, 1908). See #44b.

handiness of size, and elegancy in general get-up, will be combined in such a way as to render them ornaments to the bookcase, or suitable as a series of pocket volumes, while the price will place them within the reach of every reader, however humble in circumstance." Scott's scheme was to combine old favorites with authors not previously available in a cheap series, therefore known "only to a select few." One wonders how exactly a publisher could specify that group of patrons who, familiar with a Herrick, Poe, or Keats, had never heard (but was willing to learn) of Chatterton or Blake. One assumes that in fact this category consisted of a large, general group of middle-class readers and lecture-goers desirous of a pleasant, low-key way to absorb culture, and to enrich their environment with it, by way of elegant, pocket-sized books, fashionably decorated. Among the laboring classes, such works might appeal only to those for whom material circumstances and sectarian piety no longer dictated unostentatious frugality and/or to those who had become aggressively upward-mobile.

Whoever bought cheap editions of Herrick, often for as little as a shilling or fifty cents, enjoyed clever small-format book design, although imitative of the styles of more expensive books. As Grant Richards admits, fashion's bandwagon left in its wake many over-decorated title pages, "fidgety endpapers," and "precious adornments."[44] Osgood's *Favorite Poems* (#40; see

Figure 1-4) has wood-engraved capitals, vignettes, and illustrations (after earlier-published drawings). Macmillan's *Chrysomela* (#41) carries on cover and title page a medallion specifically engraved for the edition (see Figure 2-6b). In Scott's Canterbury Poets Herrick (#43), abundant white space is created by having each poem begin on a separate red-bordered page. The sheets or stereotype plates for this series seem to have been sold to even more distributors than were those prepared for the Jack, Newnes, or Richards volumes, subsequent impressions being bound, as was usual, in a variety of fashions: leatherette, suede, vellum, cloth with paper labels or gold-stamping, leather or half-leather. The Century Classics volume's "beauty of external form" consists of a green cloth binding blind-stamped in an arabesque pattern reproduced in green on the endpapers (#45). Designed by T. L. deVinne in old face with generous margins and ruled running heads, it is pleasant to read as well as hold. The most attractive covers, however, are the work of the Scottish designer Talwin Morris for Blackie's Red Letter Library (#47). The typography succeeds as does DeVinne's, by providing a graceful simplicity.

The editorial methodology of the cheap series is also noteworthy for its adherence to prevailing tastes. F. T. Palgrave selected those "Chrysomela" (golden apples), listed under headings such as "Idyllica," "Nature and Life." "Amores," "Graviores," which exclude Herrick's "blemishes" and best display his wit and sweetness, for the poet should be admired by general readers "whilst the love of beauty, and the magic of the past, two strong powers, retain their hold upon Englishmen" (p.vi). Palgrave's appreciation is obvious from the first edition of his famous *The Golden Treasury* (1861). Feeling that "passion, color, originality cannot atone for imperfections in clearness, unity, and truth...,"[45] he excludes Donne, accords Vaughan and Herbert one poem apiece, represents Lovelace, Suckling and even Jonson by only three, while Herrick merits seven. Palgrave's strategy focusses on ease of comprehension (aided by thematic rather than strictly chronological grouping), propriety, familiar names and titles, and consensus opinion of his peers, all in the service of recreative reading, and "the Wisdom which comes through Pleasure." That such a plan was enormously appealing, and, most importantly, a formula, is shown by the numerous editions of both *The Golden Treasury* and *Chrysomela*, and by the commendations of later anthologists. Henry Morley was one of these, as well as a physician, a lecturer, a journalist and one of the first professors of English Literature. He recommends Grosart's edition of Herrick for scholarship, Palgrave's for "choice extracts," and asserts that his Universal Library *Hesperides* (#42) assures "free reading of Herrick in our English homes" while excluding very little of the poetry: "precisely 728 lines," and two "trivial" changes in wording. The latter prevent mention of "legs" and "thighs" from intruding upon the serenity of parlors; this passage is softened to "height" and "size" ("Upon some Women," l.9).

The Canterbury Poets Herrick is notable for the influence of the Century Guild of Craftsmen in its preparation. Herbert Horne called upon his friend Ernest Rhys; upon Selwyn Image, whose help in editing Horne acknowledges; and upon Miss Beatrice Horne, who, according to Rhys, also had a hand in the editing. This early example of the Arts and Crafts movement's concern for improving public taste was perhaps necessitated by the distinctive approach of the edition, which was to arrange the poems from the carefree early ones, with their "supreme daintiness and touch of Elizabethan conceit," to the later occasional "piercing cries" of "delicate pathos." Horne admits the effort is "fanciful," not scholarly; its excuse is that it is "eminently suggestive." Even more so is John Masefield's, which, although it appears in a bibelot (#27), should be mentioned here. He imagines that Herrick's dream house, nearer London than is Dean Prior, would have a fragrant garden, bouquets in most rooms, and a study—much like that of a Victorian drawing room—with "a few choice books," a wine-cup, "a bronze Bacchus," "a chair for a poetical friend," and a Julia singing in the garden. This does for the seventeenth-century poet what Alma Tadema's genre painting did for ancient Rome. A final editor of note is the Century Classics' T.B. Aldrich, a prime representative of the American genteel tradition and a life-long admirer of Herrick's lyrics, which he praises as "polished as the bosom of a star."[46]

Such were the enthusiasms of those editors (and their publishers) who tried to make their particular cheap editions stand out from others. They and their book designers deserve more credit than they are given. Their volumes, and the gift books and library editions, not only successfully resurrected Robert Herrick, but did so in the course of publicizing a great national literature on a scale never attempted before—or since. The attachments which such bookmen brought their readers to feel for their volumes is clearly stated by Edward Hutton, introducing Palgrave's *Golden Treasury* for Everyman in 1906. He specifies its aura by listing the occasions during which the book brought him personal pleasure and relaxation:

> ...To make beautiful a weary stretch of the road or "when the small rain down may rain," in the inn parlour, or by the fireside in the winter evenings, or best of all in the summer fields among the spring flowers....[47]

Dignity and repose: ideals of aristocratic security put in the service of an upwardly-mobile middle class. The literary appreciations and book designs which incorporated these ideals helped confer status, and, consequently, raised self-esteem. They therefore took strong hold on the imaginations of many readers, creating for them an appropriate setting for the enjoyment of literature.

Notes

[1]Quoted in Frank A. Mumby, *The House of Routledge* 1834-1934 (London: Routledge, 1934), p. 30.

[2]A. S. Collins, *The Profession of Letters: A Study of the Relation of Author to Patron, Publisher, and Public, 1780-1832* (1928; rpt. Clifton, N.J.: A. Kelly, 1973), pp. 195-97; Altick, pp. 281-82.

[3]John Tebbel, *A History of Book Production in the United States* (N.Y.: Bowker, 1975), II, 485; Tomsich, p. 18.

[4]Donald Sheehan, *This Was Publishing. A Chronicle of the Book Trade in the Gilded Age* (Bloomington: Indiana University Press, 1952), p. 16.

[5]Jack, p. 41; James J. Barnes, *Free Trade in Books. A Study of the London Book Trade Since 1800* (Oxford: Clarendon Press, 1964), pp. 107-10, 111-17.

[6]Barnes, pp. 99-100.

[7]James P. Wood, *Magazines in the United States*, 2nd ed. (New York: Ronald Press, 1956), p. 76; Sheehan, p. 41.

[8]Louis Dudek, *Literature and the Press. A History of Printing, Print Media, and Their Relation to the Audience* (Toronto: Ryerson Press, 1961), Chapter 11; see also J. W. Saunders, *The Profession of English Letters* (London: Routledge and Kegan Paul, 1964), p. 214.

[9]Dudek, p. 183.

[10]Sources for this paragraph are as follows: Altick, *Common Reader*, pp. 294-317; Hudson, pp. 307-19; Dudek, pp. 155-60; Barnes, pp. 109-20; Tebbel, II, 481-87; Raymond L. Kilgour, *Estes and Lauriat: A History 1872-1898* (Ann Arbor: University of Michigan Press, 1957), pp. 130-34.

[11]Saunders, p. 202.

[12]Quoted in Mumby, *House of Routledge*, pp. 3-132.

[13]Michael Sadlier, *Bulwer: A Panorama* (Boston: Little, Brown, 1931), I, 113.

[14]*After the Genteel Tradition*, quoted in Tomsich, p. 5.

[15]Application of Veblen's theories to fashion are discussed by Quentin Bell, *On Human Finery*, 2nd ed. (New York: Schocken, 1976), pp. 16-24, 29-42; James Laver, *Modesty in Dress* (Boston: Houghton, Mifflin, 1969), pp. 24-38.

[16]Bell, p. 33.

[17]Frank Luther Mott, *Golden Multitudes. The Story of Best Sellers in the United States* (New York: Macmillan, 1947), p. 83.

[18]Altick, *Common Reader*, p. 308; Mott, p. 84.

[19]Russell Lynes, *The Domesticated Americans* (New York: Harper and Row, 1963), pp. 238-41; Amy Cruse, *The Englishman and His Books in the Nineteenth Century* (London: Harrap, 1930), pp. 210-12.

[20]Andrew Lang, *The Library* (London: Macmillan, 1881), p. 31.

[21]Elsie De Wolfe, *The House in Good Taste* (New York: Century, 1920), p. 154. (First published in 1913.)

[22]Nicholas Cooper, *The Opulent Eye: Late Victorian and Edwardian Taste in Interior Design* (London: The Architectural Press, 1976), p. 17.

[23]Lynes, pp. 231-45

[24]"Herrick," *Every Saturday* (Sept. 18, 1869), pp. 378-80.

[25]*The Academy*, Nov. 25, 1876, pp. 513-15.

[26]*The Athenaeum*, July 23, 1892, p. 124. See also *The Nation*, May 19, 1892, p. 217.

[27]*The North American Review*, April 1857, p. 491.

[28]Geoffrey Keynes, *William Pickering, Publisher: A Memoir and a Checklist of His Publications* (1924; rpt. London: Galahad Press, 1969), p. 8, 14-15.

[29]Keynes, p. 27.

[30]Cooper, p. 15.

[31]Clifton J. Furness, ed., *The Genteel Female: An Anthology* (New York: Knopf, 1931), p. xvii; Ola Winslow, "Books for the Lady Reader, 1820-1860," in George Boas, ed., *Romanticism in America* (New York: Russell and Russell, 1961), pp. 96-97; Cruse, pp. 276-87.

[32]"Everybody's Books: Popular Taste and Clever Enterprises," *The Times (London) Literary Supplement*, May 1, 1937, p. 328-29.

[33]Quoted in Cruse, p. 280.

[34]"Introduction," *The Drawing-Room Table Book*, ed. Mrs. S. C. Hall (London and New York: George Virtue, n.d.).

[35]Llewellyn E. Foll, "Nineteenth Century Gift Books: A Curious Combination of Popular and Elite Arts," in Russell B. Nye, ed., *New Dimensions in Popular Culture* (Bowling Green, Ohio: Popular Press, 1972), p. 25.

[36]Colin Clair, *A History of Printing in Britain* (New York: Oxford University Press, 1966), pp. 231-36; John Russell Taylor, *The Art Nouveau Book in Britain* (London: Methuen, 1966), pp. 37-54.

[37]James G. Nelson, *The Early Nineties: A View from the Bodley Head* (Cambridge: Harvard University Press, 1971), p. 270.

[38]"Herrick," *Every Saturday*, Sept. 18, 1869, p. 380.

[39]*Atlantic Monthly*, Nov. 1877, p. 630.

[40]Richard Altick, "English Printing and the Mass Audience in 1852," *Studies in Bibliography* 6 (1957), pp. 4, 16; Barnes, pp. 116-19.

[41]Tebbel, II, 483-84; Gross, p. 206.

[42]Quoted in Sheehan, p. 36.

[43]Ernest Rhys, *Everyman Remembers* (New York: Cosmopolitan Book Corp., 1931), p. 232.

[44]Richards, p. 33.

[45]"Preface," *The Golden Treasury* (London: Oxford University Press, 1916), p. x.

[46]The phrase occurs in one of Aldrich's letters, quoted in Tomsich, p. 145.

[47]"Introduction," *Palgrave's Golden Treasury* (London: Dent, 1914), p. x.

Chapter 3

> Mr. William Combes of Henley...is the fortunate owner of Joseph
> Warton's OWN COPY of Herrick's *Hesperides*—and he carries this book in
> his right hand coat pocket, and the first edition of Walton's *Complete
> Angler* in his left, when...he enjoys his favourite diversion of angling on
> the banks of the Thames. A halt—on a hay-cock, or by the side of a cluster of
> wild sweet-briars—with such volumes to recreate the flagging spirits, or to
> compensate for luckless sport!
> —Thomas Frognall Dibdin, *The Library Companion, or, The
> Young Man's Guide, and The Old Man's Comfort, in the Choice of a
> Library* (1824)

Nineteenth-century parlor-table books charmed an audience which
associated with chivalric gallantry its own tastes for amatory fantasies, and
looked admiringly (and nostalgically) at the Cavalier age's freedom from the
noise of cities and grime of machines. Imaginations were fired by its
spontaneity of behavior, easy tolerances of quaint eccentricities of character,
and what Herrick called "the harmlesse folie of the time." Here are some very
revealing lines concerning nostalgic reconstruction of the English past,
about "A Gentleman of the Old School" named John Leisure:

> He lived so long ago, you see!
> Men were untravelled then, but we,
> Like Ariel, post o're land and sea
>   With careless parting;
> He found it quite enough for him
> To smoke his pipe in "garden trim"...
> ....
> Not that his "meditating" rose
> Beyond a sunny summer doze;
> He never troubled his repose
>   With fruitless prying;
> But held, as law for high and low,
> What God withholds no man can know,
> And smiled away inquiry so,
>   Without replying.

The poet is Austin Dobson, a close friend of the first, and greatest, period
illustrator we will consider, Edwin A. Abbey, who designed the poet's
bookplate, drew frontispieces for some of his works, and collaborated with
him on *Selections from the Poetry of Robert Herrick* (1882; see #12).

55

E. A. Abbey: "Truth and Poetry"

Dobson's introduction offers the reader an elegant tableau (a fantasy, for Abbey worked in the English countryside, carefully collecting materials during a two-year period) of how the book was created:

> Such an anthology as might grow up in a painter's studio, where, through some sunny afternoon, one reads aloud while the other works, would be the fittest image of the present selection. Suppose afterward that the whole were printed together—the pictures which were drawn, the poems which were read, and the volume before the reader is sufficiently explained. To explain it more fully or more precisely would be to detain him needlessly—nay even discourteously, from the dainties before him. For who but an Ancient Mariner would button-hole a bidden guest when the host is ROBERT HERRICK!

These insouciant sentences, reminiscent of Wilde's description of the "proper temper" for an afternoon's work in roundel and troilet, capture the temperamental affinities between Abbey and Dobson. The book had marvelous reviews on both sides of the Atlantic, and, judging by the printings, an appeal of at least thirty years. Its design (especially "Ye Leaden-halle Presse's" fanciful italics, which equaled for "old-fashioned" quaintness Abbey's calligraphic lettering) and its illustrations kept the tenor of romance, refinement, and appreciation of nature represented in the Annuals and Keepsakes. Also conventional was the choice of poems, which, as Dobson put it, "lean[ed] somewhat to those pieces which deal with the rustic pictures, the old-world pleasures, the simple folk-lore of an earlier and less progress-ridden *England*." However, thanks to Abbey's talents, his training as an illustrator at *Harper's Magazine,* and his exposure in its New York office to the English illustrators of the sixties,[1] these *Selections* relaxed the moral stridency, the sentimentality, and the clutter of decorative detail of the earlier gift books, thus providing a volume in accord with the aesthetic tastes of the eighties.

The binding has recently been described as follows: "Beige cloth, probably designed by Abbey with radiating sun blocked in gold, floating flowers in light olive-green extending around spine and lower cover, lettering in red and black."[2] The art nouveau motif and color scheme is especially noteworthy because it is so early an example and because the illustrations themselves are in the representational mode (although the mixture of styles is in itself not unusual). One explanation is Abbey's membership, while still in New York, in the Tile Club, the *raison d'etre* of which was to carry on innovations in the decorative arts as practiced in England by Morris, De Morgan, and Alma-Tadema. Another is the influence of Macmurdo and the Century Guild. Abbey showed no interest in the Arts and Crafts movement, but he prepared the Herrick book in England, a country whose contemporary artists he had supremely admired since viewing their work at the Centennial (1876) exhibit in Philadelphia. Conversant with London artists and writers, he could hardly have avoided knowing about Japanese prints, Arts and Crafts teaching, and Rossetti's creative designs for cloth-bound books, which substituted simple floating-flower motifs for the then-fashionable clutter of scrollwork, lettering, onlays, and geometric devices.[3] Whatever its genesis, from a practical standpoint the Herrick binding is fashionable and eye-catching, making "gallanty show" in a bookstore or parlor-table display.

Harper's itself advertised this book as a display of "sweet coqueteries and bewildering graces of lovely women, the simple habits and peaceful scenes of rural life,...the social pleasures, the holiday rites and sports, and the fairy and folklore of the times, and a multitude of delicious vagrant fancies, romantic and amatory."[4] This is as accurate as most blurbs (there are some deeply serious poems and illustrations). It is also a strong enticement for those who have leisure to dream about luxurious pleasures, and the resources to buy and to show off elegant books which incorporate such "fancies." This particular blurb is similar to the tenor of Dobson's introduction. As well it should be: Dobson was a popular poet and a shrewd man of letters who knew what people wanted.

The aspects of seventeenth- and eighteenth-century life which successful popular illustrators (Caldecott, Greenaway, Thomson) stressed from the seventies through the nineties focussed on archaic styles of social interaction unavailable to middle-class readers.[5] But popular art gives its patrons the chance to empathize with what they read and see illustrated. Abbey's figures do not wear their clothing or move about in it as do the ladies and gentlemen of veiled eyes and formal gestures in portraits by Van Dyke or Lely. Instead he portrays them as "pretty people" (often with nineteenth-century hairstyle) with whom his audience can identify. Genteel middle-class folk were as fond of dressing up in costumes of the past as they were of looking at historical paintings. A patina of romance transformed the everyday. It is this imaginative sympathy or "masquerading" tendency[6] which Abbey exploits so incisively, not only in his seventeenth-century ladies but in his classical settings and figures. There are only a few of the latter, illustrating brief vignettes such as "A Short Hymn to Venus" and "Upon a Virgin Kissing a Rose." In these one notices the rhythmic balance and statuesque poses of figures drawn by painters Abbey knew and admired such as Alma-Tadema, Leighton, and Albert Moore. In their work, depicting more often domestic idylls than great events, the figures were identifiably contemporary: "everyday Rome," said one critic of Tadema's canvasses.[7] "Drawing-room Cavaliers and rustics," one might say of the figures in Abbey's wood engravings. The mixture of romantic distance and domestic familiarity aids the narrative quality, and allows the viewer to identify with the situation and figures. Mr. Richard Jenkyns notes the "fancy-dress" nature of Tadema's paintings.[8] The viewer can put himself into the picture and imagine people like himself or herself doing what the figures in the paintings do, from the safe distance of the galleries. In the case of Abbey's book illustration, let us substitute for the gallery the living room. What happens in each place is fantasizing, a recreative process like that induced by a fancy-dress ball in which people can assume costumes and roles, without endangering themselves or compromising their social status.

Jenkyns comments, disapprovingly ("too great a concern with roles and costumes might enfeeble the imagination of intelligent people") on the balls Tadema enjoyed hosting: "the artists who painted fancy-dress pictures tended to live fancy-dress lives."[9] Abbey's audience did not, of course, dress in Cavalier costume, but it did put itself in the picture. It could have read aloud or sung some verses, been reminded of its own tastes and attitudes by the words and pictures, or, in a playful moment, mimicked the pose of one of Abbey's figures. Aristocrats (of wealth and/or birth) had not only their fancy-dress balls but their *Tableaux vivants* (in which ladies recreated scenes from antique history and literature) and their amateur theatricals to bring art and life a bit closer to each other.[10] For such people, but especially for their middle-class counterparts, a more sedate but similar response to drawing-room books was possible. Abbey's work provides the kinds of details, and creates the kind of ambience, which can amuse people, or strike them as curious, elegant, or romantic; a facial expression, an attractive window-seat, a beautiful gown, or a picturesque landscape. These details mirror what one sees, or wishes to see, in the people, furniture, or decorations of the drawing room, that carefully cultivated setting for genteel social conduct. What transpired there could be stultifyingly artificial and insincere. There was, however, the potential for intimate communication and for a sense of beauty. The colors, furniture, floral arrangement, music, and pictures with which one feels at ease are expressive of personal identity (as are the illustrations and decorations in books). One can be very comfortable with them, as the designers of volumes for the Muses' Library, the Everyman's Library, the Temple Classics, and the Golden Poets show. Perhaps, this is why Abbey only once (in "To his Muse"; see Figure 8-6) uses a portrait of the poet, although often the speaker of a poem is "Herrick" (i.e., his persona). Abbey could hardly help but be aware of the revulsion Victorians felt at those gross features, which were as notorious as the "indecent" epigrams. The latter make no appearance, and the former are softened by avoiding profile. Abbey's knowledge of his audience is as practical as it is creative. The people he draws are easier to identify with than a chubby, double-chinned man with the air of a "prosperous English butcher."[11]

The media which invite one to playful fantasizing must have social acceptance. As we have seen, volumes of selections from Herrick, introduced by respectable men of letters and edited to replace "legs" and "thighs" with either mentionable parts of the body, or elliptical dots (see Figure 1-1), are such media. Illustrated for drawing-room browsing, such books require of the artist a discretion which does not serve the poet as faithfully as it does drawing-room rectitude.

Study first propriety: for she is indeed the Pole-star

Which shall guide the artless maiden through the mazes of Vanity Fair;
For verily, O my daughter, the world is a masquerade
And God made thee one thing, that thou mightest make thyself another:
A maiden's heart is as champagne, ever aspiring and struggling upwards,
And it needed that its motions be checked by the silvered cork of Propriety:....[12]

The way Abbey is bound by such dicta is evident in his conventional attitudes toward female roles (his women are smiling, elegantly dressed, obliging and chaste), his exclusive use of men in drawings with philosophical point (see "His Poetrie his Pillar" and "The Bell Man"), and his strict avoidance of prurience in his treatment of love. "Corinna's Going a Maying" is a good example of the first and third propensities. In one of the five illustrations, the lover watches from a safe distance as Corinna picks a bouquet of white-thorn from a tree, looking over her shoulder directly at the reader. In the background a man chases a woman through a meadow (see Figure 3-1). An amusing costume drama becomes poignantly familiar to any courting couple at this point. Here is where the viewer's imagination, and his or her fantasizing, comes in. Here, too, the illustrations discreetly end (as do many others in this book, at a crucial point where response to the situation Herrick creates or to the description he uses is inevitable, to be guessed at, and usually amusing). However, "green-gowns" are not given, nor "locks pickt," in an upright position. Abbey's boy and girl must face the rest of their outing unillustrated, and the poem is only half over. Herrick is much franker. His poem is a persuasion to enjoy; its final stanzas deal with the realities of love and death as a reason for love-making. The poet is "pagan" as Abbey does not dare to be. His drawings complement only the innocent vivacity of the first two stanzas. One is reminded of Dobson's statement in his introduction regarding idyllic reveries about "merrie" England. They induce "...a certain obliquity—a certain dishonesty—in our mental photography. One ignores life's dilemmas and limits his perceptions to that pastoral personage...who never lived but in the *Nomansland of Arcadian* unreality." In this kind of popular publication, Abbey's art is a high point of achievement, as one can see by attending to representative illustrations of poems dealing with local color, women, and the ubiquitous nineteenth-century theme of innocence *vs.* experience.

Joseph Pennell thought Abbey the founder of a "school" which included Hugh Thomson and the Brock brothers.[13] What his followers most often imitated was his delineation of "local color," wherein he stressed behavior and charaterization rather than a story line.[14] A good example is the illustration accompanying "To Be Merry" (Figure 3-2). The poem is a lucid, six-line statement of *carpe diem* in monosyllables, with key words repeated ("old, old Age," "evill, evill dayes"). Herrick speaks plainly and directly to his reader, for to waste words is to waste time. Abbey draws a group of open-hearted men and women broadly smiling, and making various gestures of welcome. Two of the three in the front row look, as does Corinna, directly at

Fig. 3-1 "Corinna's Going a Maying." Source: E.A. Abbey, ils., *Selections from the Poetry of Robert Herrick, with Drawings by Edwin A. Abbey* (New York: Harper and Bros., 1882), p. 77. See #12, Appendix.

Fig. 3-2 "To Be Merry." E.A. Abbey, ils., *Selections from...Herrick*, p. 67.

the viewer; the lady on the far left may be just looking askance as a friend taps her on the shoulder. The illustration is as full of quick, sharp movements as is the poem's diction. The folds of the clothing suggest this, as do the hands waving hats, holding skirts from the mud, and lightly intertwining with arms or shoulders of neighbors. The graceful, uninhibited benevolence—which the floppy, flower-bedecked hats, butterfly ruffs, pantaloons, breeches, and flower-decorated pumps make possible as bustles and stove-pipe hats do not—depicts the result of imagining one can take the poet's advice. Abbey conforms perfectly to readers' expectations as created by the literary histories of Gosse:

[Herrick] continues, almost more than any other poet, to fill his lyrics with the warmth of sunlight, the odor of flowers, the fecundity of orchard and harvest field. This Christian cleric was a pagan in grain.... He writes of rustic ceremonies and rural sights with infinite gusto and freshness.[15]

and Lang:

His delightful poems are full of the country life.... His book is like a large laughing meadow in early June...Everything is sweet, spontaneous, glad and musical.[16]

If this was all one could say about this particular illustration, it would be an example of how the artist reinforces conventional tastes in a simply decorative way, without attempting reference to more than the first two lines:

> Lets now take our time;
>> While ware in our prime;
> And old, old Age is a farre off:
>> For the evill evill days
>> Will come on apace;
> Before we can be aware of.

However, this is not the case. For Abbey's dancing men and women, is "old, old Age afarre off"? They are certainly old enough to be experienced, to have known some "evill dayes," and that the same will "come on apace." Their vivaciousness seems a conscious choice, and more becoming for that, since contentment with one's lot is a constant human fascination. As a Horatian, if not as a pastoral, motif, it is based on a mundane experience. In Victorian parlors, where—for the ideal lady—that basic principle of politeness, equanimity, was preached aggressively and practiced (by both men and women) to a point somewhere on the far side of smugness, the philosophy of Abbey's figures is on one hand easy to understand and to identify with. On the other hand, the uninhibited behavior it results in is so different from sober Victorian gentility as to command active curiosity and amused detachment. Imagine frolicking about like that! But it is amusing to see and wonder at, especially when presented with Abbey's refreshing, low-key playfulness. "To

Be Merry's" seventeenth-century people, however primitive, are very real, and are not easily dismissed. Very worldy, they have accepted a basic truth about human experience with equanimity. This brings us back to the tone of Herrick's poem and makes us realize how much Abbey has done with it. For people with the time and imagination to read, and look carefully at, not just display, the Harper's edition, he could start with conventional wisdom and end by liberating imaginations.

Abbey rather self-deprecatingly spoke of his "pretty people,"[17] but even his drawings of young women are individualized in a way that deftly relates picture to poem. This in itself testifies to his originality when one considers the conventional steel engravings and pen drawings of aristocratic fashionable ladies which dominated the Annuals, later the ladies' magazines, and later still the illustrated weeklies, stereotypically displaying the latest "fashionable fair," whom Ralph Thompson describes as "great-eyed, smooth-cheeked, straight-nosed, little-mouthed, small-waisted."[18] For an example used as frontispiece to an edition of Herrick, see Figure 2-6a. A nineteenth-century drawing room audience had a long-standing interest in the gestures and attitudes beautiful maidens were called upon to strike. Thus, in part, the popularity of Tadema paintings, in which "girls whisper together and read letters from young men rather as Keepsake beauties had done in narrative pictures thirty years before."[19] There were also the elegant portraits of Cavaliers, and their ladies, and of fashionable contemporaries in period costume, by Ferdinand Roybert and others,[20] and a low-key domestic scene like Horsley's *A Pleasant Corner* (c. 1869), in which a pretty young woman seated near a fireplace in a room with gothic decor looks up from her book with a half-smile of curious amusement, as if responding to a greeting. I find this and other works by Horsley, "painted...from rural and domestic life with sweetness and elegance,"[21] similar to Abbey's work with the female figure. He meets such popular criteria as these:

Sweetness is to a woman what sugar is to fruit. It is her first business to be happy—a sunbeam in the house, making others happy....

Girls and women are willing enough to be agreeable to men if they do not happen to stand to them in the relation of father, brother, or husband; but it is not every woman who remembers that her *raison d'etre* is to give out pleasure to all as a fire gives out heat.[22]

Abbey's females are often caught in graceful informal poses, and seem to be responding to a reading of the relevant Herrick poem. This tactic and its effect on the Victorian audience is well suggested by Forrest Reid, novelist and chronicler of the illustrators of the sixties. Good illustration had the same effect on him as did poetry; both allow the audience to imagine "that something more which cannot be said, but only suggested, communicated in some secret way, as by the whispering of spirit to spirit."[23] Abbey's work "whispers" engagingly to attentive drawing-room readers, especially women, who, in many illustrations, see their seventeenth-century counterparts responding to situations which they themselves might encounter. "Upon Sappho, Sweetly Playing, and Sweetly Singing" shows a lady in a sunny window-seat, one leg tucked under her, playing a lute and singing with an air of concentration and distant satisfaction, as if obliging the speaker of the poem's pretty compliment. Abbey's figure is accomplished and obliging, and she has a relaxed informaltiy which makes her elegance, and the refinement of costume and decor, much more natural than the magazines' and Annuals' fashion plates. This drawing "whispers" convincingly to its audience about a theme quite relevant to them, female social grace and its effect on men. Whatever the Pre-Raphaelites' "truth to nature" motto might mean, Abbey, who admired their work, certainly does replace formulae with "individual realization," and "sensitive appreciation of moods."[24]

He always does so with a careful eye on his audience. For example, consider Abbey's version of Little Bo-Peep, a pretty shepherdess standing in a copse of trees. She is informally posed like Sappho, but, an outdoor girl, she makes a pleasing contrast to the artificial qualities of furniture and costume in most of the other drawings. See Figure 3-3. Her response to the miniature blazons on her cheeks, eyes, and feet is amused distraction; as she stares at the reader, some of her sheep amble off in the background. Abbey suggests the effect of most drawings and Herrick's poems on the reader of this particular edition: a pleasantly distracting escape, the enjoyment of which may make one a bit silly but which results in no real harm. Another example is the girl in "Delight in Disorder," whose scarf and bows flutter in a wind gust. Her interested but slightly aloof stare is aimed directly at the viewer and works well as a response to an oral recitation of the poem. Suppose a man had just read to his ladyfriend that "A sweet disorder in the dress / Kindles in cloathes a wantonnesse" and that wind-blown petticoats "bewitch" him; the expression on the face of Abbey's maiden may be so much like that of the lady to whom the poem had been read that she and her suitor could share an intimate laugh. Such a response would certainly please the whimsical parson Robin Herrick visualized by nineteenth-century men of letters, as well as bringing out the feminine "sweetness" which "gives pleasure to all."

Herrick's most illustrated poem is "The Night Piece: To Julia."[25] Abbey's version depicts another response of a young woman to the poem itself. It also contrasts innocence and experience: "the theme itself of persons listening to and caught in the reflective mood of a domestic concert is of course common internationally during the 1880s. Abbey's interpretation of this *topos* is his emphasis on the contrast between the innocent enjoyment of the music and the troubled response evoked in experienced older persons."[26] In keeping with the mood of Herrick's poem, he avoids pathos or didacticism. See Figure 3-4. Julia leans forward to hear the song as it wafts toward her through the star-lit night. Both her response and that of the elderly Cavalier at her feet are inscrutable. The clearest contrast is between her youthful

Fig. 3-3 "Upon Mistresse Susanna Southwell..." E.A. Abbey, ils., *Selections from Herrick*, p. 107.

Fig. 3-4 "The Night-Piece, To Julia." E.A. Abbey, i *Selections from ...Herrick*, p. 123.

complexion and alert posture, and his lined face and relaxed pose. He, the aging dandy, has heard such things before. The song is for her alone, and she is capable of being entranced by the magical, benevolent forces of nature (elves, glow-worms, stars) which are its theme. The "Night-Piece" itself is a perfect vehicle for capturing those forces for an ingenuous female sensibility in the nineteenth-century drawing room as well as the seventeenth-century Great House.

R.E.D. Sketchley described Abbey's work as "...a sensitive appreciation of many moods, lyrical, whimsical, humorous, idyllic, but—intellectually, no more than this."[27] This is the prevailing impression of the *Selections*—reinforced, as I have noted, by the introduction, and also by the binding. There *is* more, however; it is as wrong to assume that Abbey is capable only of playful exuberance as it is to assume the same of Herrick. Mortality, for example, was a constant preoccupation of both artist and poet, and was approached by both with dignity and piety (while eschewing preachiness). An example of Abbey's versatility as an illustrator is "His Poetrie His Pillar" (see Figure 3-5). A variation on the eternizing conceit, this figure-poem stands on the page as a pillar-like memorial (a miniature "Pyramides"). The speaker—as so often in *Hesperides,* despite its gaiety and sensuality—feels death's presence ("Onely a little more / I have to write"), and his brave declaration is tinged with irony, for such artifacts as marble and lines of verse are equally vulnerable to natural decay and changing tastes:

> How many lye forgot
>   In Vaults beneath?
>   And piece-meal rot
> Without a fame in death?
>
> Behold this living stone,
>   I reare for me,
> Ne're to be thrown
> Down, envious Time by thee.
> Pillars let some set up,
>   (If so they please)
>   Here is my hope,
> And my *Pyramides.*

The poet lightly suggests that the speaker's blind insistence increases his fallibility, and this increases reader's sympathy, because the speaker has everyman's capacity for self-deception. Abbey reproduces the verses calligraphically, but in two columns, thus spoiling the emblematic effect Herrick intended. The poet's vulnerability is highlighted by having him write by candlelight. An hourglass near his left elbow mirrors that in the decoration below the drawing. In both, the sands are winding down. The candle and hourglass are complemented by the large moon outside the window, its light illuminating details such as window panes and folds of

Fig. 3-5 "His Poetrie his Pillar." Source: E. A. Abbey, ils., *Selections from ...Herrick,* p. 63.

Fig. 3-6 "How Heartsease Came First." Source: E.A. Abbey, ils., *Selections from Herrick,* p. 153.

clothing. Here is an insistent symbol of death and time from the world of nature, bisected by a bare tree and reflected in the still waters of a lake. All this is ignored by the poet himself, preoccupied with writing his poem: ironically, because these icons of "envious time" are just what he is trying to conquer. A careful observer of the illustration, therefore, might become a perceptive reader of Herrick's poem. Both focus on the personality of its creator. He is an attractive figure, although for the Victorian audience quite different than for the Cavalier. For the former he is to be regarded with awe, not whimsical affection. Once again, despite the period furniture and costume, the figure is a nineteenth-century aristocratic gentleman, sure to be admired by those of middle-class status. His dignity, equanimity, and resolution are not exercised with good-humored Cavalier acceptance of fate but in the service of a noble cause. One can adapt Gibbon's famous aphorism to Abbey's nineteenth-century version of nobility, and say that this illustration delineates "the ghost of aristocracy standing bareheaded beside the grave thereof,"[28] and already remembering the deceased not as he was but as the mourner wishes him to have been. Herrick's speaker is a vaguely self-indulgent figure in a very short poem. In the illustration we see the kind of gentleman whom Young England's idealism placed in the pre-industrial past: resolute, intelligent features, weary but proud head, hooded eyes, firm-set lips. We do not smile indulgently at his self-delusion, or even feel that there is delusion involved. There is too much of serious import to take in. In this sense, although the illustrator has thoughtfully attended to his source, he has shifted the focus from the Cavalier ironic wit to Victorian speculations on mankind's destiny and purpose. The romantic past of gallant action and graceful manners becomes, as elsewhere in historical art (and as elsewhere in Abbey's work) vigorously alive because it is made to embody the aspirations of the present.

Abbey leaves open the question of whether in fact a poet can cheat envious time in a different way than does Herrick. There is a romantic sublimity about the picture, and this forces consideration of the quite possible success of the high-minded individual seated at his writing desk, who is a poet like Herrick, whose work had, after all, attained immortality for Victorians. However pleasant and witty Abbey's other drawings are, this one is not to be taken lightly. Nor is it an inconsistency on Abbey's part. The contrasting values of spartan obligation to better self and society on the one hand, and genteel amusement on the other, can both be entertained when one is engaged in comfortable home reading, especially when both are *de rigueur* for ladies and gentlemen.

The *chiaroscuro* effects of "His Poetrie his Pillar" are the more striking for its border, with its vague grey tones. The artist's use of icons, and the clear integration of border with illustration, recall Pre-Raphaelite techniques[29] and even point forward to those of art nouveau graphics. In this example the border's greyness forces concentration on the relation of the sharply-defined poet to the immortal shades who "lye forgot." The scythe, just below his chair, enclosing an hourglass, suggests either that the latter is the Platonic ideal, or the ghostly shadow, of its model, which lies on the poet's desk. He will take his place among the shades, of course, but what of his poem, his "Pillar of Fame," inscribed to the right of the procession of ghosts, in rich blacks like those used to delineate its author? That has survived, to become important to posterity, as much a reminder of the dignity and achievement of the past as are its more tangible architecture, furniture, and manners.

Another delineation of a complex relationship between man and nature, but one which does not encourage viewers to identify with the characters but merely to wonder at them, is "How Pansies or Hearts-ease Came First" (see Figure 3-6). Here the "Frollick Virgins" are shown in an Ophelia-like madness. Abbey adheres to Renaissance notions of pansies as symbolizing fragility, melancholy, and love-fantasies. The women are in classical dress (the poem describes a pagan metamorphosis), with staring eyes and "restless," contorted postures. Their gowns are rumpled, and the elongated diagonal folds contrast to the shadowy background of tree-trunks and bare branches. The effect is one of mysterious imbalance, an impression heightened by the strange perspective of the drawing (an effect noted in Pinwell's work[30]). The trees seem very near the women's heads, and both trees and women seem to be floating just above the indistinct surface. Abbey suggests the fading of the women into nature, an art nouveau effect. One senses an unnatural, ineluctable process of transformation, taking place possibly by moonlight, which catches the folds of the gowns in the foreground and casts most of the maidens, and the foliage, into a greyish haze. Abbey captures the fantastic process Herrick describes. Its benevolence, which the poet emphasizes, the illustrator leaves the reader to accept on faith. He focusses, not on the pathos and sentiment for which Herrick won praise, nor on quaint legends, but on ghostly wonder.

The foliage in this drawing, with its slightly curving tree trunks and sinuous branches, which seem to grow and move from right to left, might adorn a volume of poetry published by John Lane in the nineties. Abbey's study of Burne-Jones and Rossetti is probably its source. Millais' *Ophelia*—the configuration of tree trunks and branches, as well as the theme—also comes to mind. The drawing is another example of the illustrator's versatility.

His most striking, and I think his most serious and resonant interpretation of Herrick's "moral-pathetic" vein, is "The Bell Man" (see Figure 3-7). In this remarkable illustration (which suggests techniques of several Pre-Raphaelite paintings[31]), Abbey creates details of a specific place and time in the central panel, and complements it with smaller rectangular panels above and below, in the manner of Rossetti when, in *The Blessed Damosel* and *Paolo e Francesca*, the painter used the technique to make contrasts between sublunary and eternal time and space. Abbey's central panel calls attention to itself by its inscribed title and white vertical borders,

Fig. 3-7 "The Bell Man." Source: E.A. Abbey, ils., *Selections from ...Herrick*, p. 185.

the left of which shows the suggestion of a frame-like design. The shaft of the Bellman's pike bisecting the composition (as in Rossetti's *Tune of the Seven Towers*) also focusses attention on the detailed night scene and at the same time points toward the top panel. The night watchman is the poem's speaker:

> Along the dark, and silent night,
> With my Lantern, and my Light,
> And the tinkling of my Bell,
> Thus I walk, and this I tell:
> Death and dreadfulnesse call on,
> To the gen'rall Session;
> To whose dismall Barre, we there
> All accompts must come to cleere:
> Scores of sins w'ave made here many,
> Wip't out few, (God knowes) if any.
> Rise ye Debters then, and fall

To make paiment, while I call.
Ponder this, when I am gone;
By the clock 'tis almost *One*.

The first four lines are most relevant to the central panel, and the last four lines also, in a striking manner, for this herald is crying out not only an hour, but a plain, solemn warning which is all the more compelling because of the unexpected implications (for the seventeenth-century villagers, and the nineteenth-century browsers who find themselves at this last illustration in the book). The message of lines 5-10 is carried by Abbey's top and bottom panels and the manner in which they interact with the central one. To take the top first, it looms out abruptly from the darkness with its moonlit bell tower, perhaps tolling the hour as the Bellman calls it out, and its single bird and tree-limbs fragile against the night. Here are universally recognizable symbols of the past, strongly juxtaposed against the detailed particularities of the central panel. The way in which Abbey's audience is made to feel kinship with a distant age is much different in "The Bell-Man" than in the idyllic vein of "To Be Merry" or "The Night-Piece," and equally different from the weird, fantasy-inducing vein of "How...Hearts-Ease Came First." The technique of the illustrator here is like the one he uses for "His Poetrie his Pillar." There is a universal and profound message ("Death and dreadfullnesse call on") to which attention must be paid. Abbey is very much a suggestive artist, not an insistent moralist trading in the guilt or anxiety he could call up with a heavy-handed sentimental treatment. His meaning is carried subtly and elegantly (as Herrick's is by the poem's plain diction and verse rhythms) by the juxtapositions between the immediate and the universal, the domestically recognizable and its symbolic counterpart. These contrasts are completed by the bottom panel with its stars set against the blackness of space, its hourglass, and its curving scythe which sweeps from left to right and back again against the three linked cartouches in which the verses are inscribed. The purpose of the top and bottom compartments is to add symbolic decoration to the realism of the middle panel. The illustrator forces the reader to see the Bellman in the same symbolic, unsentimental light that Herrick attains: as a herald of "Death and dreadfullnesse" to all sinning "Debters." Abbey could have learned these compartmentalizing effects from Rossetti's *Dantis Amor* as well as from the other paintings mentioned above.[32]

"The Bell Man" is from the *Noble Numbers*, and has an implied Christian message: *memento mori*. But Abbey uses no Christian message in his drawing. As in "His Poetrie his Pillar," he stays completely secular, not only reinforcing contemporary feeling about the "pagan" poet he is illustrating, but giving the illustration more strength by eschewing—in this case—conventional symbols and their concommitant emotions. He achieves an open-ended suggestiveness which is of a piece with his drawings of people listening to music, and equally relevant to nineteenth-century broodings.

Abbey's illustrations are suggestive and serious complements to the poems. Above all they show how many kinds of appreciation the nineteenth century, with its unique preoccupations, could bring to *Hesperides*. The artist, a Philadelphian who fell so much in love with England when sent there to gather material for the *Selections* that he stayed the rest of his life, aspired to historical accuracy about his adopted country: "the representation of events not as they might be supposed *poetically* to have happened, but as they might really have happened."[33] But it is neither his delineation of behavior, nor his antiquarian recreation of costume and furniture, from seventeenth-century England that makes his work so much more than a social document. Rather, it is his "poetry": his sensitive delineation of Victorian values and fantasies which attach themselves so closely to these events and artifacts, and to Herrick's lyrics.

Some Imitators of Abbey's Herrick Illustrations

Abbey's ingenious costume dramas and the variety of moods they incorporated engaged the fancy of many readers, but the extent to which they encouraged interest in Herrick himself is difficult to determine, in view of the number of editions, and essays in popular magazines, which had previously appeared. Abbey quite certainly heightened Herrick's appeal for other graphic artists. The best evidence for this, in addition to the illustrated editions which followed as a mass reading public materialized, is the full-page designs which appeared in magazines. James Thorpe, in his *English Illustration: The Nineties,* states that "in looking through these old magazines it is interesting to note how often Herrick supplies a theme for a page drawing, and considering this popularity, it seems strange that so few fully-illustrated complete editions of his poems have been published."[34]

From 1884 to 1917, eleven such books came out, not including reissues of the editions in which the work of Abbey, Elizabeth Forbes, Florence Castle, Charles Brock, and Charles Robinson appeared. This is more than a few—more than one large drawing-room table-full, in fact. The various styles and techniques used to illustrate books like these are foreshadowed by artists working for such magazines as *The English Illustrated, The Sketch, Pall Mall,* and *The Windsor.* Some of this work is influenced by art nouveau, and will be alluded to in the next chapter. The representational mode predominates: country lanes, quaint architecture and costume, and, especially, pretty young women and their Cavalier suitors. Thorpe mentions the work of Stephen Reid, who, "very much under the influence of Abbey, illustrated Herrick in Georgian setting and costume."[35] The most interesting drawings I found were by Cecil Aldin and Robert Sauber.

The former's work reflects Abbey's technique not only in costume-drama setting but in calligraphic reproduction of the text of the poem. Aldin approaches verses such as "Upon Sappho Sweetly Singing..." and "A Ring Presented to Julia" with an anti-romantic wit marked by humorous reactions of domestic animals to what is happening. A basset hound lies patiently at Sappho's feet, either entranced or asleep; for the exotic aura of the verses the dog is either an abrasive or apt antidote, depending on one's tastes. As Julia gazes at her ring, her pet dog fetches a stick and her cat sneaks in at the mullioned window. The animals (jealous of the suitor?) do not erase the poignancy of the moment but rather give it a lively immediacy. When the tenor of the poem admits of no humor, as in "The Mad Maid's Song," Aldin is far less successful.[36] His love-lorn maiden—accompanied, so great is this artist's (and his public's) love of animals, by two geese—wears an expression of vacant-eyed yearning. The goose nearest the viewer may be soliciting pity by staring directly at him or her, slightly open-beaked. Poor Maiden! Poor Herrick!

Some eighteen drawings by Robert Sauber appeared in the *English Illustrated Magazine* between 1893 and 1895. They deliberately mirror Abbey's in choice of poem, and, in six cases, in the poses of the figures and the historical detail.[37] However, Sauber lacks Abbey's depth of characterization and his thematic richness. "Local color" is limited to Stuart furniture and costume (which shows little of Abbey's historical correctness). The poems themselves, or stanzas from them, are reproduced in letterpress, not calligraphically. His women often simper and stiffly pose rather than respond naturally to the good-humored attention of Herrick's speakers. There are some good effects. His "To Phyllis" has an original country setting and a middle-aged pair of lovers. "The Rock of Rubies" dramatizes well the moment of the speaker's comparison of Julia's lips and teeth to rubies and pearls. He captures the fun of the moment and provides an accurate "merrie England" tavern interior.

Sauber, Aldin, and the other period illustrators in the realistic mode do not approach Abbey's subtleties. Their work would satisfy the dilatory interest in culture one might find in those drawing rooms which contained art and literature out of a sense of social duty on the owner's part. They aim merely to amuse in a superficial way by appealing to conventional notions of elegant old fashions, chivalric courtship, and humorous sketches of "high life." It is what one would expect considering the practical exigencies under which the drawings were executed. To rise above these would take an artist of real imagination—one who found commercial illustrated books perfectly congenial to his talents and who respected the tastes and imaginative abilities of their purchasers.

Period Illustration: Decorative Cliche and Caricature

In Harper Brothers' *Selections*, Abbey's illustrations take their place with the other decorative elements which, together with the drawings, recreate the "aura" of seventeenth-century England for Victorian tastes. There are the Leadenhall Press' Old Face type, a variety of headpieces and tailpieces on floral or *memento mori* themes, wood-engraved vignettes of Herrick's church, moonlit reeds, and Devonshire villages and hills. The "greenery-yallery" binding with its floating flowers on a bright, sunny background is as inviting as the title page, on which the book itself is offered the reader by a smiling, elegantly-dressed woman standing before the ornate stone steps of an enormous country house which promises as rich a reward for inspection as does the book itself. As a witty version of the architectural title page, this is an accurate suggestion of the richness of the illustrations. Most of these are full-page, placed recto from the text of the poems they complement, with "plenty of white space"[38] around them. The verso of each illustrated leaf is left blank, so that typeface impressions do not deface them. Their isolation from the pages of letters is absolute; one must remember that most of them appeared first in *Harper's New Monthly Magazine,* where they had to stand alone.

The work of Herrick's other period illustrators was made for the books in which they appear, very largely for the purpose of decoration. They are very indirect comments on the poems (which are mostly verses on love and flowers). However period-accurate the clothing and setting depicted, the figures themselves do not have the individuality Abbey gave his. Instead, they, and the drawings in which they appear, could complement many kinds of love poetry with conventional, universal statements on courtship. The illustrators conceive their assignments in a more general and less imaginative way than did Abbey. They try simply to set before the reader an idyllic view of earlier English history and a general background for the universal allure of "women, love, and flowers."

The first of these, and from some stand points the most interesting, is *Favorite Poems of Herrick,* published in Boston in 1877 (see #40). Of "vest pocket" size, it nevertheless finds room for old face type, decorated initials, vignette headpieces and tailpieces (flowers, vines, wreaths) which, like the initials, are reminiscent of Chiswick Press devices for the Aldine series of Pickering and Bell and Daldy. The publisher's advertisement suggests that the book was made for reading while on a train, or sitting before a fire. The reviews cited praise the Vest Pocket Series as "dainty" and "companionable." One blurb proclaims that "queen Mab could be fancied wisely perusing such fairy-like tomes, as she lazily lounges in a white lilly hollow." This may be especially silly, but it does suggest that the design is in keeping with the kinds of experiences poetry represents—intriguing, exotic, or pleasantly recreative. The book's presswork and decoration adapt a time-honored format for poetry to a pocket-sized volume. The four scenes depicted in wood engravings are easily recognizable accompaniments for Herrick's poems, or for those of many another author. In fact, they probably were part of Osgood and Company's office stock. Three of these simply set the poetry with generally relevant designs. Interestingly, even so casual a practice fulfills Charles Ricketts' concept of illustration as "an accompaniment of gesture and decoration, perhaps also an added element of visual poetry."[39] The frontispiece, a scene of sheep grazing in a sunny meadow, is inscribed with a few lines from "The Country Life, To...Porter...," but not related to that poem any more than to any other praise of country security. The illustration for "A New Years Gift...," showing "Jacobethan" conviviality and the "groaning board" theme, however familiar to Victorian audiences as embodying the spirit of Christmas generosity, no more closely relates to the poem it accompanies than does the frontispiece (see Figure 1-4). The same is true of the decoration for "To the Rose": the two Cupids laboring under an oversized rose wreath are copied from Sampson and Low's *Shakespere's* [sic] *Songs and Sonnets* (1863), illustrated by John Gilbert.

The other wood engraving is for "To the Willow Tree." Here the illustrator tells a story which "carries a little further" (as Abbey would put it) the theme of the poem and is interesting to consider in the context of the 1882 *Selections* and of the earlier, drawing-room books of the Keepsake variety. See Figure 3-8. It is modelled after Francis Danby's "Disappointed Love," and shows a woman sitting, hands on knees, weeping by the bank of a stream. Moonlight is on her back, on the trunk of the willow, and on its leaves, which hang down toward the weeping figure, focusing attention on her and on the natural benevolence of the willow tree as a source of comfort for deracinated lovers.

> And underneath thy cooling shade
> (When weary of the light)
> The love-spent Youth, and love-sick Maid,
> Come to weep out the Night.

The engraving is well executed and suggestive. It does more than decorate; it specifically aids a "moral-pathetic" interpretation by suggesting a healing power in nature and the submerging of grief in "favour and prettiness." It is for an audience which, like Abbey's, appreciated refined sensuality and a fanciful view of the purity of nature. Wherever these sentiments are indulged, around fireplaces or in railway carriages, old face type and wood-engraved decorations further help produce an aura reminiscent of the gallant Stuart times. The significant difference between all of the *Favorite Poems'* illustrations and Abbey's is that the former retain more of the emphasis on social duties (the groaning board), emotive intensity (the weeping maiden), and romantic commonplaces (Cupids bent under loads of flower-wreaths). This is the *ethos* of the Annuals, the Keepsakes, and the Ladies' Magazines; Abbey's work (as we have said) is in a more low-key, "aesthetic" style. The Edwardian period illustrators, although much less ambitious, follow his lead in this respect.

Bessie Nicoll's *Let's Go A-Maying* (see #14), also reminiscent of Keepsake sentiment, consists of only a few pages of calligraphic text. There is an over-abundance of flowers, birds, and tree-limbs interwoven with the letters, and a few picturesque country landscapes and half-timbered houses, out of which come dancing and singing boys and girls. Nicoll avoids, as Abbey does in this

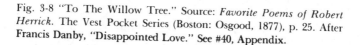

" And underneath thy cooling shade
When weary of the light."

Fig. 3-8 "To The Willow Tree." Source: *Favorite Poems of Robert Herrick*. The Vest Pocket Series (Boston: Osgood, 1877), p. 25. After Francis Danby, "Disappointed Love." See #40, Appendix.

case, any implications of Herrick's final stanzas. This is the artists' version of the editors' expurgations, and is honored in Edwardian editions as well. But this is all Nicoll has in common with Edwardian illustrators. Their touch is lighter and their sense of design more sophisticated.

The "Laurel Wreath" Series had been running for almost twenty years when C. E. Brock contributed four color illustrations for its *Love Poems from Herrick* (1910; see #31). The liberal decorations (flowers, bells, globes entwined with vine-leaves, laurel wreaths, flaming hearts) suggest that love is both joyful and sorrowful, in any event sensual and irresistible. They are symbols of the triumph of Love the Conqueror. The book's half-title motto is "let me ever dwell in your remembrance." Brock's illustrations, done with a playful light touch, keep love and its exotic fantasy-world clearly in view. His art is in the tradition of Caldecott, Abbey, and Thomson, and his period costume is meticulously exact. He specialized in literary subjects, and was especially good at picturesque manners and costume.[40] All of these qualities serve him well in the Herrick book. His figures are not Abbey's individuals, but types of young lovers, posed against the colors of sunlight and moonlight, and the flowers, stone benches, and footpaths of an old garden: a universally-suitable, even mythological setting for lovers, whose grace, dignity, and costume are perfect for a Garden of Venus and embody the spirit of romantic love, with its trials and promise of fulfillment. In this way, the figures symbolize what the decorations themselves do: love's trials, and Cupid's triumphs.

Brock interprets "The Night Piece: To Julia" much as Abbey does, by suggesting the magical qualities of the song. He shows the sprites pointing the lady's way and summoning a star-shower as one of their number bows before her. The lover lurks in the background, behind a balcony railing. Julia's expression is inscrutable, but exotic moonlit beauty sanctions romance. Brock's "The Wounded Cupid" is not about a bee-stung child complaining to his goddess-mother but about how forlorn and half-comic is the disappointed Cavalier who knows (to quote the legend) "how great's the smart / Of those thous woundest with thy dart." A pink-covered book languishes in the lover's hand as a pink cupid peeks over the wounded one's shoulder. The scene should give any courting couple a good laugh; perhaps if so, they will read the poem, which evokes a similar spirit of fun, but with which the artwork has little in common save its playfulness. The same can be said for "Gather ye rosebuds while ye may" (see Figure 3-9a), which phrase the gentleman whispers into his lady's ear. The illustration carries no hint of *carpe diem*. Like the others, it is not meant as interpretation, but as a picture in which all lovers can envision themselves, for it depicts what all lovers do, and hints at how they feel.

Brock's drawings provide witty decorations, and that is all they were meant to be. In the same vein are Elizabeth Stanhope Forbes' watercolors for T. C. and E. C. Jack's "Golden Poets" edition of 1907 (reissued in part in 1910; see #18 and 19), except that the Golden Poets Series has frontispiece and title page vignette by another hand and a largely undecorated text. Edwardian commercial editions usually did not emphasize a harmoniously designed book for which a single artist could take credit.[41] Mrs. Forbes specialized in realistic figure and landscape, and in literary and historical subjects. She was one of the contributors, along with Ricketts, Du Maurier, and Thompson, to the first issue of *Black and White* (Feb. 1891).[42] Her talents are similar to those of Abbey and Brock; as an illustrator for the Golden Poets she was also in good company. Jessie M. King did the series' Spenser and Shelley editions. Mrs. Forbes, however, worked in the representational mode.[43] Most of her eight illustrations are for love poems with floral imagery. They feature graceful girls, in costume less meticulously period-accurate than Brock's, receiving the compliments of Herrick's poems. Her "Gather ye rosebuds..." makes the female figure more active, and also a bit more the center of the picture, due to posture and the color of the dress. See Figure 3-9b. The drawing's rhythms are a compound of the contrasting colors and the girl's graceful, yielding posture. For both artists the background is important, but flattened and stylized: in Brock's case by the lettering in scroll-work, in Forbes' by the indistinct perspective (just where, in relation to the house, are the couple standing?) and neutral tones. In fact, Brock's garden looks like a stage backdrop. The book's purpose as a lover's gift, and the masquerading or play-acting tendency to which such volumes lend themselves, is well served thereby. A lady and her lover, coming across this poem, and putting themselves in either Brock's or Forbes' picture, are responding as would actors on a stage, and making the poem relevant to their own mood.

Even with their legends, both water-colors, as universally acceptable decorations to love poems, are not particularly related to *carpe diem* and Herrick's insouciant acceptance of mortality. "Gather ye Rosebuds," more than any other phrase in Herrick, has worked its way into the popular imagination, as is evidenced by Figure 3-9c, a stained glass window executed in 1906. The illustrations of Forbes and Brock evoke universal images of love and beauty (not ephemerality). For this purpose it is right that they be just as tangential to the poem itself as is the window. Both surround a graceful and somewhat aloof woman with delicate colors and flowers, and, with their flatness of background, move in the style of decoration that the art nouveau window does.

"Herrick's Women, Love and Flowers," an apt title for any illustrated collection of *Hesperides,* would have been equally relevant to a group of introductions by W. E. Henley, Lang, Alice Meynell, Swinburne, and Agnes Repplier, as it would have been to Florence Castle's *Flower Poems* (see #17, and Figure 2-4b). For gift-books, the subject of flowers has been almost as popular as the subject of love,[44] and Routledge's "Photogravure and Colour Series" makes itself special by its thick, imitation-vellum pages and a typeface similar to Morris' Golden. The poems are set with large leads between the lines, and with large margins. Other volumes in this series have art nouveau illustrations (Jessie King, Gilbert James). For the purposes of Messrs. Routledge and Jack, the difference in philosophy and technique between artists they commission for their series is apparently not important. For the kinds of decoration the gift-book style requires, both are suitable, and the techniques do tend to merge (as the example of the stained-glass window shows). Castle employs costume and Garden of Venus setting as do Brock and Forbes, but with less antiquarian detail and period color. Four of Castle's illustrations use art nouveau techniques and will be considered in the following chapter. A fair example of the other eight is "The Primrose" (see Figure 3-10). The poem's speaker suggests the too-early ripeness usually associated with this flower, and the tenuousness of his own plea for his lady's favor. That "the sweets of love are mixed with tears" is not connoted by the illustration, the lady of which seems to be thinking of perpetrating the "he

Fig. 3-9b Elizabeth Stanhope Forbes, ils., *Poems of Herrick*.... The Golden Poets (Edinburgh: T.C. and E.C. Jack, 1907), facing p. 54. See #18.

Fig. 3-9a C.E. Brock, ils., *Love Poems by Robert Herrick*, The Laurel Wreath Series (London: Nister, [1910]), facing p. 24. See #31.

Fig. 3-9c Stained-glass window by Alex Gascoyne, 1906. Source: Geoffrey Warren, *All Colour Book of Art Nouveau* (London: Octopus Books, 1972), p. 9.

Fig. 3-10 "The Primrose." Source: Florence Castle, ils., *Herrick's Flower Poems,* The Photogravure and Colour Series (London: Routledge, 1905), facing p. 38. See #17.

loves me, he loves me not" ritual upon the daisy she is holding.

None of the period illustrators except Abbey are capable of doing the kind of work which fills the 1882 Harper's volume. The latter has, nevertheless, many of the kinds of decorations the other books we have been discussing feature. They are used as vignettes to lend an air of sumptuousness, while the illustrations complement the poems with imaginative narrative *tableaux*. The contrast, and Abbey's priorities, are made clear by considering page 28, on which appear the texts for "Upon a Bed of Tulips" and "Upon a Virgin Kissing a Rose." Abbey did decorate the former poem (in *Harper's* for April, 1879), but for the book he uses on the facing page a drawing of a statuesque young woman bending over a wreath of flowers, an illustration which suggests carefully the spirit of ingenuous fancy and ethereal beauty which the latter poem inspires. This artist consistently seeks, and attains, a dimension that other period illustrators in the realistic mode seldom aspire to.

Notes

[1] Lucas, I, 26, 29.

[2] Eleanor Garvey, *The Turn of a Century* (Cambridge, MA.: Houghton Library, 1970), p. 108.

[3] Ruari McLean, *Victorian Book Design and Colour Printing* (London: Faber and Faber, 1963), p. 158. For a Herrick binding similar to Abbey, submitted to a competition, see *The Studio* 13 (1898), p. 115.

[4] *Harper's New Monthly Magazine*, January 1883, p. 315.

[5] Percival Muir, *Victorian Illustration Books* (New York: Praeger, 1971), p. 199; Simon Houfe, "The Return of the Eighteenth Century," *A Dictionary of British Book Illustrators and Caricaturists 1800-1914* (Woodridge, Suffolk: Baron Publishers, 1978), 184-201.

[6] Helen Roberts, "Victorian Medievalism: Revival or Masquerade," *Browning Institute Studies*, 8 (1980), p. 38.

[7] Robert de la Sizeranne, quoted in Jeremy Maas, *Victorian Painting* (New York: Putnam, 1969), p. 182.

[8] Richard Jenkyns, *The Victorians and Ancient Greece* (Cambridge: Harvard University Press, 1980), pp. 317-26.

[9] Jenkyns, p. 320.

[10] James Laver, *Modesty in Dress* (Boston: Houghton-Mifflin, 1969), pp. 93, 104.

[11] Marchette Chute, *Two Gentle Men: The Lives of George Herbert and Robert Herrick* (New York: Dutton, 1959), p. 246.

[12] C. S. Calverley, "Of Propriety," *Verses and Translations*, quoted in James Laver, *Victorian Vista* (London: Hulton Press, 1954), p. 25.

[13] See Houfe, p. 194.

[14] Frank Weitenkampf, *The Illustrated Book* (Cambridge: Harvard University Press, 1935), p. 195; G. Mortimer Marke, "Edwin Austin Abbey: Painter or Illustrator," *Arts and Decoration*, December 1911, pp. 60-62.

[15] Edmund Gosse, *English Literature, from Milton to Johnson* (New York: Macmillan, 1903), p. 58.

[16] Andrew Lang, *History of English Literature from Beowulf to Swinburne* (London: Longmans, Green, 1913), p. 344.

[17] Kathleen Foster, "The Paintings," *Edwin Austin Abbey: An Exhibition Organized by the Yale University Art Gallery* (New Haven: University Printing Service, 1973), p. 5.

[18]Ralph Thompson, *American Literary Annuals and Gift Books 1825-1865* (1936; rpt. New York: Archon, 1967), p. 48.

[19]Geoffrey Hemstedt, "Painting and Illustration," in Laurence Lerner, ed, *The Victorians* (London: Methuen, 1978), p. 148.

[20]Louise D'Argencourt and Douglas Deruick, *The Other Nineteenth Century* (Ottawa: National Gallery of Canada, 1978), p. 176.

[21]Maas, p. 233.

[22]Rev. E. J. Hardy, *Manners Makyth Man* (1887), quoted in Laver, *Victorian Vista*, p. 29.

[23]Allen R. Life, ' "Poetic Naturalism': Forrest Reid and the Illustrations of the Sixties," *Victorian Periodicals Newsletters*, 10 (June 1977), 53.

[24]R. E. D. Sketchley, *English Book Illustration of Today* (London: Kegan Paul, 1903), p. 66.

[25]The other illustrators are Paul Woodroffe (1897), Reginald Savage (1903), C. E. Brock (1910), Daphne Allen (1917), and George Wharton Edwards (in *A Book of Old English Love Songs* [N.Y.: Macmillan, 1897], facing p. 94).

[26]Michael Quick, "Abbey as Illustrator," *Edwin Austin Abbey: An Exhibition*, p. 34.

[27]Sketchley, p. 66.

[28]See James Laver, *Victoriana* (New York: Hawthorne Books, 1966), p. 18.

[29]See Quick, p. 26. Sketchley, p. 67, says "Abbey's drawings represent traditions brought into English illustration by the Pre-Raphaelites and developed by the freer school of the sixties."

[30]John Russell Taylor, *The Art Nouveau Book in Britain* (London: Methuen, 1966), pp. 46-48.

[31]The date is 1878, when Abbey was working and studying in New York, before he was sent to England. His enthusiasm for the Pre-Raphaelites must have been at its height at this time.

[32]Timothy Hilton, *The Pre-Raphaelites* (New York: Abrams, 1970), pp. 97, 105.

[33]Lucas, I, 189.

[34]James Thorpe, *English Illustration: The Nineties* (London: Faber and Faber, 1935), p. 142.

[35]Thorpe, p. 176, reports these to be in *The Windsor*, Vol. 11. I did not find them there, or in any other of the first 20 volumes.

[36]See, in *Pall Mall Magazine:* "The Mad Maid's Song" and "Upon his Spaniel Tracie," 2 (Nov. 1893 — April 1984), p. 480 and facing p. 85; "Upon Sappho Sweetly Playing," and "A Ring Presented to Julia," 7 (Sept. — Dec. 1895), p. 469 and p. 311. "Christmas Eve A Ceremonie" is in the Christmas number of *The Sketch.* It is reproduced in Thorpe, plate 19.

[37]These poems appear as follows: In Vol. 11, 1893-94: "To Phyllis," Dec., p. 206; "Mrs. Eliz. Wheeler," Dec., p. 242; "The Shower of Blossoms," Dec., p. 252; "To the Rose," Jan., p. 376; "Upon Julia's Clothes," Jan., p. 434; "To be Merry," Feb., p. 22; "Delight in Disorder," Feb., p. 506; "Mad Maid's Song," March, p. 576; "Rock of Rubies," July, p. 990; "Apron of Flowers," Sept., p. 1108; "Parcae," Sept., p. 1198; "Bracelet to Julia," Oct., p. 64.

In Vol. 12, 1894-95: "To be Merry" ("The Toast"), Nov., p. 50; "To Dianeme," Dec., p. 41; "Born was I to be Old," Jan., p. 40; "Corinna's Going A Maying," Feb., p. 31.

In Vol. 13, 1895: "To his Muse," May, p. 146; "Love Lightly Pleased," April, p. 56.

[38]David Bland, *A History of Book Illustration* (Cleveland: World, 1958), p. 301.

[39]Quoted in Taylor, p. 84.

[40]Geoffrey Holme, *British Book Illustration Yesterday and Today* (1923; rpt. Detroit: Gale Research, 1974), p. 32.

[41]Walter de la Mare's article ("Robert Herrick," *The Bookman*, May 1908, pp. 51-56) reproduces in black and white several illustrations from this edition. For commercial illustrated editions, see Taylor, p. 140.

[42]Thorpe, p. 78.

[43]Ralph Peacock, "Modern British Women Painters," in Walter Sparrow, ed., *Women Painters in the World* (1905; rpt. New York: Hacker Art Books, 1976), p. 70. See also Christopher Wood, *Dictionary of Victorian Painters* (Suffolk, England: Antique Collectors Club, 1971), s. v. "Forbes, Mrs. Stanhouse (Miss Elizabeth Armstrong)."

[44]Thompson, pp. 16-17. See, for example, two color plate books, Frances S. Osgood, ed., *The Poetry of Flowers and Flowers of Poetry* (New York: Riker, 1848), with an epigraph from Herrick and Susie Skelding, ed., *Flowers From Sunlight and Shade. Poems Arranged and Illustrated* (New York: White, Stokes, Allen, 1885), with "To Daffodils," accompanying the illustration of this flower.

Chapter 4

Herrick and Art Nouveau: A Discreet Ramble through a Fashionable Elysium

> Robert Herrick...pursued the uninterrupted and serene tenor of his
> pastoral way, and produced charming, flower-bedecked madrigals, dreamy,
> half-pagan warblings, little heeding that his native land was being swept by
> the violence of war.... One cannot conceive of Milton...reclining, as a
> Sybarite, on a bed of rose leaves, while fairies and sprites and classical
> divinities, with wands and garlands and crowns, flitted through groves of
> emerald verdure...redolent with subtlest perfume, and illuminated by a
> light that never was on land or sea.'
> —Charlotte Newell, "A Seventeenth Century Singer," *Sewanee
> Review*, 13 (April 1905), 200.

One might expect to find Herrick much appreciated by the *avant garde*
poets of the nineties (Dowson, George Moore, Lionel Johnson, Wilde), by
writers from whom they drew their inspiration (Swinburne, Pater), and by art
nouveau book artists (Charles Ricketts, Beardsley, Laurence Houseman,
"Alastair"). Herrick's lapidary effects were common knowledge, and analysts
of poetic genres acknowledged his "pure" lyric intensity[1] (an example of art
for art's sake, in that discursive irrelevancies were avoided). Decadents as well
as Roundeliers praised disinterested formal precision, exemplified in the
Emaux et Camees (Enamels and Cameos), published by one of their masters,
Theophile Gautier, during the Siege of Paris. Pater's fascination with a
languorous, tenuous sensuality, and his intense appreciation of rare
moments of beauty inspired by flowers, gems, patterns of sunlight, and the
sounds and movements of pagan ritual, remind us of Herrick. Lionel
Johnson's and Ernest Dowson's interest in the sensuous beauty of religious
ritual is somewhat analogous to Herrick's use of Roman ceremonies to teach
his mistresses to partake with him in "cleanly-wanton" lovemaking, and to
care for him *in extremis*. The *fin de siecle* dandy cultivated detachment from
moral idealism and heroic intensity, and a stoic acceptance of the
ephemerality of all human effort and attainment. Could he not have found
congenial Herrick's equanimity, and his dalliance at Dean Prior while his
king and country were losing the Civil Wars? Pagan mythology was
important to Swinburne and George Moore, who, to achieve idiosyncratic
and very sensual effects, synthesized from a variety of antique sources.
Probably no statements from nineteenth-century critics are more common
than those regarding Herrick's pagan sensibility, and his original uses of
Catullus, Anacreon, Horace, and Martial. The freedom of the Renaissance

artist in adapting Greek and Roman themes inspired Lucien Pissarro, Charles Ricketts, and Walter Crane to illustrate editions of Jonson's poems, Marlowe's *Hero and Leander,* Spenser's *Faerie Queene* and *The Shepheardes Calendar,* and Drayton's *Nymphidia* with a special concentration on pastoral motifs and faerie. Herrick's ability to locate mankind in a pristine natural setting would make him, one would think, a similarly attractive subject, as would his use of folklore and both English and Roman ceremonials.

The parallels are inexact, of course, as any analogies between poets of different periods are bound to be. One does not find Herrick drawn to a love of decay and morbidity. He is an active pursuer of "love, liking, and delight," not a passive diletante, and his sexual fantasies are exclusively heterosexual. He projects the temperament of a happy, simple, healthy man, as opposed to, for example, Dowson, of whom Prof. Miyoshi remarks "had he been born a couple of hundred years before, he might have passed for Robert Herrick, celebrating the joy of passing beautiful things, but being in and very much of his time in the late nineteenth century, he simply could not resist violating these lovely things before they came to flower."[2] These contrasts in themselves would not preclude the Decadents being interested in Herrick. Posterity always sees what it needs or wishes to see in the past. However, in Herrick's case, conventional men of letters had preceded *avant-garde* writers to the reshaping by about three generations. Perhaps for this reason, poets of the nineties did not pay much attention to him, although they could have found parallels to their own stylistic and temperamental affinities at least as provocative as the ones they did seek in Villon, Blake, and Keats. Only a few "decadent" references to the author of *Hesperides* exist. The first is in the 1894 *Yellow Book,* on "Parson Herrick's Muse,"[3] celebrating drunkenness as particularly winsome in a clergyman. Another is Richard Le Gallienne's wierdly funny "Julia's Clothes," in which the girl takes off her dress and petticoats only to find the speaker in the poem doting not on her nakedness but rather on the sight and odors of the garments themselves.[4] In the same coy *epater le bourgeois* spirit is Ernest Rhys' introductory "Toast" in *The Book of the Rhymers' Club,* where he defiantly advocates the moral supremacy of "queen Rhyme" in the spirit of "roystering" attributed to Jonson and Herrick.[5] All three poems are but passing nods to what Taine, William Allingham, and Lionel Johnson ("Lovelace, adorable and vile") noted as "Cavalier blackguardism."[6]

It was with more "respectable" intentions than those of the Decadents that Herrick was approached. When investigating his art nouveau illustrators, we need to keep in mind that they were aware of the middle-class tastes of their late Victorian and Edwardian audience. In the case of *Hesperides, avant-garde* attitudes were tempered (if not completely submerged) by "conventional" aesthetic standards (i.e., acceptable to polite society). In order to understand how these operated, we need to consider the literature and book design in the context of fashions in furniture, bibelots, and clothing; the appurtenances of genteel manners which can be classified, in 1880, 1895, or 1910, as "aesthetic." As we have seen in the case of Abbey and other period illustrators, with their delineations of Cavalier gallantry, courtship rituals, and quaint furniture and costume, social aspirations become entangled with, and help define, aesthetic values. This is true especially when drawing-room gift books, and the ways they focus attention on accepted values in literature and graphic art, are at issue.

"Aesthetic" Fashions: Furniture, Dress, Bibelot, and Books

"Aestheticism," during the last three decades of the nineteenth century, meant harmony, order, and simplicity associated with Japanese and ancient Greek art, and British design of the Queen Ann period. These three were often haphazardly mixed together. Max Beerbohm speaks of 1880-84 as a time when "...the spheres of fashion and of art met" and when "Peacock feathers and sunflowers glittered in every room, the curio shops were ransacked for furniture of Annish days,... [and] a few smart women even draped themselves in suave draperies and unheard-of-greens."[7]

"Japonaiserie" included prints with flat colors, two-dimensional perspective, and asymetrical arrangement, elegantly crafted lacquer and metalwork, blue and white porcelain, decorative arrangements in fan shapes and diaper patterns, and floral ornaments featuring stylized lilies, sunflowers, and cherry-blossoms.[8] Rossetti designed bindings with spiral shapes asymetrically arranged (Swinburne's *Atalanta in Calydon*, 1865) and with floating flowers superimposed upon rows of disks for his own *Ballads and Sonnets* (1881). Such designs were probably based on Japanese motifs in lacquerware and porcelain.[9] Abbey's cover for the 1882 *Selections* is worth mentioning in this connection. These efforts would have pleased Owen Jones, whose *Grammar of Ornament* (1856) advocated symbolic as opposed to naturalist representation in architecture and interior decoration.

Greek design was popular for some of the same reasons as were the Japanese: its elegance was another way of reducing the clutter and somber hues of Victorian interiors.

To Mr. Owen Jones, Mr. Morris, Mr. Cottier, who is a Pupil of Ruskin's, we owe a debt of gratitude.... The stained glass, the ceilings, the stencils designed by them are very beautiful. The forms are studied and adapted from the finest examples in Roman and Greek decoration, and their colors are all exquisite in themselves and delicately harmonized. Queer blues, that are neither blue, nor green, nor lilac, queerer greens and yellows, and all varieties of tertiary tints, are tenderly united and mixed....."[10]

The lyrical diction here is like that with which dresses were advertised: "The flower of a dream," "the transition from red to black passed through a hint of blue."[11] The simplification of women's garments advocated by the Dress Reform Movement is relevant here. Its practical implications for liberating women from the drawing room were significant, but was this alone what made it popular? DuMaurier's cartoon "Modern Aesthetics" (see Figure 4-1a), which satirizes the mixture of Greek, Japanese, and Medieval styles, acknowledges that dresses with Grecian styling are hardly suitable for outdoor sports. As far as style is concerned, a *desideratum* of nineteenth-century women's clothing is that it be non-functional, thus aristocratic and designed for leisure hours. "It was not hard for an English girl to adopt the straight nose and clear cut features which [Alma-Tadema and Albert Moore] had rendered more attractive than had Phidias and Praxiteles; to look as aloof and unapproachable as the caryatid of a temple on the Acropolis."[12]

Further evidence of Greek fashion may be found in the journal Oscar Wilde edited, *The Woman's World* (1887-89), in *Aglaia, the Journal of the Healthy and Artistic Dress Union*, and in Walter Crane's illustrations for children's books in the 1870s and '80s, which featured Greek dress and setting as often as they did tapestries, vases, and prints with peacocks and sunflowers. Wilde's "New Hellenism" was dedicated to improving taste by adhering to the purity of Greek line,[13] but in practice Greek and Japanese influences were so mixed together that one could hardly tell them apart.[14] This is true of the architect E. W. Godwin, and evident in a painting such as Whistler's *Symphony in White, No. IV: The Three Girls* , in which the figures pose in Greek style, wear Attic headress, and stand on Japanese mats near which are cherry-blossoms.[15] Figure 4-1b reproduces an art nouveau sideboard in a setting which includes Japanese flatness of perspective and asymetricality, Greek vases and goblets, and, in the sideboard itself, medieval styling.

A third ingredient in this jumble was the fascination for the English past, provided by Queen Ann style red brick houses (decorated with sunflower reliefs, gothic bay windows, gables and balconies[16]), William Morris wallpaper, bibelots with eighteenth-century or medieval motifs, chests and pianos decorated with Pre-Raphaelite maidens and languid knights in elegant black armor.

This was the state of perceptions of the "aesthetic" at a time when, as William Gaunt puts it, "art was important enough...to be confused with fashion."[17] But to deprecate popular affectation of these styles may obscure one's understanding of the period's attitudes toward art and literature, and prevent giving credit where it is due. An example of aestheticism in book decoration—demonstrating the richness with which its diverse motifs could be employed—is Figure 4-2, which reproduces vignettes from title pages in the Early English Poets (1876) and Golden Treasury (1877) series. One can see Greek and Japanese influences: flatness of perspective, Greek symbols of natural fecundity, love, and death, and an attempt decoratively rather than realistically to reproduce patterns of natural growth and movement. The vignettes unpretentiously suggest the timelessness and refreshing elegance of *belles-lettres*, which are as life-enhancing as are flowers, fresh air, and love itself. Aesthetic style in commerical books—large margins, small, old-style typeface, restrained use of ornament, plain binding—reinforces this effect.

George Du Maurier 'Modern Aesthetics'
From *Punch* 14 December 1877

Fig. 4-1a "Modern Aesthetics." Source: Robin Spencer, *The Aesthetic Movement* (London: Studio Vista, 1972), p. 102.

'Old Studio' sideboard, designed by Liberty's, 1903.

Fig. 4-1b An Art Nouveau Sideboard. Source: James Laver, *Edwardian Promenade* (Boston: Houghton Mifflin: 1958), facing p. 97.

The Herrick editions in the Early English Poets (#7) and the Muses' Library (8,9) series are good examples.

For a large number of newly-affluent people, aestheticism was a first recognition of what art could do to enrich one's environment. Its attractions were escapist, and showed a smug disregard for the squalor and injustice in which the less fortunate were enmeshed. What was the goal of this escape? One answer is Walter Hamilton's response to a "home of the aesthetes," which he described in an epilogue to his *Aesthetic Movement in England* (1882). Along with the neo-Gothic architecture, he remarks the "comfort and elegance, without ostentation; books, flowers, and pictures, china and glass ornaments...whilst through the open casements, views of the sunlit lawn, the hawthorn trees in full bloom, golden laburnum and sweetly scented lilac could be seen...."[18] He is reminded of lines from Thomson:

> Was nought around but images of rest;
> Sleep-soothing groves, and quiet lawns between;
> And flowery beds that slumbrous influence kest [cast]
> From poppies breathed....

> There eke the soft delights that witchingly
> Instil a wanton sweetness through the breast;
> and the calm pleasures always hover'd nigh;...

It is not the moral and social virtues of "merrie" England (magnanimous generosity, open-hearted communal wholeness) which are stressed here. Rather, it is a restful, Edenic *joie de vivre* which need not be justified by the obligation to help the poor or by the illusion of a near-Utopian social structure. In fact, to such a frame of mind a sense of social obligation was irrelevant.

As Professor Jenkyns shows, diverse groups of Victorian writers and artists found ancient Greece, especially, a source of mythic freedom not only from the grime, materialism, and disputatiousness which made Young England advocate Christian responsibility, but also from all institutionalized conventions of social conduct. Therefore, writers and artists found it possible to touch on unconventional moral standards, and more freely to treat amatory and erotic themes, by situating a poem or a painting in pagan times,[19] or, in the case of a Japanese setting, by allusions to a contemporary land as exotic, remote, and Arcadian as ancient Hellas.[20] As Walter Hamilton, as well as several Pre-Raphaelites, show, the medieval ages could also be used in this way.

Herrick's illustrators in the art nouveau decorative tradition used for the most part Greek settings, along with images of the pre-industrial English past (when appropriate), for suggesting carefree sensuality or faerie-haunted moonlit vistas. By turning to classical icons, and, especially, by avoiding costume-drama settings, graphic artists were in a position to both appeal to

Fig. 4-2a A.B. Grosart, ed., *The Complete Poems of Robert Herrick,* The Early English Poets (London: Chatto and Windus, 1876). See #7, Appendix.

Fig. 4-2b Francis T. Palgrave, ed., *Chrysomela: A Selection from the Lyrical Poems of Robert Herrick,* The Golden Treasury Series (London: Macmillan, 1877), See #41.

fashion and, as well, to make something different of the notion of freedom from modern restraints than were period illustrators working in the representational mode. The latter did focus on Greek settings but only occasionally, and then not with the mythic cast possible in decorative art.

They were more interested (as were the great nineteenth-century genre painters of "everyday Rome") in a realistic social milieu, however distant in time, and in depicting social contexts which Victorians could imagine as similar to those in which they sometimes found themselves.[21] With fantasizing of this particular kind even popular art nouveau illustrators working for commercial publications had little to do. Contrast Henry Ryland's design for "Division By A Daffodil" (Figure 4-3) with Abbey's treatment of "His Poetrie his Pillar" (Figure 3-5). Both poems treat the speaker's impending death. Abbey's period-piece is full of high seriousness; his writer burns the midnight oil, a model of Victorian commitment. In this

Fig. 4-3 Henry Ryland, illustrator, *The English Illustrated Magazine*, May, 1891, p. 575.

role Victorian men could easily see themselves. By contrast, Ryland's impassive women and serene meadow (the Greek maiden is posed against a medieval walled town; the medieval lady against an Attic grove) connote equanimity of spirit and comfortable repose. The consolation his women feel is mysterious, and has reached them through another vehicle than heroic effort or conventional moral platitutdes. They are harder to identify with than is Abbey's figure, with whose determined, active response the admiring nineteenth-century viewer is more familiar. But illustrations like Ryland's were ubiquitous from about 1880 to 1910; the kind of escapism they presented had definite "aesthetic" appeal. Clearly, middle-class readers with widely varying degrees of sophistication in literature and art enjoyed them with a "modern" aloofness from modern squalor.

The English aesthetic movement is especially interesting for the way artists associated with it reworked radical concepts in the service of bourgeois respectability. Men such as Burne-Jones, Moore, Whistler, and Sickert[22] relied on the patronage they received, even if, like Whistler, they despised the Philistines who gave it. In their paintings one finds, as one does in illustrations such as Abbey's "How Heartsease Came First" and "The Bell Man," symbolic overtones, sophisticated treatment of line and form, and predominance of mood over narrative, as well as easily recognizable subject and background. If English aestheticism was a muddle, it was also a richly imaginative current from which artists and public alike drew inspiration. It standardized art and literature so that a wide audience could appreciate them. In the process it lost its appeal for the exclusive group which originated it.[23] Its importance as popular culture lay in the ways people could identify it with their tastes and aspirations. The application of this standardization process to late Victorian (and Gilded Age) illustrated books, insofar as it is relevant to "aesthetic" fashions which separate the respectable classes from the masses, is clear from the practice of "conspicuous consumption" and from the equation between dignity and repose stressed by writers and artists delineating the attractions of poetry, and the art of reading in general. Gentlemanly endeavor does not serve practical ends. Even the most hard-driving successful financier can convince himself of this, if he aspires single-mindedly enough to be genteel. This notion of gentility is clearly reflected by Hamilton's passage in favor of restful recreation reproduced above, and in the tenor of his book as a whole, which was written to defend the "manners and customs of a very exclusive section of society"[24] from Philistines who had learned about aesthetes, he felt, only from the satires of Gilbert and Sullivan and *Punch* "...Aesthetes are supposed to belong to the "Upper Crust.' One of the characteristics of the lower middle classes is an intense desire to know, or to profess to know, all that goes on in aristocratic circles."[25] That is very true, but Hamilton underestimates the extent to which aestheticism had by 1882 permeated society, and had therefore lost its avant-garde stigma. Many respectable men, although they worked hard in the City, had their houses decorated with Japanese fans and Grecian vases, leaving to their idle, artistic wives the task of demonstrating their own and their family's ingenuous love of art and literature.,

The outside of a book, as Thomas Love Peacock has said, is an exquisite pleasure as long as one knows it needn't be opened unless curiosity or *ennui* dictate. But if a lady or gentleman has a fancy to do so, he or she finds that illustrators and decorators have provided an aura for the poetry which is very relevant to social and personal aspirations. These decorations and illustrations show medieval, Japanese, and Greek motifs, suggesting light, purity, and repose, making an *au courant* aesthetic style relevant to the poetry. The graphics reflect nineteenth-century fashions in dress (the Greek style) and behavior (Herrick's mistresses as visualized by Paul Woodroffe or Robert Anning Bell are most often just as graceful, ornamental, and obliging as Abbey had depicted them). This is especially interesting in relation to, once again, the dress reform movement. The lightly-robed women in the illustrations may be somewhat more active and free than they would have been in medieval or seventeenth-century costume, just as their late Victorian and Edwardian counterparts are less completely the prisoners of the drawing room, a bit freer from hobbling skirts and corsets, than they were twenty years before.[26] However, female roles remain much the same, in society and in commercial book illustration, as they were in the mid-Victorian period,[27] and illustrators focus on the conventional themes: innocence, love, faerie, and idyllic nature.

One may easily doubt the motives and credentials of artists who make such concessions to fashion. But, if Mozart could produce great music for sleepy German princelings, skilled graphic artists could execute imaginative illustrations which threw new light on Herrick's poetry for languid young ladies, attentive suitors, vivacious matrons, and even respectable breadwinners. This audience was ready, eager, even capable: certainly attentive. Fashion, to quote Quentin Bell, is not "just the product of a light weight emotion":

Fierce and at times ruthless in its operation, it governs our behaviour, informs our sexual appetites, makes possible but also distorts our conception of history and determines our aesthetic valuations.[28]

Hellenism and Hesperides: *Youth, Purity and Sweetness*

The epigraph to this chapter echoes Edmund Gosse's even more eloquent homage to *Hesperides* (quoted in Chapter 1): the strong young men, "loose-draped nymphs," the sunny valleys and "silent woods with their melodies and dances," the "world rearisen to the duty of pleasure." There is a popular notion here about ancient Greece which was much more generally appealing at the turn of the century than that of Swinburne or George Moore. See Figure 1-7 for Dent and Company's title-page advertisement of the pleasant pagan gods of love and song. The *avant garde* fantasy shared with the popular one the unabashed celebration of desires, but the former would define these only in a "decadent" way. For Swinburne, cruelty was deeply involved in pleasurable sensations welling from the uninhibited psyche; Moore states in his *Pagan Poems* that his fleshly satisfactions involve letting loose his pet python, after having denied it food for a time, so that....[29] Walter Pater is closer to the "acceptable" view. His *Marius The Epicurean* (1885) suggests that the most fundamental tenets of paganism are as morally wholesome as those of Christianity. The most attractive features of each are ceremonial beauty (as opposed to doctrinal greyness), and primacy of physical sensation over ratiocination (the former nourishes, rather than obscures, a vibrant moralism; the latter is the letter without the spirit). Marius is for a time a part of the Aesculapian cult, which preaches bodily health and refined perception of "beautiful phenomena" as a pathway to salvation, for which repose and security (lifelong obsessions with Marius and Pater) must be abundantly available.[30] Repose and security; these qualities were thought by nineteenth-century *belles-lettrists* to be more easily apprehended in pagan times because the following conditions then applied: an idyllic climate and rustic simplicity, the spontaneous celebration of natural instinct, an absence of social inhibitions (which among Victorians made a guilty prurience commonplace), an unpremeditated blitheness, and a graceful dignity unhampered by confining clothes.[31]

Some commitment by a vicar to churchly duties and vestments being assumed, these are the qualities chosen by turn-of-the-century men of letters to characterize Herrick's "paganism" for the sizeable audiences of such publications as *The Edinburgh, The Fortnightly,* and *The Bookman.*[32] In Herrick's case the operative terms are "spontaneous," "frivolous," "playful," and "humble." Gosse describes his "easy-going callousness of soul," which makes it impossible for him to "feel very deeply." Conviviality was intrinsic to his habitual idleness—both resulted from the security provided during college years by his uncle, then by his Dean Prior living, and, in bad times, by the charity of friends. The situation fostered an "airy frivolity" (eat, drink, and be merry), a determinedly placid attachment to "youth's unfading roses," and a complete freedom in expressing not only joyous *elan* but pathos and sentimentality.

Since Herrick himself made much of the man/muse analogy, he probably deserves to be made a prime example of the nineteenth-century practice of domesticating a poet by equating the tenor of his verses with his personality. This was especially easy in the case of a writer of lyric, a form "temperamental in origin and emotional in effect."[33] The kind of man who created for himself the pagan ethos described above was just the sort to produce "pure" lyric: cameo-like[34] in its attachment to surfaces, non-discursive ("the cadence is the thought"[35]), and quintessentially musical (Swinburne's "the greatest song writer...ever born of English race"[36]). Such appreciations account for his popularity for anthologists such as Palgrave,

Locker-Lampson, Saintsbury, Edward Hutton, W. E. Henley, and even George Moore,[37] although in the latter case a Greek "innocence of vision" meant an objectivity created by a poet with the ability to stand, in the act of creation, "outside his own personality" and its moral scruples.[38] Herrick's paganism also stimulated erudite source-hunting. "It is interesting speculation to consider from what antique sources Herrick, athirst for the pure springs of pagan beauty, drank the deep draughts of his inspiration."[39] One such scholar, Rev. C. C. Phinn, who annotated the *sententia* for the 1898 Muses' Library edition, chose to remain anonymous because such work seemed indecorous, or at least too time-consuming, for a clergyman.[40]

Hellenistic youth, sweetness, and grace are visualized in graphics which remind one of illustrations for children's books. Robert Anning Bell did work in this genre; his drawings for *Midsummer's Night Dream* are especially suitable for children. In those accompanying poems for *English Lyrics from Spenser to Milton* (G. Bell, 1898), young people take a remarkably significant part. His tailpiece for "To the Virgins," for example, consists of a little girl reaching languidly into a trellis full of roses. R. E. D. Sketchley acknowledges Bell's "fairy gift of seeming to improvise without labor and without hesitancy," and his "shapes of delicate sweetness, pure, graceful—so graceful that their power is hardly realized."[41] These are qualities upon which children's-book artists build. In Bell's case they are supplemented by complementary talents. Bell started his career in an architect's office, which was a good apprenticeship in that, as John Russell Taylor points out, British art nouveau is largely a matter of arranging designs built up out of white space.[42] He also studied Renaissance Florentine design in bas-relief and book illustration, as did Ricketts and Shannon, who, like Bell, specialized in Grecian figures and setting.

The full-page illustration of "To Meadows" picks up the many pagan motifs transparently suggested by Herrick's verses. See Figure 4-4a. With her dishevelled hair crowned by honeysuckle, each virgin is as young as springtime; together they dance with a dreamy-eyed determination, spending a summer day placidly intent on the music with what Gosse might characterize as "airy frivolity." The pose, costume, and theme suggest the tradition of the dancing graces, and especially Botticelli's *Primavera*. Bell forces the viewer to see startlingly graceful shapes by cutting one of his figures against the right-hand edge (an effect, like the flat perspective, used in Japanese prints) and by his use of line and white space. The intertwined hands and arms on the right and the folds of the clothing in the center and left of the drawing define its vertical rhythms. The white space formed of hands and heads contrasts with the closely-spaced alternation of black and white in the rest of the foreground and harmonizes the undraped part of the figures with the outlines of tree and sky. Despite the sense of rhythm, the drawing is very much a frozen tableau of child-like sweetness and pastoral repose.

**YOU'VE HEARD THEM SWEETLY SING
AND SEEN THEM IN A ROUND**
Fig. 4-4a R.A. Bell, "To Meadows," *English Lyrics From
Spenser to Milton* (1878; rpt. London: Bell and Hyman, 1979),
p. 149.

THE COUNTRY LIFE

R. HERRICK

Fig. 4-4b R.A. Bell: ils., *English Lyrics from Spenser to Milton*, p. 126.

You have beheld how they
      With wicker arks did come
To kiss and bear away
      The richer cowslips home.

The poem ends in winter, with the meadows no longer "fresh and green."
The consequences of pagan attachment to mutable colors and textures, on the
part of nature herself as well as humanity, is clear in Herrick's final couplet,

You're left here to lament
      Your poor estates alone.

These implications are all the more poignant for Bell's facing illustration
and the couplet he prints beneath it.

    Henry Ryland's decoration of "Gather ye Rosebuds" (Figure 4-5) is
successful in a similar way. His calligraphy suggests Greek simplicity and

Fig. 4-5 Henry Ryland, illustrator, *The English Illustrated
Magazine*, June 1891, p. 677.

delicate beauty in the same way his impassive, virginal young girls do. Posed against a floral background which involves thorns as well as roses, they are themselves rosebuds: at once subject of the poem and object of its advice. Ryland makes a fuller comment on the poem than do Brock or Forbes (see Figure 3-9a and b) because the symbols inherent in the Greek motifs carry the universality of the theme in a way realistic period costume does not.

Bell's headpiece (see Figure 4-4b) for "The Country Life" shows a heavy-lidded young woman in a full, loose gown reclining under a tree while a child shows her a flower. The tailpiece presents a girl reading a book while a boy naps beside her. These vignettes of "sunshine holiday" are only very generally related to the poem, but some lines in what starts as a sober Horatian epistle show Herrick's own playful sensuality:

> This done, then to th'enamelled meads
> Thou go'st, and as thy foot there treads,
> Thou see'st a present God-like power
> Imprinted in each herb and flower;
> And smell'st the breath of great-eyed kine,
> Sweet as the blossoms of the vine....
> (11. 29-34)

Playful dalliance is the specialty of Paul V. Woodroffe in his decorations for Joseph Moorat's *A Country Garland of Ten Songs Gathered from the Hesperides*...(1897; see #15). This artist was a disciple of Laurence Houseman; in the mid-nineties he was modelling his work on Walter Crane's example,[43] especially for two books of fairy tales, also edited by Moorat. For these he drew realistically, using Queen Anne or medieval settings. The Herrick illustrations are a bit more stylized. His full-bodied, half-smiling Greek ladies, with their heavily-folded robes and upright postures, are similar to Crane's for *Echoes of Hellas* and *The Baby's Aesop*. In "Her Pretty Feet" a barefoot girl playing a lute is posed against a background of enormous blossoms. The folds of her robe are intricate and rich, like the petals of a flower. Her cap is like the center of a flower itself, and her bearing is as graceful as the stems. The drawing blithely complements the frivolous miniature blazon with the ethereal beauty of music, flowers, and poetry, without becoming an exercise in the ways feet can inspire love poetry (ankles are kept discreetly covered). See Figure 4-6a.

Man and Nature: English Faerie and Pagan Gods

The carefree ingenuousness of the above illustrations makes it totally unsurprising that Bell and Woodroffe, along with many other art nouveau illustrators (in Herrick's case most notably Reginald Savage and Charles Robinson), worked often for commercial publishers of children's books. Therefore, the appearance of English fairies is as expected as it is welcome. In Woodroffe's "Night Piece: to Julia" (Figure 4-6b) one misses the allure of romantic moonlight and faint music which Abbey creates, especially since

Fig. 4-6a Paul Woodroffe: ils, *Country Garland of Ten Songs Gathered from the Hesperides of Robert Herrick, Set into Music by Joseph Moorat with a Cover and XV Drawings by Paul Woodroffe* (London: George Allen, 1897), p. 28. See #15.

Fig. 4-6b Paul Woodroffe,: ils., *A Country Garland of Ten Songs...*p. 16.

Woodroffe is illustrating a song book. His focus is all on Julia as a kind of Snow White framed by heart-shaped stalks of foxglove and laughing at a panoply of elves who mischievously sport with her. One puts a petal on her thumb, another lights the way, a third plays a flute, and a fourth, astride a vine, imitates a despatch rider whipping a horse. To see the poem as a fairy-tale is not to see it as trivial, but to suggest its restorative vitality. The hero of Kipling's *The Light That Failed,* morose and unlucky in love, hears a friend sing the Night Piece and is refreshed in mind and spirit, and momentarily re-armed to battle with life,[44] perhaps by the romantic fantasy the poem offers— as Abbey would have it—but perhaps instead by its vigorous natural benevolence (which Woodroffe represents).

Late-century aestheticism encouraged a fantasy of unification with an idyllic nature inhabited by generous (if mischievous) spirits. Such an intuition of the fairy-infested English forests and meadows was fancied to be disorienting but uniquely recreative to any heart-sore adult, nostalgic for the pride of youth, with the luck or daring to confront them. An example is Andrew Lang's Mr. Kirk. Abducted by fairies to be their chaplain, he experiences "Of Fairyland, the lost perfume / The sweet low light, the magic air."[45] Closely related to faerie is the notion of pagan Gods in English settings. Professor Jenkyns cites Ruskin's concept of the power of imagination to refresh itself by "creat[ing] for itself fairies in the grass and naiads in the wave."[46] W. E. Henley describes a spell cast by Pan's "ancient Music" in Piccadilly on May-Day

> By the persuasion of his mighty rhyme,
> Here in this radiant and immortal street
> Lavishly and omnipotently as ever
> In the open hills, the undissembling dales,
> The laughing-places of the juvenile earth.

> The enormous heart of London joys to beat
> To the measures of his rough, majestic song;
> The lewd, perennial, overmastering spell
> That keeps the rolling universe ensphered,
> And life, and all for which life lives to long,
> Wanton and wondrous and for ever well.[47]

There are slight echoes of "Corinna" (where parks and streets turn to open fields) here. Much louder ones occur in an earlier poem:

> The Universal Pan
> Still wanders fluting—fluting—
>   Fluting to maid and man.
> Our weary well-a-waying
>   His music cannot still:
> Come! let us go a-maying,
>   And pipe with him our fill.[48]

Since no one would label Kipling or Henley "aesthetes" (unless from the safe side of an unfordable river), for further evidence of the prevalence of nineteenth-century British fascination with pagan vitality I turn to Alice Meynell, who cultivated the fugitive hints of "savage savour and simplicity" in poets (as diverse as Herrick and Matthew Arnold) who wrote "a little wildly and with the flower of the mind."[49]

Literary critics and poets were equally taken with such themes. In fact, as passages cited in the previous section show, a fashionable title page for *Hesperides* could be designed from their musings. It would include—if large enough—a stately muse with a rose crown and lily sceptre,[50] English fairies and pagan nymphs, and a shallow stream whose shore is graced with willowy trees, flowers, birds, and Cupids:

> And mark how Cupid bends his bow,
> A-Maying with Corinna go,
>
> Or weep beside the silvery streams,
> Or pleasure find in fleeting dreams....[51]

One of the birds should be from Jerome K. Jerome's fable of the seventeenth-century thrush who composed "Gather ye Rosebuds" as a dirge for an ant killed by a grasshopper:

It was a very pretty song, and a very wise song, and a man who lived in those days, and to whom the birds, loving him and feeling that he was almost one of themselves, had taught their langauge, fortunately heard it and wrote it down, that all may read it to this day.[52]

Room must be found for "Amaryllis going home to the farm with an apronful of flowers,"[53] for "brown lads and lovely girls, crowned with daffodils and daisies,"[54] dancing on Devon hillsides, for sunshowers, maypoles, and glow-worms, with perhaps a frontispiece showing the poet, with his Roman nose, bull-throat, voluptuous mouth and chin, as "the last laureate of fairyland."[55]

...visiting us in our leisure moments, [*Hesperides*] can lap us in the happiest of dreams, make our hearts beat cheerily, and render us at peace with all the world. Would we quit Fleet Street to while away an hour in Fairyland, among Titania and her maids of honour?—we have only to take up *Hesperides*. It is merely a piece of sweet and careless dissipation.... It is redolent of ambrosia, nectar, and all the tipple of the gods. An idle, dreamy, treasure of a book: Aphrodite without her veil, Thalia without her mask, Diana cutting capers as mysterious as the necromancy of Cornelius Agrippa![56]

One can cite several illustrators of *Hesperides* who, by focussing on English fairies and pagan gods, complement its delineations of a life-enhancing vivacity unavailable in modern times ("little we see in nature that is ours"). Reginald Savage's line-drawings for Newnes' edition in the Caxton series came out in 1903 (see #16). The twenty-six full-page illustrations show great range, although the majority delineate attentive men and aloof or simpering (but sometimes independent) women in courting roles. He is the only illustrator except Abbey to tackle the epigrams and he does so with humor and a fine sense of the grotesque. He deals in the same way with Herrick's facial expression and imagines those of his brother as well. (see Figure 8-2). Some of his women are robust country girls, a few are wistful Pre-Raphaelite damsels, some are willing coquettes, and still others are proud and aristocratic. The girl in "Upon Love" (Figure 4-7a) is a damsel in distress. A rose-crowned, androgynous Cupid with sensuous mouth has applied a flame-tipped arrow to her head, demonstrating for the apprehensive male, the speaker of the poem, that

> Love's a thing (as I do here)
> Ever full of pensive fear.

The horror of love, he fears, would make him impotent, but, since love is irresisitible,

> Then the next thing I desire
> Is to love, and live i'th'fire.

The power of Cupid in the poem is like that attributed to Pan by Henley: "lavish," "omnipotent," "lewd, perennial, over-mastering." Savage embodies it in Cupid's impassivity and his powerful (not dainty and diaphanous) wings. He is not sinister, but a potent natural force.

Interestingly, Savage is able to associate with the pagan god the compelling, unsettling erotic qualities indecorous for a popular illustrator to portray in mortal, fashionably clad ladies and gentlemen, however fanciful the milieu. Another example of this is "His Cavalier,"[57] where the poem's speaker, again a mute observer, watches a sinuous, naked figure drive a monstrous, scaled, fierce-eyed steed though a raging current.

Vibrant natural rhythms also dominate "Oberon's Palace" (Figure 4-7c) and "To Phillis to Love and Live with Him" (Figure 4-7b): the graceful poses of the languid women and active, gesturing men, the sinuous curves of vines, flowers, trees, costumes, and flowing hair. The fairy-tale atmosphere of both drawings further emphasizes the connection of sentient beings with trees, rivers, plants, and animals. This is suitable for both the English fairies and the English lovers. The Englishness of the latter is part of the pastoral Herrick imitated from Ralegh and Marlowe, which Savage provides with a crowded background of tangled foliage and rocky streams reminiscent of a Pre-Raphaelite painting. The illustrator works into both drawings many fancies of the kind Herrick's critics praised for their playful use of pagan myth, faerie, and rural ceremonies.

Walk in the Groves, and thou shalt find
the name of *Phillis* in the Rind
Of every straight, and smooth-skin tree;
Where kissing that, Ile twice kisse thee.
To thee a sheep-hook I will send,
Be-prankt with ribbands, to this end,
This, this alluring Hook might be
Lesse for to catch a sheep, then me.

("To Phillis...," 11. 39-46)

...and now he finds
His Moon-tann'd *Mab*, as somewhat slick,
And (Love knowes) tender as a chick.
Upon six plump *Dandillions*, high-
Rear'd, lyes her Elvish-majestie:
Whose woolie-bubbles seem'd to drowne
Hir *Mab-ship* in obedient Downe.

("Oberon's Palace," 11. 83-89)

Savage's Phillis is exotic but sweetly languid and not affected with decadent spleen. His Oberon is not, as Herrick has it, about to exercise his drunken lust upon Titania. Phallic imagery and double-entendre are as prominent in the poem as is the description of the queen's bed-chamber with its canopied bed

...all behung with those pure Pearls,
Dropt from the eyes of *ravisht Girles*
Or writhing Brides; when, (panting) they
Give unto Love the straighter way.

(11. 108-11)

Although Savage's queen is a seductive and mature woman and his king a commanding presence with an inscrutable expression, a rape-fantasy should not be called attention to in a commercial publication. The artist's avant-garde connections, the Essex House Press and Ricketts and Shannon, are not his models for the Newnes Herrick.[58] He also eschews the themes of violent death, dismemberment, and sexual perversity treated by Frederick Sandys, an artist whose techniques Savage seems to have studied carefully. The motifs and draftsmanship of his Herrick illustrations are very much in the style he used for the six black and white illustrations, and colored frontispiece, he contributed to Newnes' story-book, *Queen Mab's Fairy Realm* (1901).

A final approach to situating mankind in nature is represented by two decorated pages in *The Studio*. These are academic examples of art nouveau, submitted to competitions the magazine was fond of running. Here a basic principle of the style (in Britain) is used:[59] the arrangement of white space and "surface bodies" against flat perspective. Both figures and inanimate shapes are held in a balance suggestive of the abstract patterns of natural movement which human life shares with primitive forms.[60] In Kate Light's "The Bag of the Bee" (1896), this theme of integration is carried out in great formal detail

UPON LOVE

Fig. 4-7a Reginald Savage, "Upon Love," *Hesperides Or Works...Together with His Noble Numbers or Pious Pieces*, The Caxton Series (London: Newness 1903), I, facing p. 160. See #16.

Fig. 4-7b Reginald Savage, "To Phillis," *Hesperides or Works...*, I, facing p. 267.

OBERONS PALACE

Fig. 4-7c Reginald Savage, ils., *Hesperides or Works, I,*
facing p. 229.

(Figure 4-8a). The interlocking vines enclose one illustration for each of the
poem's three stanzas, thus unifying calligraphy and drawing. Even the
serpentine lines which separate the stanzas are similar in shape to the vines.
The rectangular frame of the picture, with its small triangles, reflects the
triangular shape of the white dots in the background. One might also
mention as calligraphy the bee, which becomes a sort of Whistlerian
punctuation mark, in the lower right corner. "Isca's" decoration for "The
Wounded Cupid" (1900; Figure 4-8b) shows more substantial harmonies.
Curving organic shapes are common to the vines, river, folds of Venus' gown,
and her curly hair. The black river and sky give the effect of a negative print; it
is easy to sustain the illusion that white figures and shapes have been sketched
on a black ground. The artist suggests the primacy of what appears to be
background; this furthers the impression of an integrated whole. The thick
black lettering of the poem's title and decorated initial unify calligraphy and
illustration.

Fig. 4-8b "Isca," ils., "The Wounded Cupid," *The Studio*, December 15, 1900, p. 220.

Fig. 4-8a Kate Light, ils., "The Bag of the Bee," *The Studio*, Oct. 1896, p. 35.

Fig. 4-9 Paul Woodroffe, ils., "To the Virgins, To Make
Much Of Time," *A Country Garland of Ten Songs...*,
frontispiece (#15).

Sensuality, innocence, and spontaneity are present in both illustrations
if one wishes to see these qualities. or the carefree ingenuousness which
inspired Gosse, Henley, Woodroffe, or Bell. However, as is the case with the
erudite wit of Herrick's text itself, these qualities are not insisted upon. They
are only suggested by the cool detachment of the decoration. Isca makes this
point especially well, by having her Venus and Cupid appear on a fore-
shortened stage. Beyond binding together the stylized forms of boy-gods,
goddess, flowers, trees, and river by the basic configurations of line and form,
suggesting the common springs of all life, the artists give no message, but
rather a frozen tableau which liberates the imagination. In the *Studio*
drawings—as in Ryland's work for the *English Illustrated Magazine*—a
chaste (not decadent) art-for-art's-sake detachment has discreetly permeated
illustrations for *Hesperides*.

A Few Steps Toward the Modern Sensibility

The Fanfrolico Press, in 1927, and the Golden Cockerel, in 1955, published editions of Herrick which gave full play to erotic fantasies. Two fine illustrators, Lionel Ellis and William Russell Flint, openly realized an aspect of "cleanly-wantonness" which was very delicately implied by turn-of-the-century artists with their motifs of immersion in natural rhythms, childlike spontaneity, and freedom from modern social and moral restraints. That the implications were there is significant. They would not have been, without a Savage, a Bell, or a Woodroffe. We have mentioned that the kind of fantasizing which period illustrators (and genre painters like Tadema and Poynter) could stimulate with their historically accurate representations was different from that which decorative art nouveau illustrators could induce. The former project viewers into familiar social milieu, but distant in time, thus allowing one to believe that noble or virtuous conduct was more possible or appreciated then. One can imagine taking part in public, universal situations calling for graceful courting techniques, generous abnegation, and heroic efforts to cope with evil or misfortune. On the other hand, art nouveau illustrations such as those reproduced in this chapter are more limited in scope. Except when courting is the subject, they do not deal with situations in which people prove to others their character or social accomplishments. The setting is usually pastoral. The clothing, when not Hellenic, is Caroline, but vaguely, for costume drama (despite the popularity of Greek motifs in *tableaux vivants* and fancy dress balls[61]) is not the goal of these stylized graphics. They steer one's imagination into different channels, complementing Herrick's "paganism" with images very different from those suitable for the romance of "merrie" England. They stimulate fantasies (involving physical and spiritual liberation from restraints) which are more personal and asocial than those of period illustrators working in a representational mode. The Greek maidens of Bell and Ryland, the elves of Woodroffe, the pagan deities of Savage and the *Studio* illustrators, as wholesome and respectable as they all are, represent a further step in the relaxation of Victorian high seriousness. Much of Abbey's work does also, but the aforementioned artists (Abbey's exact contemporaries, of course) do not emphasize, as he often does, the correct performance of conventional social duties. In addition, they suggest, tentatively, an expansion of women's roles. Some freedom from the bondage of confining clothes, drawing-room accomplishments, and passive sweetness is evident, as it is in Elizabeth Forbes', as opposed to C. E. Brock's, version of "Gather ye Rosebuds" (Figure 3-9a and b). Also, at least in Reginald Savage's case, the young women being courted not only flirt or blush but kiss, simmer with restrained desire, and sometimes appear bored—they take an independent part in determining their fate. Ryland and Woodroffe add to this a sense of freedom, adventure, and in Woodroffe's case, overt sexuality (see Figure 4-9). This may be a tame antecedent for between-the-wars eroticism, but when a man begins to see, in

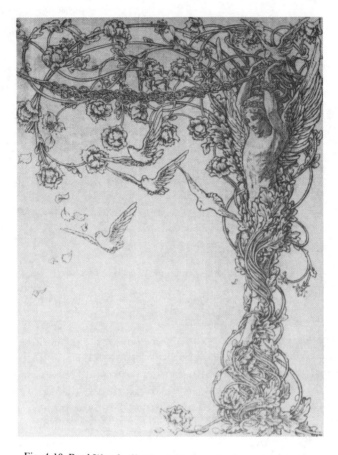

Fig. 4-10 Paul Woodroffe, ils, *A Country Garland...*, endpapers
(front: flyleaf; back: pastedown)

respectable magazines and books, a woman's body as more than a tightly-
laced ornament of conspicuous leisure, his sexual libido more directly
expresses itself. There is, then, some timid progression toward the ideals of
Jack Lindsay, editor of the Fanfrolico Press: to drop "all ethical and social
falsities and find the individual in all his candid rights"; to project a
"blitheness" and "emotional expansiveness" characterized as "hellenistic."[62]
This being so, I would like to close this chapter by citing a few examples of
Edwardian decoration which, however fashionable, approach an avant-garde
sensibility.

A few of Woodroffe's illustrations do for women in Greek dress what
Savage does for Titania in his "Oberon's Palace." "To the Virgins" displays a
girl in a clinging robe whose pose is calculated to show the curves of her
thighs, hips, and breasts, a maiden for whom sexuality is as natural as sleep or
air. His endpapers (Figure 4-10) present, with the help of Japanese technique
and Greek motifs, a fecundity of natural forms, rose-tinted and arranged

Fig. 4-11 *Love Poems of Herrick,* The Lovers' Library
(London: John Lane, 1903). Endpapers. See #25.

asymmetrically along the top and side edges of the paste-down and fly-leaf. A garlanded male nude half-emerges from the foliage and supports vine leaves stretching across the page. Along either side of the leaves are flowers, stems, and birds, all promising a fantasy of music and graceful sensuality. Woodroffe seems freer here to use abstract symbolic patterns than he does in the illustrations themselves, with their laughing maidens and blooming flowers. The endpapers, as an example of "high" art nouveau, use the hybrid form: the male figure entwined in the plant shapes. It is an example of "the human figure subjected to an alienation that create[s] something non-human, non-anthropomorphic, a self-impelling ornament...."[63] The artists we have been considering never took such symbols far enough to create a "total work of art" which refined perception and synthesized genres such as poetry and book design, as did Charles Ricketts. This did not happen because commercial publishers were content to use avant-garde art incidentally, as eye-catching devices. But one of Ricketts' most suggestive concepts, that of "document," is clearly enough exhibited by Woodroffe's endpapers to be noted here. This is a design neither rational, discursive, or narrative, "...a thing [as Ricketts says] easily imagined away from a picture, but authoritative there, as a gesture, or poetical recollection...." It is a symbol which, "by its cunning spontaneity, will give the emotion that sudden movement adds to nature—the ripple of grass in a summer landscape, for instance—and so become Document—that monument of moods."[64]

Perhaps an even better example of high art nouveau is the design by Phillip Connard for the endpapers of "The Lover's Library" edition of Herrick, published by John Lane in 1903 (#25, see Figure 4-11). The thick writhing lines of these rose-tinted flowers make them vibrant, primitive life-forms. A description by Robert Schmutzler of a drawing for Wilde's *Salome* is relevant: "Half ornament, half still life, the picture somehow conveys an uncertain meaning, a hidden symbolic content."[65] Symbols of inexorable natural rhythms could be provocative for poetry which deals with **metamorphosis of women into flowers and streets into fields and parks,** which transforms "wantonness" into "cleanly" love by fanciful use of classical ceremonies, and which frankly acknowledges the power of sensual impulse. Bell, Savage, and Woodroffe treat such themes by the creative use of white space, sinuous flowing lines, and flat perspective. However, theirs are not symbolic drawings. Their moods are defined not by symbol but by the figures, their costume, and the pastoral background. They are thus acceptable to the same genteel audience for which men of letters described Herrick as a "genuine Old English poet" and a "saint of flowers."

This brings us to an illustrator most of whose work we have considered in the previous chapter. A few of Florence Castle's designs do not use period costume but instead wraith-like females clad in flowing robes and set against a stylized background of sky and parkland. She therefore is our final example of the variety of *avant-garde* motifs put into the service of popular appreciation. To emphasize the point we should refer to Abbey's "How Heartsease Came First" (figure 3-6), reminiscent in technique and theme of art nouveau and also concerned with transformation of anxious mortals to primitive and quiescent forms of life. Castle's women, who first make their appearance gold-stamped on the binding (see Figure 2-4b) may be considered nymphs, or, in some of their moods, Herrick's own mistresses, who share with flowers delicacy, grace, ingenuousness, and a fairy power to bewitch and entice. There is little *joie de vivre* in these women. As the "flower poems" bid them, they weep over the poet's grave, solemnly consider a bed of tulips as an emblem of their own "frailties" (for they shall be "lost like these"), or, in the frontispiece, embody the evanescence of daffodils. This drawing (Figure 4-12) uses colors combined experimentally by art nouveau painters (especially blue and green)[66] to create horizontal contours which alternate from white to blue to green to white again, and finally become dark green at the bottom right. The gently undulating irregularities of the landscape are evocative, especially the river, which, vaguely suggested by the brownish wash that represents its banks, reflects with unnatural clarity the white and blue of the sky. Against this background are the dominating vertical rhythms, the tree in the left foreground starkly rising very near the girls' heads as they run into **the shade of a copse of trees. They seem not to be escaping the daffodils' fate** but rather to be ingenuously representing their natural affinity with the flowers.

> We have short time to stay as you
> We have as short a spring;
> As quick a growth to meet decay
> As you, or anything.

Fig. 4-12 "To Daffodils." Source: Florence Castle, ils., *Herrick's Flower Poems*, frontispiece. See #17.

From epigrammatic suggestion Castle creates a watercolor both restful and vaguely disturbing, rich in symbols of nature's evanescence and metamorphic power.

Notes

[1]Ernest Rhys, *Lyric Poetry* (1913; rpt. London: Dent: 1933), pp. 208-09; Felix Schelling, *The English Lyric* (1913; rpt. Port Washington, New York: Kennikat Press, 1967), pp. 89-91.

[2]Masao Miyoshi, *The Divided Self: A Perspective on the Literature of the Victorian* (New York: New York University Press, 1969), p. 324.

[3]C. W. Dalmon, "Parson Herrick's Muse," *The Yellow Book*, October 1894, pp. 241-42.

[4]When Le Gallienne had a four-page leaflet of three erotic verses "loosely laid" in some copies of his *English Poems*, he used the first two lines of Herrick's "Argument" as an introduction. See Grant Richards, *Author Hunting*, p. 82. The third poem in this leaflet is "Julia's Clothes." It describes her dress "fallen in a snowdrift round her feet./Then, bending low, I take the sweet cloud up,/Stained through with sweets from arm and breast and thigh,/And.../Upon the hoarded fragrance sup and sup."

[5]Ernest Rhys, *A London Rose and Other Rhymes* (London: Elkin Mathews and John Lane, 1894), pp. 90-91. See Hoxie N. Fairchild, *Religious Trends in English Poetry* (New York: Columbia University Press, 1962), V, 156.

[6]H. A. Taine, *History of English Literature*, trans. H. Van Laun (New York: Burt, 1891), p. 240; William Allingham, *Varieties in Prose*, I, 135. Rhys attributes to Marlowe ("wine and blood

and wit and deviltry") what Johnson does to Lovelace. Johnson's phrase is found in Graham Hough, *The Last Romantics* (London: Methuen, 1961), p. 213.

[7]*The Yellow Book*, January 1895, quoted in Charles Spenser, ed., *The Aesthetic Movement: Catalogue of an Exhibition at the Camden Centre London* (London: Academy Eds., 1973), pp. 14-15.

[8]Charles Spenser, pp. 20-22; Peter Selz and Mildred Constantine, eds., *Art Nouveau: Art and Design at the Turn of the Century*, rev. ed. (New York: Museum of Modern Art, 1975), p. 14.

[9]Robert Schmutlzer, *Art Nouveau* (New York: Abrahams, 1962) p. 185.

[10]Mrs. H.R. Haweis, *The Art of Beauty* (1870), quoted in James Laver, *Victorian Vista* (London: Hulton, 1954), p. 234.

[11]Maurice Rheims, *The Flowering of Art Nouveau* (New York: Abrams, 1966), pp. 378-79.

[12]Gaunt, p. 62.

[13]Rodney K. Engen, *Walter Crane as a Book Illustrator* (London: Academy Eds., 1975), p. 6.

[14]Jenkyns, pp. 316-17.

[15]Schmutzler, p. 185.

[16]Charles Spenser, pp. 23-24.

[17]Gaunt, p. 61.

[18]Walter Hamilton, *The Aesthetic Movement in England* (London: Reeves and Turner, 1882), pp. 113-14.

[19]Jenkyns, pp. 136, 304.

[20]Charles Spenser, p. 20.

[21]Jenkyns, pp. 317-19.

[22]Graham Reynolds, *Victorian Painting* (New York: Macmillan, 1966), p. 195.

[23]Renato Poggioli, *The Theory of the Avant-Garde,* tr. Gerald Fitzgerald (Cambridge, Mass.: Belknap Press, 1968), pp. 79-83.

[24]Hamilton, p. viii.

[25]Hamilton, p. 8.3

[26]Geoffrey Squire, *Dress and Society, 1570-1970* (New York: Viking, 1974), pp. 166-69; Mary Lou Rosencrantz, *Clothing Concepts: A Social and Psychological Approach* (New York: Macmillan, 1972), pp. 154-56, 286-90.

[27]Rheims, pp. 377-78.

[28]Quentin Bell, *On Human Finery*, 2nd ed. (New York: Schocken, 1976), p. 62.

[29]Karl Beckson, *Aesthetes and Decadents of the 1890s*, rev. ed. (Chicago: Academy Chicago, 1981), p. xxxiv.

[30]Richmond Crinkley, *Walter Pater: Humanist* (Lexington, KY.: University Press of Kentucky, 1970), pp. 143-53.

[31]Jenkyns, pp. 315-16, 304, 168-73.

[32]A. H. Garstang, "The Love Songs of a Bygone Day," *Fortnightly Review*, Dec. 1908, p. 988; Thomas Seccombe and W. R. Nicoll, *The Bookman Illustrated History of English Literature* (London: Hodder and Stoughton, 1907), p. 159; [J.C. Squire], *Books in General by Solomon Eagle* (New York: Knopf, 1919), p. 123 (reviews contributed to the *New Statesman)*; Walter de la Mare, "Robert Herrick," pp. 52, 53, 56; Gosse, "Robert Herrick," p. 180.

[33]W. E. Henley, ed., *English Lyrics Chaucer to Poe* (London: Metheun, 1897), p. ix.

[34]J. C. Squire, p. 125.

[35]De la Mare, p. 155.

[36]Algernon Swinburne, "Preface," *Robert Herrick: The Hesperides and Noble Numbers*, ed. Alfred Pollard, I ix.

[37]F. T. Palgrave, ed., *The Golden Treasury* (London: Macmillan, 1861), 8 poems; W. E. Henley, ed., *English Lyrics Chaucer to Poe*, 23 poems; George Moore, ed., *An Anthology of Pure Poetry* (New York: Boni and Liveright, 1924), 3 poems; Frederick Locker-Lampson, ed., *Lyra Elegantiarum*, rev. ed. (London: Ward, Lock & Co., 1891), 20 poems; George Saintsbury, ed., *Seventeenth Century Lyrics*, 3rd ed. (London: Rivington, 1902), 21 poems; Edward Hutton, ed., *A Book of English Love Poems* (London: Methuen, 1905), 14 poems. For a large list of anthologies to 1910, see Floris Delattre, *Robert Herrick...*(Paris: Alcan, 1910), pp. 547-49.

[38]Moore, "Introduction," *Pure Poetry*, pp. 18, 34.

[39]Gosse, p. 189.

[40]E. Marion Cox, "Notes on the Bibliography of Herrick," *The Library*, 8, 3rd series (1917),

117. See L. C. Martin's discussion of Phinn in his 1956 edition of Herrick for the Oxford Univ. Press, pp. v-vi.

[41]Rose Sketchley, *English Book Illustration of Today* (London: Kegan, Paul, Trench and Trubner, 1903), p. 8. A similar style is adopted by George Wharton Edwards, an American illustrator, in *A Book of Old English Love Songs*, ed. H.W. Mabie (New York: MacMillan, 1897).

[42]John Russell Taylor, *The Art Nouveau Book in Britain* p. 19.

[43]Taylor, pp. 111-12.

[44]*The Light That Failed* (Boston: Harcourt, n.d.), p. 176 (Chapter 8).

[45]*The Fairy Minister*, quoted in Ifor Evans, p. 297.

[46]Jenkyns, p. 182.

[47]"Allegro maestoso," *London Voluntaries* (1890-92), in *Poems* (London: D. Nutt, 1916), pp. 202-03. (First published 1898).

[48]"To S. C.," *Echoes* (1878), in *Poems*, p. 150.

[49]Quoted in Anne Kimball Tuell, *Mrs. Meynell and Her Literary Generation* (1925; rpt. St. Clair Shores, Mi.: Scholarly Press, 1970), pp. 73, 179.

[50]William Allingham, "The Lyric Muse," *Poems* (London: Chapman and Hall, 1850), p. 56. See also "To the Author of Hesperides," p. 135.

[51]Charles Lusted; "Herrick," *Gentleman's Magazine*, October 1899, p. 413.

[52]*Novel Notes* (NY: Holt, 1893), pp. 6-97.

[53]W. E. Henley, "Herrick," *Views and Reviews* (London: D. Nutt, 1890), I, 112-13.

[54]Gosse, p. 181.

[55]Newell, "A Seventeenth Century Singer," *Sewannee Review*, p. 206. (See chapter epigraph.)

[56]"Robert Herrick, Poet and Divine," *Temple Bar*, January 1861, p. 167.

[57]Possibly inspired by Frederick Sandys' "The Spirit of the Storm," published 1896.

[58]Taylor, pp. 141-42; Simon Houfe, *A Dictionary of British Book Illustrators and Caricaturists 1800-1914* (Woodridge, Suffolk: Baron Publishers, 1978), s.v. "Savage, Reginald." See Stephen Calloway, *Charles Ricketts: Subtle and Fantastic Decorator* (London: Thames and Hudson, 1979), pp. 51, 53 for a drawing of a group of Vale Press illustrators, including Savage.

[59]Taylor, pp. 18-19.

[60]Schmutzler, pp. 8-11, 29-32.

[61]See illustrations for "Tableaux Vivants," *The Strand Magazine*, 2 (July-Dec. 1891), pp. 3-8; "The Latest Fashionable Fad," *Pall Mall Budget*, July 14, 1887, p. 24. [Greek Dinners]; "Jubilating at Gray's Inn," *Pall Mall Budget*, July 14, 1887, p. 17. [performance of a "Maske of Flowers"].

[62]*A Retrospect of the Fanfrolico Press* (London: Simpkin and Marshall, 1931), n.p.

[63]Schmutzler, p. 10.

[64]"The Unwritten Book," *The Dial*, 1892, quoted in Calloway, pp. 13-14.

[65]Schmutzler, p. 27.

[66]Schmutzler, p. 72.

Chapter 5

Private Presses: Daniel, Kelmscott, Elston and The Aura of Things Past

> Even in these days, however, books have been entirely produced by hand, and, for that matter, we could do no better than follow the methods of the scribe, illuminator, and miniaturist of the Middle Ages. But...the artist must make terms with the printing press if he desires to live. It would be a delightful thing if every book were different—a millenium for collectors! Perhaps, too, it might be a wholesome regulation at this stage if authors were to qualify as scribes (in the old sense) and write out their own works in beautiful letters! How it would purify literary style!
> —Walter Crane, *Of the Decorative Illustration of Books Old and New*
> (1905), pp. 294, 299.

Total control by the craftsman of all facets of presswork, and the primacy of the finished product as a unique work of art, rather than as a saleable product: these are what make private press books differ from the commercial editions we have been discussing so far. With different motives come a different audience and setting. A book printed in a run of 250 copies is a rarified work, purchased for the most part by a knowledgeable and small group, including friends and admirers of the artist. It is more likely to take its place with similar works in one's library than to be displayed indiscriminately with cheaper or more garish volumes on a drawing-room table. We are dealing here with a more austere art-object than is a commercial edition. Whether the attractions it suggests for Herrick's poetry are radically different from those suggested for a gift-book or cheap reprint is another matter. Considering the differences in audience expectation and publisher's motive, it is an important matter, both in this chapter and when we consider the private presses of the 1920s, the illustrators of which make detailed comments on the eroticism of the poetry. The editions discussed here are almost completely unillustrated, and their decorations provide a general setting for classical poetry. Even so, they make a different impression than a book issued by Harper's, Macmillan, Lawrence and Bullen, or Gay and Bird.

In the work of William Morris and his contemporaries we are concerned with the harmony of typeface, decorated initials, borders, margins, title-page opening, and size of page. The private press work displays, first, meticulous craftsmanship in all these elements, resulting in a consistent, well-made whole.[1] Second, a single artist controls all facets of design. With commercial editions this is not the case. Reginald Savage's illustrations for Newnes (#16) are combined with a title-page by A. Garth Jones, and Elizabeth Forbes' for T. C. and E. C. Jack (#18) are introduced by an engraved frontispiece portrait and title-page reproduction of Herrick's vicarage by A. S. Hartrick. These are all excellent artists, and the results are pleasing, although the uniformity of title-page design throughout a series such as Newnes' or Jack's may produce incongruities such as those John Russell Taylor notes in the Golden Poets editions of Shelley and Spenser, in which Jessie M. King's illustrations are "tucked away in each case behind inappropriate and undistinguished title page openings by another hand."[2] One might make a similar criticism of the cover of the Morley Universal Library edition (#42) of *Hesperides,* on which a spidery, elongated typeface ill suits the design of stylized sunflowers. Also, however interesting the art nouveau decorations for the Lover's Library Herrick (#25), they lose some force when the reader encounters exactly the same design in the series' Tennyson or Browning.

Artwork in commercial editions stands in relation to that of the private presses as popular fashions in furniture or clothing do to the avant-garde art from which they take root. They are the counterparts—for popular consumption—of high art. Consider the Everyman imitations of Kelmscott (see Figure 2-6c): the woodcut borders, floral decorations, caligraphic motto and title, as well as the endpaper design and typeface, project an aura (much as do Kelmscotts) of archaic dignity. The difference is that the Everyman suggestions about how to approach poetry are attractive because they reinforce popular notions of beauty and propriety. These notions became fashionable in part because of the impression made on graphic artists and publishers by the Kelmscott Press and its imitators. Everyman title pages do not present a false impression of the original models, but Morris' volumes possess a very different richness of texture created by handmade paper, specially prepared ink, woodcut decorations by Morris' own hand, and an originally designed typeface. They impress one as rarified, exclusive objects.

The 'fine arts' are definitive: they are the patrician arts. The term is a survival from a period when one small class was content to surround itself with beautiful things as a means of escape from a distasteful environment, *without any desire to impose its tastes or standards on others* [italics mine]. The 'fine book' belongs to that period, and has nothing to do with the cradle-days of printing. It became an anachronism after 1789. The 'fine books' of our time, however modern, are equally anachronistic.[3]

Thorstein Veblen's mention of Kelmscott in *Theory of the Leisure Class* is interesting for its classification of fine printing as one means of inducing in the wealthy the practice of "conspicuous waste."[4] His reason is that the archaism of such books makes them venerable, and, more difficult to find (in their limited editions) and use (gothic type, old style spelling, uncut pages) than cheaper, practical ones. I do not agree with his interpretation of the motive of their printers, or of their purchasers; the latter motive he considers solely as an example of displaying social status. Both appreciation and acquisition of a Kelmscott (or a Doves or Elston Press book) required an effort which makes this judgement simplistic. More germane is his recognition that the deliberate archaisms of the private press are a significant part of its appeal.

These remind one of the manner in which archaic clothing worn by soldiers or priests, judges or Oxford dons suggests the honor, dignity and special efficacy of their professions, and is reinforced by time-honored rituals.[5] A book based on the architectural principles of medieval manuscripts, and fifteenth-century Florentine or sixteenth-century German incunabula, shows a similar faith in the profession—or, to use a medieval guild term, the "mystery"—of printing and *belles-lettres*. Such work can evoke a charismatic aura, or magical efficacy, and so the nineteenth-century craftsman desires to imitate meticulously past practice, in order to produce, for those with similar visions of the past, a better world in one's own time. The epigraph to this chapter, although whimsically stated, is an example of this faith, expressed by a Kelmscott illustrator. So is the following passage, set in a utopian future which has recaptured the medieval aura. It concerns narrating, not reading, but the former, more basic communal activity benefits from occuring in an ambience the nineteenth century found congenial for the latter:

> ...at last we even got to telling stories, and sat there listening, with no other light but that of the summer moon streaming through the beautiful traceries of the windows, as if we had belonged to time long passed, when books were scarce and the act of reading somewhat rare.[6]

Both reading and storytelling are defined here by the imaginative reveries they induce.

In the context of fine printing, Walter Benjamin's concept of "aura" is very relevant. Remarking the reverence with which man beheld religious objects in their proper setting (the sacred places, times, and rituals in which they were displayed), he suggests that the "aura" imbued a work with "distance, however close it is,"[7] a distance which mechanical reproduction destroys by making many copies possible, and by uprooting an artifact from the original setting which gave it charismatic significance (a setting for story-telling such as Morris describes in the passage cited above). "The technique of reproduction detaches the reproduced object from the domain of tradition,"[8] from which "the uniqueness of a work of art is inseparable."[9]

Of course a private press book exists in many copies, any one of which a purchaser can take where s/he pleases. However, the archaic effects the graphic artist painstakingly creates and the limited number of copies provide a specific provenance for the book, and locate it—by the evocative power and symbolic effect of typeface, laid paper, woodcut borders, vellum binding, decorated initials—in a time and place of special fascination. It becomes a cult object. Only a few of artistic temperament can experience the results or be curious about the process. For these happy few of patrician tastes (which are so often associated, as Veblen points out, with the archaic), the book might have the properties of a fetish (just as for the artist himself, an intricate ritual is necessary to bring all the elements together so that the traditional beauty is recapitulated from the raw materials). The purchasers of such a work are likely to be *cognoscenti* who would disdain showing it off to a casual visitor. It might enrich their lives socially as well as aesthetically, but in a more subtle way than commercial editions used as aids to courting or as diversions which advertise *au courant* genteel tastes. The latter of course have their auras, imitative of the avant-garde works under discussion here, which present theirs in a more intensely formalized way, with a somewhat different effect, and certainly to a smaller audience. The fashionable commercial counterparts domesticate the process for a larger group of middle-class readers.

Daniel: *Herrick His Flowers* and *Christmas From the Noble Numbers*...(1891)

Rev. C. H. O. Daniel was a Fellow of Worcester College from 1863 to 1903, and Bursar from 1870 to 1903, when he became Provost. His chief pastimes, besides printing, were "to saunter among the streets and by the streams of old Oxford, whose 'Shadows,' quaint yet cherished, he fixed with his innocent 'black art' [a reference to a set of memoirs he commissioned from colleagues], to play chess with wife or friend, to turn over old books, to sit like Izaak Walton with pipe and angle and a favourite volume at his elbow on the deck of his houseboat or on the banks of his riverside parsonage..."[10] Such a man did not aggressively advertise his gentility. His household, in the words of a close friend, was "a product of old Oxford, where minds might be subtle but characters were simple, and great simplicity of life was combined with a beauty and exquisiteness of surroundings usually associated with wealth and luxury."[11]

Dr. Daniel identified himself closely with the ambience of Worcester College, a perfectly congenial place for him to be. He lived there when a bachelor, and was always dedicated to maintaining its buildings. As he himself wrote, "Something of the Benedictine tradition seems to linger round its ancient walls, and to imbue its members with the spirit of peacefulness and contentment...."[12] That these values were Daniel's own is best illustrated by his equanimity when informed that his first attempt to become Provost had failed: "I think I should like a pipe."[13]

The Daniel Press bibliographer, Falconer Madan, concludes that Daniel's chief purpose in printing was "to give pleasure to literary friends."[14] His books are small in scope (collections of lyric poems or memories), occasional (for birthdays, holiday greetings, or charity drives), and therefore intimate. *Herrick: His Flowers* (#53) was printed in 100 copies for an orphanage fund-raising luncheon, and was advertised with some whimsical verses in black letter:

> Stay/Buy my flowers
> While yet you may
> A few short hours/
> They pass away/[15]

Not unsurprisingly, this gentleman-scholar-printer had many talented friends. His printers' mark, Daniel in the lion's den with the motto "Misit angelum suum," was the work of two men with large interests in the "romance of the past." It was designed by E. A. Abbey and wood-engraved by Alfred Parsons (who also contributed four other ornaments, two of which are used on the back paper wrapper of *Herrick: His Flowers*).[16] Among the writers Daniel knew were Robert Bridges, John Keble, Pater, and Margaret Wood. He published works by each of these. His most renowned volume, *The Garland of Rachel,* a commemoration of his daughter's first birthday, contained poems by Dobson, Lang, Robert Bridges, Henley, Gosse, Lewis Carroll, and others. The Herrick Christmas volume (#54), containing five poems from *Noble Numbers*, was sent to thirty-six friends of his young daughters (60 copies were printed), and is prefixed with a poem by Daniel blessing the recipients ("With merry eyes undimmed by tears/Long locks unbleached by tedious years").

As far as goals and subjects are concerned, Daniel was the opposite of William Morris. Nor was he a student of typography, as the latter was. But by 1887, a year before Morris' essay on printing, Daniel had been recognized as having done something very important in reviving the art of the book. This was because, from 1877, he had been using the Fell types, which, with their "beautifully rhythmical irregularities,"[17] were very well suited to the subject and format of Daniel Press books.

Dr. John Fell found the Oxford University Press its first home, at the Sheldonian theatre. He brought from Holland several matrixes, punches, and types, which naturally were not much used in the eighteenth century. From Daniel's first use of them in 1877 his workmanship improved, probably because the "flowers" (the ornaments) as well as the letters were suited to the literature.[18] Since Daniel's time, the Press has fully realized the virtues of this type: see Quiller-Couch's *Oxford Book of English Verse* (1900, 1924), and various Herrick volumes printed by Oxford (see #11, 60, 75, 91, 95). The Fell type was a welcome addition to the old faces. By the mid-nineteenth century commercial publishers had recognized their attractions, especially the model provided by Caslon, and had been using them widely for *belles-lettres,* for which they were preferred to Modern Face. The differences lie in the pronounced, painfully thin serifs of the latter, the hooks and curls (Morris called them pear-like swellings) on its ascending and descending strokes, and its mixture of thick and squat with attenuated lines. Many of the editions discussed in the previous two chapters use Caslon old face, for the revival of which one must thank Pickering and Whittingham—as well as the interest of the period in the earlier English literature in its historical setting.[19] Without wide concern for the "romance of the pre-industrial past," neither Pickering, Daniel nor Morris would have flourished as they did.

Figure 5-1 reproduces two pages from *Herrick: His Flowers,* giving some idea of the presswork. The heavy impressions supported by the typeface

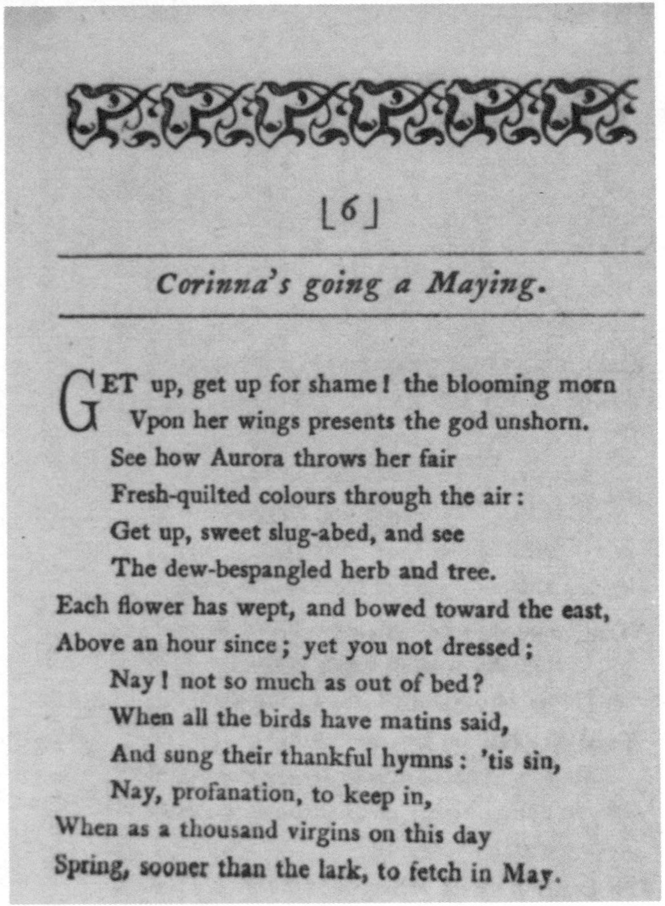

[6]

Corinna's going a Maying.

GET up, get up for shame! the blooming morn
    Vpon her wings presents the god unshorn.
        See how Aurora throws her fair
        Fresh-quilted colours through the air:
        Get up, sweet slug-abed, and see
        The dew-bespangled herb and tree.
Each flower has wept, and bowed toward the east,
Above an hour since; yet you not dressed;
        Nay! not so much as out of bed?
        When all the birds have matins said,
        And sung their thankful hymns: 'tis sin,
        Nay, profanation, to keep in,
When as a thousand virgins on this day
Spring, sooner than the lark, to fetch in May.

Fig. 5-1a *Herrick: His Flowers* (Oxford: C.H.O. Daniel, 1891), p. 6. See #53.

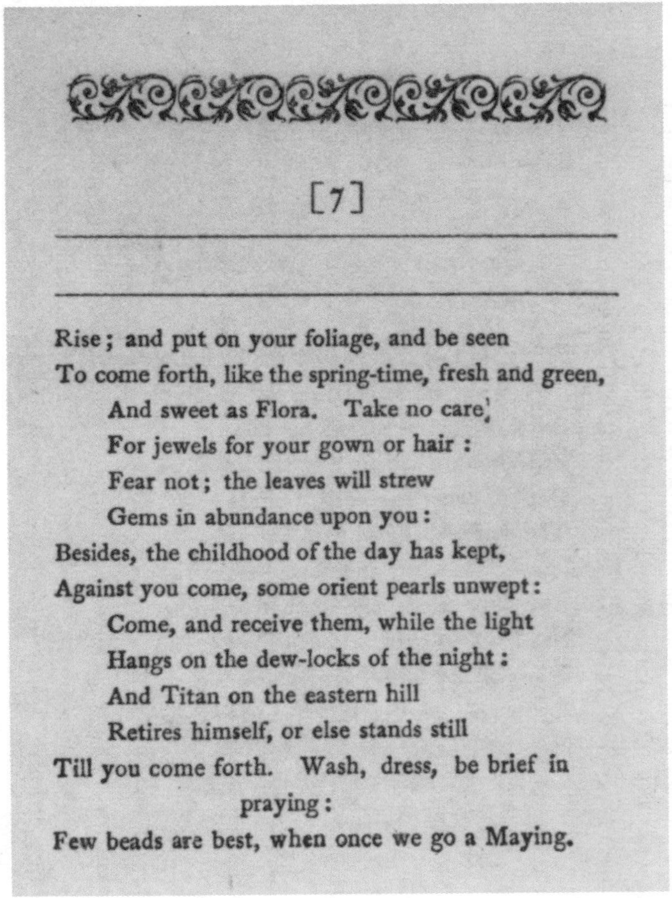

[7]

Rise; and put on your foliage, and be seen
To come forth, like the spring-time, fresh and green,
        And sweet as Flora.   Take no care,
        For jewels for your gown or hair :
        Fear not; the leaves will strew
        Gems in abundance upon you:
Besides, the childhood of the day has kept,
Against you come, some orient pearls unwept:
        Come, and receive them, while the light
        Hangs on the dew-locks of the night :
        And Titan on the eastern hill
        Retires himself, or else stands still
Till you come forth.   Wash, dress, be brief in
        praying:
Few beads are best, when once we go a Maying.

Fig. 5-1b *Herrick: His Flowers*, p. 7.

suggest a rough-hewn, vigorously serviceable book, and the variety of ornaments (different in each of the three pages) harmonize (as relief processes) with the page of letter to lend a note of elegance and a personal touch. This evokes a modern ideal of the Renaissance book. Actually, the presswork of the 1648 *Hesperides* is inferior to Daniel's and this particular Fell font (brevier roman) was cut in the eighteenth century,[20] but the illusion is what is important. Colin Franklin notes that the large ornaments, small typeface, and small page give Daniel's work a "Tudor look" and that in Daniel a scholar's taste for poetry is ascendant over the decorative instincts of Morris.[21] Even so, this thirty-page selection of 23 poems suggests the perennial beauty of the poet's "Garden of Flowers" (the volume's subtitle). Its aura is further created by touches of sumptuousity: handmade, yellow-tinted Van Gelder paper and four blank leaves inserted at beginning and end—for "restfulness", as Madan notes.[22]

This book and its companion-piece are good examples of Dr. Daniel's hallmark, which is only partly his skill and control as a craftsman (evident in the perfect harmony of typeface, ornament, paper and duodecimo format to Herrick's lyrics). There is also the individual creating the books, with a temperament sensitive to a decorous aura for Herrick's poetry. There are the equanimity, amateur eclectic spirit, and good-natured generosity of the old English gentleman who was C. H. O. Daniel.

Kelmscott: *Poems Selected from the Works of Robert Herrick* (1895)

William Morris felt that simple, useful craftsmanship in the "minor," practical modes could be as beautiful as a painting or sculpture. He had faith in his own time to recapture what he saw as the medieval social achievement: the union of all classes in mutual responsibility and respect. One would think, given his vision of the beauty of an artifact as inseparable from its practical use, and his hatred of its being idly displayed to aggrandize its owner, that all men might equally have appreciated the Kelmscott books— clerks and laborers, bankers and lawyers, professors and politicians. So they might have, if, first of all, they could afford the 30 shillings or two guineas. While this is not tremendously expensive,[23] only the most elaborate gift books cost more; a glance at the listings in the *English Catalogue* reveals few books nearly as high. Even if we admit that in this respect Kelmscotts "never stood beyond the reach of many who might have appreciated them,"[24] there is a second consideration which suggests that they were enjoyed only by an exclusive audience. Commercial editions, with their engaging illustrations (often in color), their elaborate bindings and end-papers (as fashionable as Morris and Co. wallpaper), their thick, shiny, sham-archaic paper, and their introductions by well-known men of letters, aggressively courted the book buyer's attention. Morris detested many of their tactics and designs. However, their publishers successfully established expectations regarding the kinds of aesthetic enrichment (and social advantages) which would accrue from their possession, let alone their perusal. They were also printed in much larger quantities than Morris'. The common reader would be much more likely to come across a commercial edition, for Kelmscotts often sold out by subscription. Even if presented with a choice, s/he may well have decided in favor of the more conspicuously attractive, familiar values advertised by Newnes, Jack, Harper's or Routledge. Such a reader would have been more likely to appreciate Morris' style in the cheap reprints or gift books which imitated it.

Professional writers as well as commercial publishers exploited those social aspirations which could be satisfied by some knowledge of *belles-lettres* in order to acquaint an upwardly-mobile, mass reading public with its literary heritage. From the Palgraves, Dobsons, Gosses and Henry Morleys, men like Morris could have learned how to reach large numbers of people. He chose not to. However much he wanted to enrich the lives of his fellow citizens, he would never willingly encourage conspicuous consumption and its attendant debasement of the consumer and his peers: "more and more stuffed chairs and more cushions...more and sharper differences between class and class."[25] Reality, to men of Morris' sensibility, did not admit the validity of the modes and tactics by which practical businessmen communicated.[26] His own press, as Colin Franklin notes, may be compared to his romances: "a kind of wandering in worlds which worked the way he wished."[27] It was founded in 1890, after his retirement from active involvement in socialist programs (and the movement's internecine squabbling[28]). It was a great personal consolation during his last years, and the culmination of a life-long fascination with medieval calligraphy, illuminated manuscripts, and incunabula. Kelmscott was, after all, a perfect example of a private press, which, whether it thrives financially or not, is dedicated to an artist's personal values and experiments, not profit, and does not compromise with a public whose tastes are not receptive to it.[29] In a letter to a friend who gently protested receiving Kelmscotts as gifts, Morris made his motives clear:

I do the books mainly for you and one or two others; the public does not really care a damn about them, which is stale. But I tell you I *want* you to have them....[30]

Mackail notes that Morris did turn a profit: enough to hire Sidney Cockerel as secretary in 1894. The money was used to keep materials and workmanship uniformly excellent. Morris did not seek the public, and in fact, became his own publisher in 1893 (before which time Reeves and Turner distributed the books).[31] As Colin Clair points out, his standards in craftsmanship and in poetry dictated costly books with a limited appeal.[32] Some part of the public did find him, however, and his books were in demand. Kelmscott's first secretary, H. Halliday Sparling, recalls how articles in the February and April, 1891, *Athenaeum* noted the impending appearance of the first volume, necessitating a decision, "to Morris' outspoken annoyance," that 180 copies be made available for purchase. Apparently the consternation was not solely because of doubts that the press could handle a run of this size. He also found unpleasant the use of a smaller format than planned, because the initials had been designed for a larger size and because the monotony of their task might cause carelessness among the pressmen.[33] Even the act of setting a price rankled, and he would take only what could cover the cost of copies to be sold—not for gift copies or depreciation of materials.

For Morris, as the press was his own private affair, an experimental venture entered upon for the sake of turning out books worth looking at, and not for pecuniary profit, these were matters which concerned him alone, to be paid for out of his own pocket.[34]

If Morris had refused to offer copies for public sale, he would indeed have appeared to be a disinterested aesthete. Once the decision to publish was made, his annoyance could have been occasioned not only by artistic compromise but by the realization that his public persona had trapped him into that compromise. He seems to have been pulled in opposite directions by two equally important motives: both artistc expression and social service meant much to him.

Some part of the public, then, had so much respect for the "master craftsman" as to force him to share his "books beautiful" with them. One assumes they were sophisticated connoisseurs. Some may have desired them for what Veblen calls their "honorific" display value as hand-made objects, but to accuse Morris, as one contemporary did, of producing "*bric-a-brac* [which] appeal only to a class you are continually condemning"[35] is a distortion of his motives.

Although Kelmscotts were not for the common reader, Morris' lectures throughout the last decade of his life, in which he clearly set out socialist ideals in forceful language any intelligent listener could understand, attempted to refine taste by attacking fashionable vulgarities in the minor arts, including printing. He excoriates commercial practices as sharply as, earlier, he had those of interior decoration and architecture.

America has produced a good many showy books, the typography, paper, and illustrations of which, are, however, all wrong, oddity rather than rational beauty and meaning being apparently the thing sought for both in the letters and the illustrations.

. . . .

. . . it happens to this craft [typography] as to others, that the utilitarian practice, though it professes to avoid ornament, still clings to a foolish, because misunderstood, conventionality, deduced from what was once ornament, and is by no means *useful*. . .[36]

Since the Kelmscott Press was not conceived to rectify matters as his furniture concern, Morris and Company, did, and since his strenuous efforts for social reform were in the past, he did not show the way to the middle classes by example with his book work. That was left to avant-garde designers like Ricketts, whose Vale Press books were well advertised through John Lane,[37] to the J.M. Dents and Grant Richards, and to Macmillan and Kegan Paul (for both of whom Laurence Houseman worked).Be that as it may,it is important to note what he found objectionable in commercial book design, so that we can see how even a small-format Kelmscott like the Herrick took on a unique aura. His views are contained in two short lectures, "The Ideal Book" (1893), and "Printing" (1888).[38]

First, he finds little in the way of a truly architectural sense. However fine the illustrations in themselves, modern design has no sense of "the due relation of letter to picture and other ornament." Simply to take up an entire page with an illustration (as the Routledge, Newnes, Jack, and Harper's editions do), or to surround a decoration with a small typeface which does not complement its richness (as the Harper's *Selections* occasionally does) is deplored. However brilliant Abbey's drawings, Morris would have disdained the volume itself, not only for its architectural primitiveness but for the stylishness of its cover, the elaborate curls and hooks of the italics in which the titles of poems are set, the thick paper, and the general "showiness" as an American *edition de luxe.* By contrast, as Charles Ricketts put it, a Kelmscott

is a living and corporate whole,....it is not decorated as a modern house is decorated by the upholsterer and the picture dealer.... This would differentiate a Vale book, for instance, in which each part is the result of design, from the finest and most costly continental *edition de luxe,* in which portions may be admirable, the plates, the decoration, for instance, whilst the book as a whole is casual, and a combination of common elements not exquisite in themselves nor exquisitely related to one another.[39]

A second kind of criticism involves the commercial printer's mishandling of individual elements: typeface and its disposal on the page, paper, margins, and even ink. Each of these offends Morris because its appearance is the result of an economic, not an artistic, decision. The alternatively thick and thin widths of the Modern Face letter he thought ugly; "letters should be designed by an artist, not an engineer." Based on the "sweltering hideousness" of the Bodoni type, Modern Face was also too small for legibility. But both design and size made it easier to put more letters on a page. The spaces between letters, and the "leads" between lines, were too large for his taste, regardless of design of type; if the latter had "character," and was not chosen because it allowed a lot of copy to be crammed into a page, large spacing would not be necessary. This practice caused "rivers of white" to meander across the page of letter. As for margins, the modern designer, again in the interest of squeezing as much as possible onto a small space, dumps his type into the middle of the paper, with the disorienting result that often the lower margin is less than the top. Since the ink is cheap, the black-white contrast is not as sharp as it should be, and this leads to a final deficiency which galled Morris extremely: paper. Cheap paper he saw as serviceable, if it were not disguised as expensive by the publisher's sacrificing durability to smoothness and whiteness, "which should be indicative of a delicacy of material which would of necessity increase the cost."

Morris did his own work on the assumption that honest and responsible men would produce objects both useful and beautiful. He thought medieval society had allowed craftsmen to follow these ideals, and was as enthusiastic a defender of fifteenth- and sixteenth-century printing as Charles Ricketts was of the Renaissance book. His preferences are evident in the Herrick (#55), and its companion volumes of Keats, Shelley, Rossetti, and Coleridge, which are just as reminiscent of incunabula in their design as are his reprints of his own romances, with their medieval settings. Morris does not vary his style to fit the subject as Ricketts does, nor does he recapture a seventeenth-century aura, as Daniel does. These poets do merit a Roman (the Golden) type, and an octavo format. This was not his favorite size, for as he says in "The Ideal Book," it "fidget[s] you out of the repose which is absolutely necessary to reading; whereas a big folio lies quietly and majestically upon the table."

It should be noted that Morris' feeling about Herrick is problematical. We know that most of the older English poets whom Kelmscott reprinted he highly esteemed: Coleridge, Shelley, Keats, Chaucer, Shakespeare.[40] Sparling says that he chose "authors worth reading again and again and again, and not merely skimmed through as a pastime or ephemeral refreshment...."[41] And yet, Herrick was so read if not so advertised. Also, Morris would have mistrusted on principle those qualities which made this "lyrist" fashionable: his elegant wordplay, his ethereal aloofness from the sordid and mundane, the "moral-pathetic" vein of his laments for maidens, children, and primroses, his insouciant immersion in holiday festivities and country contentment. He would disdain the nineteenth-century taste for such effusions (if not the poems themselves) as sanctioning the social injustices of one's own time by affecting an air of "dignified" (possibly self-righteous) equanimity. Illustrated single poems by Herrick were being presented by the reviews and magazines as aesthetic amusements, with the implication that they were also inconsequential: gaudy page-fillers. The number of editions, introduced by literary journalists, and bound in gold-stamped cloth (some with "gilt top," untrimmed edges, and romantic title-page vignettes), may well have confirmed any opinion on Morris' part that Herrick's verses as usually presented could hardly propagate a "useful" outlook on art or its place in society. In 1895, the most recent and available of such books would have been produced for the Muses' Library (ed. Pollard,#8), Morley's Universal Library (#42), The Canterbury Poets (ed. Herbert Horne, #43), Harper's (ils. E. A. Abbey, #12), and Macmillan (the oft-re-issued *Chrysomela*, ed. Palgrave; #41). It is possible that these editions could have led Morris to try his own version (Herrick is the only seventeenth-century poet he published). Then too, the volume's editor, F. S. Ellis, formerly one of Morris' publishers and an old friend, may have been the guiding force, wishing to try his hand at what recent scholars and men of letters had done. This is one of the motives inspiring a latter private-press innovator, Jack Lindsay. However, Lindsay was a life-long admirer of Herrick. As the Kelmscott was in press, all Morris would say, with an indirect note of disdain, was that "I like him better than I thought I should. I daresay we will make a pretty book of it."[42]

A pretty book it is, elegantly displaying most poems with large woodcut initials. Vine-leaves, sometimes printed in red, are used after words for special emphasis, as a balance to running titles (also printed in red). The reader is never allowed to forget that he is in the presence of a unique shaping of nature into art. See Figure 5-2. The Golden Type is thick and square, with each line equal in width to the others. It stands up well against the decorated initials, displays the rich blackness of the ink, and allows a solid impression upon the hand-made paper which emphasizes the pleasure of simply holding such a well-made and serviceable—as well as beautiful—object.

However fused the virtues of useful and beautiful are in Morris' philosophy of art and the social order, in his books *dulce* is paramount. The ornate, architecturally-sound contrivance of the title-page opening is the best evidence. Figure 5-2b shows a *mise-en-page* containing the title on the verso and the first poem on the recto. The title and the flowers surrounding it are printed in red. The margins are largest at the bottom and outer edges. The borders and initials were drawn by Morris himself and printed directly "from the wood," not photomechanically. As far as congruence with typeface is concerned, woodcut is the most suitable technique, for it is applied, as is the type itself, by the relief process. Solid "knitting together" of letters and decorations is effected by printing the thick, square capitals of the Golden type with little spacing between the words, small leads between the lines, and leaf decorations indicating beginning of new lines. The page of letter therefore has the same rich density as the decorations of vines, leaves, and grapes. The overall result is quite similar to that of the fifteenth-century Venetian books which to Morris represented the apotheosis of the printer's art. See Figure 5-2c.

There are so many sinuous curves in the Kelmscott borders and initials that the page opening seems more ornate than its model; indeed, to many it is cluttered and over-decorated. This suggests a high Victorian style; it is certainly devoid of the sometimes witty experiments with perspective and white space which characterize art nouveau. Despite Morris' criterion of the primacy of usefulness over display, his books seem to some "rather curiosities of book-making than real books," as the American typographer Bruce Rogers called them.[43]

While the most sophisticated art nouveau work attempts to suggest new perspectives from which to evaluate experience, Morris recreates an aura of an

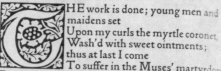

MY wearied bark, O let it now be crown'd!
The haven reach'd to which I first was bound.

ON HIMSELF.

HE work is done; young men and
maidens set
Upon my curls the myrtle coronet,
Wash'd with sweet ointments;
thus at last I come
To suffer in the Muses' martyrdom,
But with this comfort, if my blood be shed,
The Muses will wear blacks when I am dead.

THE PILLAR OF FAME.

FAME'S pillar here at last we set,
Out-during marble, brass, or jet;
Charm'd and enchanted so,
As to withstand the blow
Of overthrow:
Nor shall the seas,
Or OUTRAGES
Of storms o'erbear
What we uprear;
Tho' kingdoms fall,
This pillar never shall
Decline or waste at all
But stand for ever by his own
Firm and well-fix'd foundation.

To his book's end this last line he'd have plac'd:
Jocund his Muse was, but his life was chaste.

266

Fig. 5-2a *Poems Chosen Out Of The Works Of Robert Herrick* (London: Kelmscott Press, 1895), p. 266. See #55.

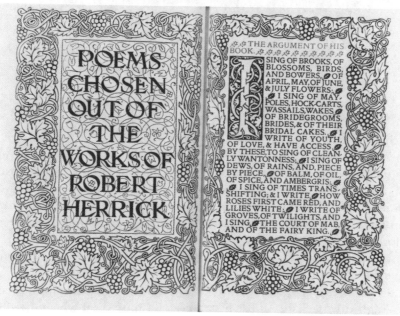

Fig. 5-2b *Poems Chosen Out Of The Works of Robert Herrick*, title page opening.

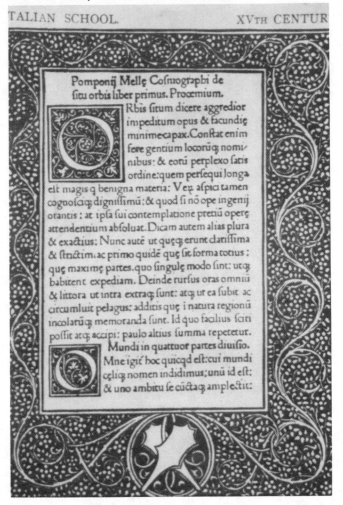

Fig. 5-2c Venetian incunabula, 1478. Source: Walter Crane, *Of The Decorative Illustration Of Books Old And New*, 3rd ed. (1904; rpt. Detroit: Gale, 1968), p. 297. By Permission of Gale Research.

archaic past, and all that Walter Benjamin meant by such a evocation of time and place applies very well to a Kelmscott. Multiple copies notwithstanding, he uses time-honored symbols (woodcut borders, pure ink, gothic-inspired typeface, handmade paper) to give his art "distance, however close it is," to locate it in "the domain of tradition," and to give it the charismatic uniqueness of a medieval altar-piece. Further, he is a consummate artist in the effort he is willing to expend in realizing his vision. For instance, the paper, based on a fifteenth-century Italian pattern, was made wholly of linen and even the wire moulds on which it was constructed were hand-woven to give an authentic irregularity to the texture.[44] The ink was made in Hanover because no English worker would use his choice of a linseed oil which, freed from grease and mixed with boiled turpentine, was then to be aged six months.[45] Naturally, a Kelmscott was a patrician, conservative work of art, not a functional object, and as such different not in kind but in degree (i.e., in the complete, not partial, sophistication of its design) from, say, *Herrick's Flower Poems* or *A Country Garland of Ten Songs From the Hesperides*. The Kelmscott creates, but in a way only an original creation by a single artist can, the aura of an aristocratic, exotic past, which is what illustrators like Abbey, Brock, Woodroffe, or Bell do in their own way, sweetening the impression by giving it a genial, humorous, or innocent tenor for popular consumption.

The final word is the bibliographer Alfred Pollard's: "To anyone who cares at all for poetry or romance, the Kelmscott books are extraordinarily attractive...."[46] As commercial publishers knew, many readers did, including the purchasers of Herrick reprints in gift books (*Flower Poems*, #17; The Lyric Poets, #22; The Chap Books, #27), and cheap series (Everyman Library, #44b and c; The Temple Classics, #44; the Red Letter Library, #47). This is why, in some details of typography, title-page design, shoulder-notes, borders and decoration, these books imitate Kelmscott. Ironically, it was just after, and partly because of, the Kelmscott Press's heyday that cheap commercial editions of literature "for the people" proliferated. The designs of such books would not have made Morris weep for joy, as he did when he saw the efforts of the Vale Press. But, although he may have despised the motives of the publishers and suspected prevailing tastes, he would certainly have noticed (if he had lived a few more years) that his teachings had helped improve the design of books for a mass reading public, largely because his popularity gave publishers a chance to do lucrative imitations. He had become fashionable, and his designs a status-enhancing token of respectable family reading. In America, the Roycrafters Institution, with a flair for public-relations gimmicks, published books and greeting cards imitating Kelmscotts. Its first "Little Journey to the Homes of the Great" was to Morris' Red House.

Elston: *Poems Selected from the Hesperides of Robert Herrick* (1903)

Elbert Hubbard, the founder of Roycroft, was a rare combination of practical philosopher, fine printer, and master salesman. The Roycroft Inn had a room named in honor of Morris, where "Fra Elbertus" gave readings. His writings on the poet included some dramatic embellishments, such as an argument between Morris and Marx. Although such tactics have, it seems, biased judgement against his bookwork, it is certainly true that many Roycroft "limited editions" (in some cases the press runs were actually several thousand) contained garish and slavish imitations of Kelmscott borders, initials, and title-page designs.[47] The Elston Press, on the other hand, produced interesting and skillful variations, under the direction of Clark Conwell and his wife, Helen Marguerite O'Kane, an excellent designer. To some extent, the Elston's choice of writers—Rossetti, Morris, Langland, Chaucer, and Herrick (an almost identical title to the one Morris chose)— mirrors Kelmscott's. But the books are chosen not to imitate but creatively to challenge the model. As Colin Franklin points out, this replication was one of the signs of the private press as opposed to one seeking practically to meet a commercial need. "That was what he made of it, now see how mine looks. It could have been a form of criticism, a hobby.... Each book was partly a technical performance, an act among friends."[48]

The Elston books got plainer as the press entered its last phase, and Franklin, who gives the Herrick (#56) high grades, praises it as "well-disciplined."[49] Its title page is not bordered as is Kelmscott's, nor is it part of a *mise-en-page* which contains the "Argument." In fact, it looks more like a half-title, printed in black and red but taking up only a small part of the page. It is followed (pp. 3-11) by the contents, which bear a Morris-like pseudo-medieval caption: "A Table of the Pieces which are Printed in this Present Edition of Hesperides." The colophon is similarly phrased. By happy coincidence the volume was "Finished this May-day MDCCCCIII." The type is not Golden, which Conwell abandoned after several early efforts ("dreary predictables," Cave calls them[50]), but a similarly solid, evenly weighted Caslon Old Roman. The running titles are printed on the shoulder of each page, in red capitals. Below them are the titles, also in red, of each poem. O'Kane's woodcut initials set each poem off from the other. A contrast between the last page of *Hesperides* in the Elston (Figure 5-3a) and the Kelmscott (Figure 5-2a) shows how the former has managed a variation on its model.

The Elston Herrick remains an Arts and Crafts production, despite the signifcant and well-conceived variations. The type and initials as well as size, title, and colophon present the stolid, earnest look of a medieval manuscript. The book does not have the lighter, more experimental look that Ricketts (who imitated Renaissance book artists) was able to infuse into Vale Press works like Drayton's *Nymphidia* or Marlowe's *Hero and Leander*. But two striking woodcuts—a rectangular one at the head of the first poem (Figure 5-3b) and a circular one placed in the center of the text of the colophon (Figure 5-3c)—are very much in Ricketts' style. The circular tailpiece is similar to the rosettes the latter used for his *Cupid and Psyche* (1897). The rectangular headpiece, in design as well as shape, is like a *Daphne and Chloe* design by him for the John Lane edition of 1893. It seems to impose its art nouveau vignette on a shape identical to that which Morris used as his Kelmscott trademark. Both O'Kane designs show what a sensibility highly attuned to the subtleties of high art nouveau could bring to *Hesperides*. The integration of foreground and background in the headpiece suggests the delicacy, grace, and ingenuousness that the women share with the flowers, grass, and the trees with their (golden?) apples. These dancing daughters of Hesperus, with their attenuated figures, flowing hair, and Greek robes, create rhythms picked up by the reeds and the tree itself in the background, and even by the lettering at their feet. Everything is subject to the same gentle movement, as simple and inevitable as that of breeze and water on a calm night. The circular device, by having the bending flowers imitate the posture of the bending maiden, achieves a similar effect. Foreground and background are perfectly adjusted to the circular frame. In both designs the women are more animated and less

PART of the worke remaines;
one part is past,
And here my ship rides
having Anchor cast.

THE worke is done: young
men and maidens, set
Upon my curles the
Mirtle Coronet,
Washt with sweet ointments; Thus at last I come
To suffer in the Muses' Martyrdome:
But with this comfort, if my blood be shed,
The Muses will weare blackes, when I am dead.

I

TO HIS BOOK'S END THIS LAST LINE HE'D HAVE PLAC'T,
JOCOND HIS MUSE WAS; BUT HIS LIFE WAS CHAST

Fig. 5-3a *Poems Selected From The Hesperides Of Robert Herrick* (New Rochelle, N.Y.: Elston Press, 1903), p. 155. See #56.

THE ARGUMENT OF HIS BOOK
SING of Brooks, of Blossomes, Birds and Bowers:

Fig. 5-3b *Poems Selected From The Hesperides...*, p. 13.

CUT ON WOOD FROM DESIGNS BY
H. M. O'KANE

PRINTED AND SOLD BY
ιRKE CONWELL AT THE ELSTON PR

Fig. 5-3c *Poems Selected From The Hesperides...*, p. 157.

languid than those of Burne-Jones, and there is none of Beardsley's sinister wit (nor any hint of a serpent). O'Kane's work could of course have been influenced by these men,[51] but the figures under discussion here and their poses are reminiscent more strongly of some of Ricketts'. They certainly are decorative in the sense Ricketts meant with his concept of "document," suggesting "what one might imagine as possible in one charmed moment or place."[52]

These woodcuts complement *Hesperides* beautifully and reflect the qualities of equanimity, sweetness, delicacy, and youthful idyllic enjoyment of nature for which the period admired Herrick. I doubt that their style would have prevented readers from understanding them, but there is nothing very much like them stylistically in all the illustrations the poet inspired in commercial book art. Existing in a private press edition of 260 copies, they synthesize calligraphy and ornament into a total work of art, making no compromise with drawing-room proprieties or sentimental courtship rituals.

Notes

[1]Colin Franklin, *The Private Presses* (Chester Springs, Pa.: Dufour, 1969), p. 85.

[2]*The Art Nouveau Book in Britain,* p. 134.

[3]Holbrook Jackson, *The Printing of Books* (London: Cassell, 1938), p. 31.

[4]"Pecuniary Canons of Taste," *Theory of the Leisure Class,* in *The Portable Veblen,* ed. Max Lerner (New York: Viking, 1948), pp. 192-95.

[5]Quentin Bell. *On Human Finery,* 2nd ed. (New York: Schocken Books, 1976), pp. 148-54.

[6]*News From Nowhere,* ch. xx, in *William Morris,* ed. G. D. H. Cole (London: Nonesuch Press, 1948), p. 131.

[7]Walter Benjamin, "The Work of Art in the Age of Mechanical Reproduction," in Hannah Arendt, ed., *Illuminations,* trans. Harry Zohn (New York: Harcourt, Brace, and World, 1968), pp. 222-26.

[8]Benjamin, p. 223.

[9]Benjamin, p. 225.

[10]"Memoir by Sir Herbert Warren, in Falconer Madan, *The Daniel Press. Memorials of C. H. O. Daniel* (1921; rpt. Folkstone, England: Dawson's, 1974), p. 6.

[11]"Memoir by Mrs. M. L. Woods," in Madan, p. 28.

[12]Madan. p. 12.

[13]Madan, p. 7. See also Franklin, p. 31.

[14]Madan, p. 44.

[15]Franklin, p. 30.

[16]Madan, pp. 159-61, 106.

[17]Will Ransom, *Private Presses and Their Books* (New York: Bowker, 1929), p. 66.

[18]Madan, pp. 157-61; Nicholas Baker, *Oxford University Press and the Spread of Learning: An Illustrated History* (Oxford: Oxford University Press, 1978), pp. 15-18.

[19]Stanley Morrison, *On Type Designs Past and Present,* New Edition (London: E. Benn., 1962), pp. 63-72; Bernard Newdigate, "British Types for Printing Books," in *The Art of the Book,* ed. Charles Holme (London: The Studio, 1914), pp. 3-9.

[20]Madan, p. 159.

[21]Franklin, p. 22.

[22]Madan, pp. 46, 106, 162.

[23]Ray Watkinson, *William Morris as Designer* (New York: Reinhold, 1967), pp. 63-64.

[24]Franklin, p. 41.

[25]"The Beauty of Life," in G.D.H. Cole, ed., p. 561.

[26]See Gillian Naylor, *The Arts and Crafts Movement,* 3rd ed. (Cambridge, Mass.: MIT Press, 1980), p. 7 on the failure of the Arts and Crafts movement to comprehend the "nature of the forces that were revolutionizing society."

[27]Franklin, p. 40.

[28]Holbrook Jackson, *Dreamers of Dreams* (London: Faber and Faber, n.d.), pp. 159-60.

[29]Will Ransom, "What Is A Private Press," *Private Presses...,* "corrected and amended" in Paul A. Bennett, ed., *Books and Printing,* rev. ed. (Cleveland: World, 1963), p. 179.

[30]Letter to Philip Webb, quoted in J. W. Mackail, *The Life of William Morris* (1899; rpt. New York: Benjamin Blom, 1968), II, 307.

[31]Mackail, II, 281-82.

[32]Colin Clair, *The History of Printing in Britain* (London: Cassell, 1965), p. 246.

[33]H. Halliday Sparling, *The Kelmscott Press and William Morris Master Craftsman* (London: Macmillan, 1929), p. 76.

[34]Sparling, p. 77.

[35]Quoted in Clair, p. 246.

[36]"Printing," in May Morris, *William Morris: Artist, Writer, Socialist* (1936; rpt. New York: Russell and Russell, 1966), I, 256, 259. May Morris attributed most of this essay to her father, although Emery Walker is usually considered co-author.

[37]Cave, pp. 136-37.

[38]*The Ideal Book, An Address by William Morris,* (New York: Calumet Press, 1899). The essay is reprinted in May Morris. For Morris' views on book design, see Susan O. Thompson,

American Book Design and William Morris (N. Y.: Bowker, 1977), pp. 23-24 and Appendix.

[39]Quoted in G.S. Tompkinson, *Select Bibliography of the Principal Modern Presses Public and Private...* (London: The First Edition Club, 1928), pp. xv-xvi.

[40]Morris' response to a questionnaire on his favorite books is summarized by Jack Lindsay, *William Morris: His Life and Work* (New York: Taplinger, 1979), p. 298.

[41]Sparling, p. 91.

[42]Mackail, II, 311. See Sparling, p. 91: "In the absence of a definite claim, either intrinsic or enforced by friendship, no book would or could have been printed by him."

[43]David Bland, *A History of Book Illustration*, p. 275.

[44]Paul Thompson, *The Work of William Morris* (New York: Viking, 1967), p. 141.

[45]Paul Thompson, p. 144.

[46]Franklin, p. 49.

[47]See the chapter on Hubbard in Susan Otis Thompson, pp. 170-84.

[48]Franklin, p. 52.

[49]Franklin, p. 159.

[50]Roderick Cave, *The Private Press* (New York: Watson, Guptil, 1971), p. 161.

[51]Noted by Franklin, p. 158; Susan Otis Thompson, p. 163.

[52]Stephen Calloway, *Charles Ricketts: Fantastic Illustrator and Designer* (London: Thames and Hudson, 1978), p. 16.

Chapter 6

British Private Presses, 1927-1955: Herrick and the Twentieth-Century "Common Reader"

> This Robin Hood the second owed homage to two worlds—the actual world of his day-
> by-day activities where he lived as a favored bachelor priest...and the world of his
> imagination, the enchanted Forest of Arden, a kind of land of Shee that any Jacobean
> Miss could in an instant conjure up for him.... These lively, lovely girls, shy and
> liquid-eyed as new born calves in his own strawy cowshed...could in a trice translate
> him body and soul into a horse-shoe fairy world substantial enough for treading, and
> for ravishing sensations, and yet ethereal too....
> —Llewelyn Powys, "Robert Herrick: Minister of Grace," *Saturday Review of
> Literature*, February 8, 1936, pp. 3-4.

The monumental social changes accompanying World War I altered
interpretations of national purpose, individual responsibility, wealth and
social status, and of human motives. Naturally, the tastes and expectations of
the post-war audience for *belles-lettres* were very different from those of its
Victorian and Edwardian counterpart. Factors most relevant to the changes
may be briefly stated as follows; they will be more fully discussed in the
context of specific twentieth-century limited editions of Herrick. These were
all produced in England; this chapter is based on between-the-wars literary
tastes in that country.

The changing status of women in society was not fully understood in
Edwardian times, but after the war females were no longer the delicate
ornamental creatures whose proper function was to be guardians of drawing-
room culture. Writers and editors could no longer expect women to be
content with tales of flowery meads, gallant cavaliers, or dewy-eyed maidens,
or with expurgated novels and lyrics. Human sexuality was no longer a taboo
subject in middle-class milieux. The twenties was the Age of Freud;
bowdlerization was in full retreat, and the vigorous prosecution of publishers
of works judged "obscene" is an obvious example that what self-appointed
but officially-sanctioned moralists thought "respectable" was no longer
identified in literary circles with education or refinement. Part of the
explanation for publishers' greater frankness with taboo subjects was that
print media no longer exclusively commanded, as in Edwardian times, a mass
audience, the latter having supplemented books with film, theatre, and radio
as ways of learning about fashions and behavior patterns. Therefore,
publishers, especially in limited editions, could legitimately appeal to a more
exclusive and tolerant audience—for whom a work threatened with
censorship piqued curiosity rather than offended sensibility. Notions of the

gentleman had not so far changed as to exclude magnanimous aloofness from anxiety and crassness, and dignity and repose were still *desiderata* of a civilized lifestyle. However, next to nothing remained, among literati at least, of Victorian ideals regarding a gentleman's duty both to lead the way in improving society and to make himself an example of aloofness from fleshly indulgences. Such an illusion was considered romantically quaint, so far out of step was it with the modern *zeitgeist*. The latter set a premium on radical philosophies of social intercourse, on a detached, "aesthetic" gaiety and wit, and especially on idiosyncratic libidinous expression and its vicarious enjoyment in erotic literature and art.

Fanfrolicing in London: The Roaring Twenties, Dionysus, and Robert Herrick

In 1926 a 26-year-old poet, literary critic, historian and fledgling polymath arrived in England to carry on in civil Bloomsbury a press he and a friend had started in their native Australia. He was Jack Lindsay; the press was the Fanfrolico; their first London success was Lindsay's translation of *Lysistrata,* with illustrations by his father Norman Lindsay, Australia's foremost artist and fearless advocate of the artist as Nietzschean hero, liberating himself from convention and testing the strength of his spiritual and sensual (especially erotic) insights. The press, as his son stated, "was established on the basis of propagandising his ideas."[1] As Norman Lindsay put it in the press' 1928 *Statement of Aims,*

...Love and Happiness must be the basis of a return to stability and order in the action of life.... I truly care to find there is a genuine return in interest for my own effort to express love and gaiety and a frank delight in lyricism, and to define once more the simple creed of youth's right to love.[2]

The press' name was a gesture of homage to Rabelais, one of Jack Lindsay's favorites (along with Plato, Sappho, Nietzsche, Freud, Rubens, Beethoven, Blake, Keats, Rossetti, and William Morris). In *Gargantua and Pantagruel* lads and wenches "fanfrelucked it at every fields end." One of Norman Lindsay's pastimes was the writing of bawdy stories about the Duke of Fanfrolico; he read one to Jack when the latter first became his disciple.[3] In London, Jack Lindsay's circle was bound by a Fanfrolico ethic: "to drop all social and ethical falsities and find the individual in all his candid rights."[4] This meant more than twitting the literary establishment (most notably with a magazine the title of which parodied the *London Mercury,* and whose opening manifesto took on Eliot, Wyndam Lewis, Gertrude Stein, J.C. Squire). It meant more than publishing literature and art of sufficient literary frankness to flirt with police action, more than engaging in wild parties and living with beautiful girls. Although fanfrolicing noticeably did include such larks, the press uniquely supplemented its typographical aims with an aesthetic sensibility based on a complex and eclectic program for combatting the impersonality and cynicism of the modern world.

As for "how to print finely," Lindsay owed much to his friend John Kirtley, whose decision it was to go to London to try his mettle as a publisher. He returned to Australia, but Lindsay, who was left in charge with his partner P. R. Stephensen (who handled the financing and advertising) found in the mecca of fine printing artists such as Harold Curwen, Bernard Newdigate, and Francis Meynell. Their own craftsmanship profited from the example. They bought types from Curwen for some books they printed on their own press. Most were prepared at commercial firms. Curwen took a special interest, and his press printed several volumes, including the Herrick, in the text of which Koch Kursive made its first appearance in England. Fanfrolico experimented with many new faces.[5] Simply as a designer of beautiful books Lindsay deserves high repute. "What to print finely," however, was the primary concern of this restless young iconoclast.

Stephensen's "Policy of a Fine Press" in *Fanfrolicana: A Statement of Aims* (1928) describes the press' "selective principle." It offered to the public literature which attempted "to redefine beauty in terms of delight": "Greek and Roman Laughter" (Petronius), "lyricism" (Sappho, Herrick), "Elizabethan Gusto" (Skelton, Sir John Harrington), "Romantic suavity" (Robert Landor). Like the sixteenth-century Italian printers, Lindsay and Stephensen edited the texts they published, quite independently—they made a point of saying—of the standards of the "venal and obtuse" critics of the day. If this protected the purity of the literature from the smug dissections of the "sensitive misery" school, who preached the absurdity of life and the compulsive fears and traumas of twentieth-century man,[6] the policy regarding illustration also attempted to repudiate the *zeitgeist* which Lindsay saw as paralyzing the literary establishment. Because illustration was "the *sine qua non* of a book with character," the press utilized not only the work of a few congenial contemporary artists but also dared to reprint "relevant masterpieces" by Holbein, Rubens, Turner, Blake, Rossetti, Delacroix, and Praxiteles. Fanfrolico was nothing if not learned; one catches Lindsay in the process of attempting what he admired Nietzsche for doing: "absorbing the whole philosophical tradition at one gulp" as well as "formulat[ing] a Dionysian philosophy."[7] Immersed in the greatest accomplishments of the European tradition in arts and letters, the Fanfrolico men were never callow or shrill in their teaching. But they were proud—that they had captured the Elizabethans' "essential concord with the Hellenes," that they had given an example to "tired" Londoners of an "anachronistic blitheness and emotional expansiveness" characteristic of energetic Australia, and that they had shown how, from Plato's time to the present, libidinous vitality had been preached by philosophers and poets great enough to be worth collecting in limited editions.

Despite all the idealism, and however much Lindsay and his circle hated the cash-nexus, Fanfrolico was shrewdly conducted as a commercial enterprise. "In point of sales we were the most substantial Press by far after the

Nonesuch."[8] Lindsay's "Retrospect of the Fanfrolico Press" compares it to Kelmscott as a "coherent" expression of avant-garde ideas.[9] But as we have seen, it was the public who found Morris, somewhat to his chagrin, and Lindsay actively sought purchasers, not only to exhibit his ethic but to make a living. In this, Fanfrolico was not different from other presses which turned to commercial printers to do their presswork. The prototype of this policy was Nonesuch (as it was in the careful editing of its texts[10]). Despite the larger size of the latter's editions (Fanfrolico usually issued about 550 while Nonesuch press runs were usually over a thousand), both presses placed a variety of subjects and styles within reach of the common reader. This is an important point to keep in mind when considering the nature of the audience for limited editions. We will deal with that audience in detail a bit later. The evidence in the next paragraph suggests that however contemptuous Lindsay and his friends were of retreat from the boisterous joy of life's raw conquests, their advertising exploited such motives as bourgeois acquisitiveness, conspicuous consumption, the gentlemanly leisure of book collecting, and prurience masked as art appreciation. No better example is Stephensen's trunkload of books, trundled along on his visit to Nice to discuss with D. H. Lawrence an edition of the latter's paintings. He thought the Riviera's "fashionable resorts" would provide a good market, but was unsuccessful. "How mad people are," noted Lawrence, "there is quite a large vogue in editions de luxe that cost two or five or twenty-five pounds. I hate it."[11]

Stephensen ends his essay on Fanfrolico policy by noting that since these books are illustrated by famous artists of the past, they will be proof against even such rigorous censorship as "the American customs" might impose. He reminds the reader that all the editions are limited, and therefore "gold spent on these books will not be gold wasted.... One of the most amusing aspects of Fine Book collecting as well as of Fine Book producing, is that the hobby satisfies the maker of beauty as well as the miser of coin. Happy dualism."[12] Jack Lindsay's contribution to *Fanfrolicana* is a witty poem entitled "Hypothesis of a Publisher":

> We have assayed, the best we can
> To temper prophesy to man;
> To tune our trumpets till our rage
> Fills the advertising page;
>
> . . . .
>
> Apollo's tailors, since we try
> To find the noblest trousers or
> Camisoles for Forms we adore,
> That other lovers may be wooed
> To possess poetry in the nude.
>
> . . . .

> We shall not dress in beauty's lace
> Some sluttish or cold-moral face,
> But maenads send, post-paid, to you.[13]

The dualism between philosophical ideals and pecuniary realities is faced (if not reconciled) with a "happy dualism" of gaiety and determined shrewdness. When one finds in Fanfrolico's magazine *The London Aphrodite* advertisements headed "Very Pleasant Gift Books," one feels the editors might be satirizing commercial book-selling practices, but this could not be the primary motivation of the appeals to vicarious consumption and conspicuous leisure which met the eye in such unfrolicsome arbiters of modern taste as *The Times Literary Supplement* and *The New Statesman*, especially when some of these advertisements quoted J.C. Squire, Desmond MacCarthy, and John Drinkwater. The Christmas Supplement of *The New Statesman* (Dec. 1, 1928, p. iii) carried a full-page notice headed "Fanfrolicsome Books Are Gifts For the Discerning." A crucified Venus, dressed only in an enigmatic smile, drew attention to *The Antichrist of Nietzsche*. A few weeks later (Dec. 12, 1928), a *TLS* advertisement suggested that "even a quite extensive private library will not contain editions" of works like the Press' fully-annotated Beddowes, thus proving its superiority as a gift-book to commercial editions of the classics. About a year earlier, the Herrick edition was announced in a notice set in Koch Kursive typeface:

The most charming edition of Herrick's poetry which has ever been issued—a book perfectly suitable, both in form and substance, for gift purposes—

Delighted Earth
. . . will take its place as one of the most elegant achievements of modern Fine Book productions
A SMALL EDITION
In view of the special demand for this revitalized HERRICK, immediate application to the Booksellers is advised.[14]

Lindsay edited *Delighted Earth* (see Appendix, #59) under the pseudonym "Peter Meadows," a name he also used for a six-part "autobiographical fantasia" of sexual conquests which ran in the *London Aphrodite*. He must have felt the word "meadows" to connote what men and women have been known to do together in them, which acts have nothing to do with the dignity and repose of conventional, respectable pastoral. Meadows' scholarly avatar[15] is evident in the inclusion of "Mr. Robert Herricke his farewell unto Poetrie," from the Ashmole MS, and in the lengthy excerpt in the second part of the Introduction from Phillip Stubbes' indignant description of rural Mayday celebrants. The latter is set down not only to give a sense of the period, but because this puritan's "righteousness transcribes itself into the lyric rush of these revellers." Therefore it is an example of the inability of a representative from what Lindsay called the "dark forces which denied life and muddied the springs of sex"[16] to root out from his own being a fascination with those forces. Censorship would have especially drawn fire from Lindsay in 1927. British authorities were ready to pounce on what they considered "indecent" literature, and a year and a half later, in the *Aphrodite,* Stephensen defended "free expression against the dominant Philistine puritans represented by Squire among the intellectuals and James Douglas among the journalists."[17]

The first part of the Introduction, which is more a narrative than a discursive essay, is entitled "Robin Herrick." Written in what the TLS reviewer acknowledged to be an "ambitious" and "enthusiastic" style, but stigmatized as "too della-cruscan artifice,"[18] it applies the Fanfrolican perspective to Herrick and thus helps us understand something of what Lionel Ellis is doing in his illustrations. Lindsay is the only critic to explain why Herrick was a happy man by allusions to that most anguished of men, Nietzsche. From this essay on "The Modern Consciousness" in the *Aphrodite*—which magazine F. J. Hoffman called "perhaps the best modern exponent of Nietzsche's position"[19]—comes a notion of the artist as hero which underlies the introductory essay in *Delighted Earth.* Such a man uses the weapons of artistic imagination and defiant individualism to fight off what social custom and conventional moral sense dictate as right. He thereby achieves a "liberated judgement,"[20] and can both contact and control his— and his universe's—natural vitalities. With unshakable commitment to his art and his sexual libido, with gaiety and courage, Herrick ignores the life-denying and abnegating attitude of "Ebeneezer" and "Jeremy." These bovine Devonians, the type who appear in Herrick's epigrams and in whom Lindsay could recognize the "wowzers" of his boyhood, grumble about the "gaudie trinketing" of their parson, a "poking-nosed rakehell" with hair "all prettified with curling-tongs." They resent his "cage-full of girls," whom, it was rumoured, he had bought from the "Grand-Turk" with "tithe-money," and who constitute the most interesting furniture in the Dean Prior parsonage.

...he turned his eyes to where all the girls were lying in a huddled naked heap, piled up against the wall in the corner, all the life soothed out of them by sleep. Only a paint of life remained, breathing, a subtle cosmetic of warmth. Julia, Anthea, Phillis, Lucia, Corinna, Perilla, Sappho, Sylvia, Dianeme, Oenone. They were growing too mischievous: he would have to get a bigger cage to hold them. (p. 3)

Herrick has shaped these daughters of earth in an idiosyncratic act of imagination—the kind of "creative effort" Norman Lindsay describes in his 1920 treatise of that title.

"Meadows' " essay does show us "Robin" Herrick the man. As bizarre and cerebral as his interpretation is, it reflects the ubiquitous admiration readers feel for Herrick's ability to project his unique personality into brief lyrics. We would expect Lindsay to share this admiration. For him, poetry and the poet's idiosyncratic character cannot be separated from each other.

One's imagination and reason must be at the service of, and build on, visceral sensation and irrational desires. A heroic, and lonely, effort is necessary, for Herrick as for Lindsay's favorite contemporaries (Dylan Thomas, Edith Sitwell, Tristain Tzara).[21] To such exemplars of creativity we add Norman Lindsay, whose profile was dominated by an autocratic nose, who was as mercurial a sensualist as "Meadows" makes Herrick to be, who enjoyed the company of simple folk ("Meadows" has Herrick buying drinks for his parishioners), and whose appearance and conversation were bird-like[22] (the introductory essay concludes with "Robin" musing, "I am a bird. The songs we sing are straight and fragile as a wisp of straw, as rich as cream eaten at dawn").

On a matter much discussed by more conventional scholars, whether Herrick's mistresses were real or imaginary, "Meadows" has a unique viewpoint: they were in a sense both. His poet-hero would not deny himself sexual gratification; one who rises "above" worldly appetites ceases to be a poet. Therefore he was able to shape earthy human experiences, and beautiful women, into ideal forms in his "liberated judgement" or imagination, and to integrate Dionysian and Apollonian, real and ideal, body and soul. These contrasts are implied in titles of sections into which the poems are divided: "Toilets [i.e., "dressings"] of a Kiss" (the only title which does not quote Herrick), "House of Flesh on Fire," "O Flame of Beauty," "Bellman of the Night." The contrasts are central in the introductory essay, especially love and poetry, body and soul.

The heathen Turks thought women had no soul, perhaps truly. But could not Julia be a soul though she had none? Your soul or mine: not dim stuff of the spirit floating like sunsets round the cherry-blossom, but kindly sirens of a man's lonely thought; for no girl exists unless she has taken the shape of a kiss. That is why there are bodies.

His girls, what were they? When they knocked at the door, naked and confident, he had not the heart to turn them out. But why should they continue to cheat his mouth, becoming a serpentine drift of flowers...? (p. 4)

There is a very beautiful poem, "Lovers how they come and part," from which Lindsay may have taken his cue (he included it on the first page of the section "O Flame of Beauty"):

A Gyges Ring they beare about them still,
To be, and not seen when and where they will.
They tread on clouds, and though they sometimes fall,
They fall like dew, but make no noise at all.
So silently they one to th' other come,
As colours steale into the Peare or Plum,
And Aire-like, leave no pression to be seen
Where e're they met, or parting place has been.

In the service of showing how these contrasting elements are integrated into the "subtle knot" that makes one man and poet, "Meadows" gives an odd interpretation of the Narcissus myth as a symbol not of solipsistic fear of life's attachments but of the necessary complement the soul must find in a localized time and place, in the "pool of matter." Here is Lindsay's description, in *Life Rarely Tells*, of his own first realization of what poetry meant to him:

> ...no simple narcissistic discovery of my own face, between the lillies, in the pool of poetry, the pool of my own senses penetrated by a single beam of light. True, the spirit-world was darkly and powerfully one with the new life seething in my loins.... The continual movement of detachment from the world had inverted itself into this discovery of a perfected sensuous essence, a nacreous bubble of light precariously united with my leaping heart. (pp. 67-68)

"Meadows" describes Herrick as identifying himself with Narcissus, and fancying it was not his own reflection but "rather Narcissa who lifted up the brown ripples of her hair to stare back into my eyes. How reach the soul's unity. In this sweet simple act of love? Yes, and in more. Julia opened her eyes and he knew it was in Poetry" (p. 5).

Lionel Ellis was a close friend of Lindsay and his beautiful drawings show his understanding of the mythic contrasts the introduction cryptically delineates. They are reproduced in collotype, so their delicate shadings come through clearly, and help make the contrasts between nature and art, nudity and clothing, mythological and naturalistic figures. They are not literal interpretations of any single poem but rather each decoration introduces one of the eight sections. One contemporary critic notes that "if Rubens had had the chance to illustrate Herrick...he might conceivably have produced something like this...."[23] Fanfrolico found in Rubens its most congenial painter of rapturous affirmation of wordly delights; his Munich *Bacchanal*, Lindsay declared, "...sends Silenus staggering into our own experience," and "makes us feel our whole life (now become drunkenness) moving into the experience of the picture and returning revitalized back into our own self-delighting."[24] Ellis' collotypes show his debt to Rubens (and also Bernini and Delacroix): *chiaroscuro* effects, powerful figures with aggressive movements or laconic, satiated postures, windblown drapery and sea-foam, fleshly female nudes, and vibrant landscapes suitable for both the pastoral frolicking of mortals and for Venus, cupids, Pan, and the fairies.

"Come, Sons of Summer" (see Figure 6-1a) introduces a section largely devoted to lyrics on holiday ceremonies. The title is from "The Hock Cart, or Harvest Home:...," a poem in which the Earl of Westmoreland's tenant farmers sportively dress themselves, their horses and the cart in incongruous finery and eat and drink their fill. The men and women in Ellis' drawing are not British peasants, although Herrick's phrase "Harvest Swaines, and Wenches" is universal enough to apply. The vehicle to which the powerful horses are yolked (although there are only two not four) is as likely to be Apollo's chariot as a wagon full of wheat. The crowned, air-borne figure at the center of the picture, whose posture may in fact parody a crucifixion, may be the sun-god himself. With a magical gesture he calls forth the energy and light in which he himself is nearly effaced and which bathes the revellers who salute him with a toast. The opening image in the first poem in this section, "Corinna's Going a-Maying," suggests the rays of the sun, i.e., Apollo's streaming hair: "The god unshorne." Ellis makes muscled limbs more evident than compliant feminine curves; thus he stresses the benevolent interaction between Apollonian heaven and vibrant, Dionysian earth.

The images of "House of Flesh on Fire" (Figure 6-1b) make a similar iconographic point. The eye is drawn from the goat (attribute of Bacchus-Dionysus) at the bottom of the drawing, through the ritual movements of the women and satyr at the center of the picture, to the female peering from the edge of a cloud at the top. The latter's pose is slightly reminiscent of that of Rossetti's *Blessed Damosel,* and both the painting and the drawing make a connection between the blessed spirit and the yearning flesh. But where Rossetti stresses the contrast between earthly and heavenly love, Ellis shows their unity. The woman in the clouds is indistinguishable in form or function from the three on earth. She reminds the viewer of "Meadows' " interpretation of the Narcissus myth as a union of the soul with the body in the "pool of matter," and also of his feeling that the mundane and the eternal are fused in life-affirming, creative acts such as that which the three venereal figures and the satyr share in. From the breasts of the seated female (as in Rubens' *Garden of Venus*) flow the source of life, nourishment, and creative inspiration. It is gathered by her attendants (either priestesses of Venus or maenads, servants of Bacchus) and fed to a satyr whose bestial nature may be tempered, but will not be eradicated, by it. The drawing suggests benevolence and gentle, formal movements, and thus belies its title. Like Ellis' other decorations, it depicts a life-affirming perspective from which readers of *Delighted Earth* can judge the poetry. Editor and artist ignore the whimsicality and playful wit with which Herrick tempers the love agonies contained in this section of the book. But its opening couplet does suggest the balance in which love and poetry, feral impulse and benign rationality, must be held:

> Love is a circle, and an Endless Sphere,
> From good to good, revolving here, and there.

The attraction of the illustrations for most readers would not lie in the manner in which they complement Lindsay's ideas but in the gracefulness of the usually naked female figures (whether in dramatic movement or sensuous repose), the sharpness with which pastoral landscape is drawn, and the variety of universally-recognizable icons of love, beauty, innocence, and creative spirit. The subjects are richly varied: wildly gesticulating fairies, a demure, buxom peasant girl with an "Apron of Flowers," nymphs and satyrs making love, a toilet of Venus in which the reclining goddess is almost devoured by kisses while cupids try to cover her with tiny flowers, and a Venus

COME, SONS OF SUMMER

Fig. 6-1a *Delighted Earth* (London: Fanfrolico Press, 1927). "Come, Sons of Summer," p. [29]. See #59.

HOUSE OF FLESH ON FIRE

Fig. 6-1b *Delighted Earth:* "House of Flesh on Fire," p. [103].

arising from the sea with such energy that the *putti* hovering over her and the mortal swimmers at her feet are thrust into the shadows by the force of sea and wind. The popularity of this "revitalized Herrick" (less than 100 copies remained by the summer of 1929[25]) would have been due not only to the erotic illustrations but to other aspects of the "deliberately pretty book."[26] The luxurious art-work harmonizes with the Koch Kursive typeface, and its graceful lines, delicately angled serifs, and open-faced upper case: one critic said of Koch's typography that it "vibrates like the air in springtime."[27] The title page, and colophon in blue and black, matching the case binding of blue balloon cloth all added to the sumptuousness. The *TLS* reviewer concluded that "Herrick might have likened it to violets and cream."

The Between-the-Wars Audience for Limited Editions

What kind of people comprised the audience for Fanfrolico books? It could hardly have been Jack Lindsay's kindred spirits, who did not number in the hundreds. Even if they had, the tenor of P.R. Stephensen's marketing tactics was not aimed at the dedicated followers of the *avant garde:* readers who found poetry and prose by Lindsay (or by Lawrence, Joyce, Woolf or Pound for that matter) congenial. Among the diverse purchasers of Fanfrolicos Lindsay reports "a bank-clerk who lived at Bromley" and "an American businessman."[28] His press catered to a broad group of general readers with tastes formed by the men of letters *The London Aphrodite* attacked, mandarins of an establishment which "politely ignored [his] noise, held its nose, and went on with its own business."[29] One of the ironies of Lindsay's situation in the 'twenties, therefore, was that he was exercised in keeping himself financially stable by serving up the "Fanfrolico ethic" to people many of whom inherited values and a conduct of life for which he had a measure of contempt. His most likely market—for which he competed with Nonesuch, the Golden Cockerel, Cresset, and The Medici Society—had to be drawn from the upper-middle-class "middlebrow" consumers who patronized the easily comprehensible "Georgian" poets whom *The London Mercury* and *The New Statesman* championed.[30] This audience's notions of gentlemanly tastes and sophistication were exemplified by John Drinkwater, **Walter de la Mare,** Edmund Gosse, W. H. Davies, and John Masefield, and by "aesthetes" who imitated those in Bloomsbury or Sitwellian circles. In the thirties, Lindsay (with many other poets) abandoned the attempt to elevate middle-class taste in favor of a socialist crusade on behalf of a proletariat he could love and respect. For our purposes, however—an understanding of how private presses between the wars interpreted Herrick for the general reader— we must clarify the interests of their audience, so we may understand how they exploited and refined those interests. I don't mean that private presses were successful because a number of fairly affluent readers enjoyed Rupert Brooke and John Drinkwater, wanted Carew's "A Rapture" on laid paper with Post-Impressionist illustrations, or emulated the life-style of Noel Coward or

Sacheverell Sitwell. I mean that the cultural ambience in which fine printing flourished can be specified by considering the sensibility which could be caricatured by such attachments.

The final anthology of *Georgian Poetry* appeared in 1922, but post-war readers had apparently not lost interest in cheerful, gentlemanly, pastoral repose. W. H. Davies (a poet, incidentally, often compared to Herrick), Edmund Blunden, Lascelles Abercrombie, and **Walter de la Mare continued** to describe the magic of childhood and moonlit downs, the contemplative pleasures of rural life in contrast to urban agitations, and the consolations of a gracious optimism.[31] This body of verse includes work by T. F. Powys, Edward Thomas, and Thomas Hardy, written with colloquial diction and "a thoughtful receptivity before the poet's environment, especially nature seen in a somewhat domestic way, by the cottage not on the mountain."[32] Such verse could lapse into easy whimsy, but it was written in language readers could understand about experiences which refined members of the urban middle classes could appreciate. These people found that elite writers unceremoniously lumped them with the bourgeois and saw their moral standards, literary expectations, occupations, and pastimes deprecated by young, experimental, and difficult-to-read poets and novelists. With a Davies, a Drinkwater, or a J. C. Squire—who also wrote Georgian verse[33]—a large group of "middlebrow" general readers could share a literary heritage and a sense of community. The same is true of the critical essays of Squire, Augustine Birrell, Edward Hutton, and Desmond MacCarthy, who succeeded Squire in 1920 as literary editor of the *London Mercury* and who brought (possibly by way of his Bloomsbury connections) a "tradition of breadth, enlightenment, rational sociability, civilized forbearance."[34] The values that the *Mercury*, or *The New Statesman and Nation*, projected for their readers seemed superficial to writers like Eliot, Wyndham Lewis, Lawrence, Pound, or Jack Lindsay. The Squirearchy and the "literary bolshies" of the 1920s confronted each other with a belligerence that could not but do harm to the state of English culture. "The best art becomes available where there are fewest stratifications of public taste, when, in fact, the elite of society and society in general share, broadly enough, the same tastes."[35] As for the popular poetry of rural contentment just described, we might say with Ifor Evans that "it no longer answers the new, strange, harsh shape in which the world and civilization show themselves. It is the product of minds which still live in the pattern of a past which is no longer there."[36] But the conviction of a common literary heritage which this poetry and the magazines which championed it kept alive was not an illusion for private press executives like Meynell, Robert Gibbings, and Bernard Newdigate, who advertised in these periodicals and arranged to sell their volumes in bookstores the owners of which also took out notices therein. Publisher and distributor alike knew that readers of these magazines needed them.

The appeal of fine books very much depended on the conviction that literary classics could offer refreshment and strength of purpose because of their broad-ranging power to communicate to literate people. Thus Christopher Sandford's Golden Cockerel is interested in "old tales of adventure," "old people and their poetry," "the masterpieces of English and French literature and classical literature. He is really a very human bird, kind and sometimes very amorous, never spiteful, never morbid, never cruel."[37] Francis Meynell asserts that "we intended to choose our books to suit our tastes.... But fortunately, many other people also wanted these books. For our taste proved to be a normal contemporary taste."[38] Meynell's family lived in Bloomsbury and were acquainted with, but not a part of, Virginia and Leonard Woolf's circle. The difference in philosophy of publishing, and perhaps of sensibility, is evident in Meynell's reminiscence:

Virginia Woolf was only once a party guest. Undistracted by the clamour, she gazed fixedly into my eyes and with a firm grip of my hand said: "The Hogarth Press may not make any money— but at least [the grip on my hand tightened] at least we did not publish *The Week-End Book*." She was surprised when she heard me guffaw this to the rest of the company.[39]

The Week-End Book was a compendium of helpful and recreative poetry and prose for British travellers, one of Nonesuch's unlimited editions, but Woolf's comment, however genial, indicates a disdain on the part of the publisher of Eliot, Auden, and Spender for catering to popular taste. It suggests a feeling similar to D. H. Lawrence's for the late-twenties vogue of expensive "editions de luxe" and all they implied about the persistence of middlebrow attachment to conspicuous consumption and books as furniture.

In his review of the early twentieth-century literary scene, John Holloway states that the new poetry, written "by, and for, a metropolitan intelligentsia," repudiated "the broad city middle class" and therefore "affords a link between the new poets of the 1910s and those of the Aesthetic Movement."[40] Part of the appeal of private presses was to help give a positive sense of identity to many literate members of this "broad middle" class, who did not patronize "gift verse" by Ella Wheeler Wilcox, and did not see in themselves the *betes-noires* whom the Rhymers Club, George Moore, or T. S. Eliot pointed to as boorish slaves of the "cash-nexus." Instead, they aspired to be well-read, tolerant, industrious citizens, comfortable with their leisurely pastimes (good conversation, appreciation of the fine arts, the "reading habit"). In buying Nonesuchs, Cockerels, Fanfrolicos, and Cressets, one could luxuriate in the restrained, sophisticated beauty of volumes bound, illustrated, printed, and decorated so as to be pleasant to hold and—as Meynell insisted—meant "for reading, for reference, for the elucidation of textual problems, and for hard wear."[41] Nonesuch books provide pleasure in the reading, not in the mere collecting and showing off. One could thereby disassociate oneself from bourgeois crassness.

Also desired was aloofness from life-denying "respectability," that death-in-life very well delineated by the popular poet Humbert Wolfe in his

"The Respectable Woman":

> I have not heard nor seen them,
>   I have not danced nor sung,
> and when love passed between them
>   he left my heart unwrung.
> They have wasted their lives by spending,
>   and are with death rewarded,
> but I shall find no ending
>   of the life that I have hoarded.
> I saved the source of living,
>   Thou knowest at what cost,
> and, therefore, All-forgiving,
>   now give me what I lost!

The "them" of the poem are free spirits who, daring to cultivate romantic feeling and ignore prudence, are capable of a vital, adventurous life. Wolfe's poem reflects a Fear of Respectability inevitable among sensitive people bombarded by self-righteous censors and advertisements identifying success with good taste in motor cars, soap, and whiskey. The fear surfaces even in the penchant for heroes of detective fiction such as Dorothy Sayers' ultra-sophisticated Lord Peter Whimsey (collector of incunabula as well as abstruse clues) and in the fascination with fictional "aesthetes" in novels by Nancy Mitford and Evelyn Waugh. There was also interest in flesh-and-blood gentlemen like Sacheverell Sitwell, who with his brother and sister was responsible for making several aspects of *avant-garde* literature and art fashionable.[42] Admiration for the sort of social role such figures exemplify owes something to the ability of the person assuming it to live an elegant, vivacious life unencumbered by conventional moral strictures. It owes something also to admiration for the traditional equanimity and independence of the English gentleman, and especially to the desire to be secure enough in one's own self-esteem to express curiosity and delight at what respectable people shun.

An example of a graphic artist known for gracious and benevolent dandyism as well as his work for private presses is Lovat Fraser. He was a man of unfailing, playful good humor (despite ill health), whose creative response to his World War I service was fashion-plate drawings of fancy uniforms. He decorated with gaiety and delight not only poetry by friends like Ralph Hodgson, John Drinkwater, and Walter de la Mare, but toys, envelopes, and children's stories.[43] His ambition, as Drinkwater records it, was to reach the common man with "gay colours and brave ruffling figures.... When someone complained that he made his Shakesperian people like figures from a pack of cards, he could not see how this could be other than a compliment...."[44] Fraser's use of line and color reflected perfectly the "returning gaiety and sparkle of the post-war decade."[45] His designs appeared throughout the period on a variety of advertisements, and in printers' decorations for the Curwen Press. That his tastes in literature coincided with those of private press executives and readers is clear from the following:

I love the ballads because they were the voice of a great lusty England that was naked and crude in its patriotism and yet was unashamed—the proud hearted England of before the birth of tolerance, a land whose fervid limited vision gave us Shakespeare and Milton and Herrick with all his golden company....[46]

A final characteristic of the private press audience—having much to do with contempt for respectability and deference for the vibrant individualism celebrated in great literature—is its interest in the sensual and erotic. Here again, readers' (and artists' and editors') sense of identity is involved. The publisher William Jovanovich has some very perceptive comments on why, apart from prurience and its exploitation, sexual explicitness in literature is so important to twentieth-century readers. Sex is an "unremittingly individual" experience, which tests a person's physiological and emotional capabilities and allows one to understand oneself in a way that very often one's occupation, income, and social obligations do not.[47] Also, and most relevant for twentieth-century private press editions of Herrick, eroticism satisfies "nostalgia for a past state of innocence, [a need for] celebration of the life of nature, [and] a desire to experience simple physical activity—aesthetic and romantic."[48] This is similar to Havelock Ellis' assertion that "obscene" literature for adults serves the same purpose that fairy tales do for children, providing "relief from the oppressive force of convention."[49] Well worth appending to these explanations are two observations. First, erotic art provides a vicarious experience and as such has the potential to stimulate imagination and contemplation. Second, possessing a finely printed novel or poem signifies the taste and intelligence to appreciate good literature whatever its theme or setting. After a century of bowdlerizations accepted when drawing-room respectability was a viable part of their culture, middle-class people in the Age of Freud require a license maturely and passionately to respond to any erotic stimuli, however explicitly or even brutally and violently expressed.

There is a tradition in British letters of printing erotic literature in limited editions, under the assumption that wealthy, educated people can be safely exposed even to writing which, in the words of the British Home Secretary in 1929, "would tend to corrupt and deprave the public mind."[50] As mentioned above, the threat of censorship hung heavily over British and American publishing in the late twenties. Francis Meynell's reaction in his 1929 Prospectus to recent actions by the Director of Public Prosecutions struck for his clientele just the right note of insouciant equanimity:

...no publisher can be positive in his announcement that he will issue such and such a book. Chaucer? Fie, his language is coarse. Plato? The less said about Socrates and his young friends, if you please, the better. Shakespeare? He will perhaps pass unchallenged, for "Lamb's Tales" doubtless exhausted the censor's interest in this prurient author. Farquhar? *Don Quixote* even—?

[These were two current Nonesuch publications.] These too may corrupt the corrupt, which is the current legal test of obscenity.[51]

That is as astute and elegant a combination of social comment and sales pitch as ever a gentleman-publisher who knew his audience devised.

Limited Editions and Robert Herrick, 1928-1968

Lovat Fraser died in 1921, and published very few decorations of poems by Herrick.[52] However, the style and influence of this friend of Albert Rutherston, Oliver Simon, and Harold Curwen is significant. Fraser's affection for *Hesperides* epitomizes the upper-middle-class attitude toward the English literary tradition, recreative reading, and independence from tight-lipped respectability:

He was a voracious and cultured reader; but his reading ran always toward the dandies of the pen, living or dead. Above all, it was toward the writer of the musical phrase, to the lyrical sense in the man, that he was most drawn—Herrick was ever his love—and they that wove their art of words akin to Herrick. The neat epigram, the condensed epitome of life, phrased with the musical lilt of words, tuneful, colourful—these ever drew Lovat's homage.[53]

Fraser's decorations of poetry—often for seventeenth- or eighteenth-century lyric—are line drawings suggestive of the crude, vigorous woodcuts which characterize eighteenth-century chapbooks and Tuer and Crawhill's revival of their primitive style. To some tastes, Fraser's quaint milkmaids, eighteenth-century dandies, half-timbered buildings, and miniature stylizations of billowy fields under fleecy clouds are "mawkish," "sentimental" retreats to an imaginary rural past of sweet tempers and neat cottages.[54] However, as J. R. Taylor states, his two-dimensional sketches (sometimes done in broad, flat colors) and their fanciful irregularities are "none the less charming for all [their] evident determination to charm."[55] They add a stylized, playful naivete to the long-standing fascination with "merrie" England to which Abbey, Thomson and the Brock brothers, each in their realistic manner, responded with enthusiasm.

Holbrook Jackson compares Fraser's drawings to pictorial marginalia such as those in letters to friends, and to personal remarks that a poetry-lover might scribble next to a favorite line of verse.[56] A taste for such self-contained impressions about poetry is necessary to appreciate Lovat's work. Any one sketch being very lightly related to the poem it ornaments, it can be transferred easily to other contexts; for his admirers such a process would not be thought of as distorting the spirit in which he drew. From one of Fraser's last books, *Poems from the Works of Charles Cotton* (The Poetry Bookshop, 1921), Haldane McFall took three decorations from the poem "Winter" and used them in a Christmas pamphlet "printed, not published" for Earl Fisk (see #61). It contains three poems by Herrick: "A New-years gift sent to Sir Simeon Steward" (with a headpiece of a snow-covered house), "Ceremonies

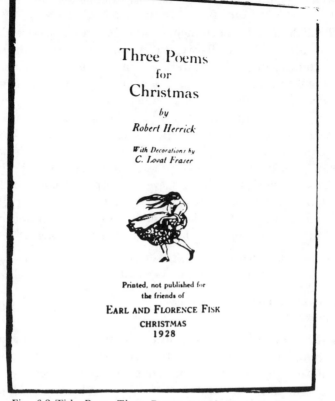

Three Poems
for
Christmas
by
Robert Herrick

With Decorations by
C. Lovat Fraser

Printed, not published for
the friends of
EARL AND FLORENCE FISK
CHRISTMAS
1928

Fig. 6-2 Title Page, *Three Poems for Christmas by Robert Herrick*. (1928). Decoration by Lovat Fraser. See #61.

for Candlemass daye" (headed by a man smoking a pipe) and "Ceremonies for Christmasse," decorated with a girl with hair and skirt blown by the wind. The latter figure is reproduced on the title page. See Figure 6-2. These decorations are unobtrusive, cameo-like gestures between friends who feel as comfortable with their happy spontaneity as with Herrick's poetry itself.

Fraser's pen-names, "Richard Honeywood" and "Felix Folio, gent.," with their slightly archaic, playful tenor, complete the persona his drawings, his manners, and his preferences in literature imply. One senses a witty, self-sufficient gentleman without large-scale ambitions, who cheerfully endures the contempt of earnest, respectable folk, and who is sure enough of his own character to enjoy frivolous pastimes and appreciate the subtle tonalities of minor poetry and cameo art. Such a sensibility is attributed to Herrick himself by essayists of the 'twenties and 'thirties, and it would therefore be natural to find it in his illustrators of the period: certainly not in Jack Lindsay, but definitely in Fraser and his friend Albert Rutherston, whose style owes much to Fraser. Although judgements of Herrick's character are the subject of my final chapter, I would like to mention here the introduction to the four-volume Cresset Press edition (#60) by Humbert Wolfe, in which he strives to secure an impression of the poet suitable both to the poetry and, possibly, to the four frontispieces contributed by Rutherston.[57] Wolfe sees a tranquil and dignified temperament behind the sensual features. Herrick, he says, loved "all the quiet spells of earth" so much that he remained aloof from sensual commitments and lived the life of imagination "...self-sufficient to the point of selfishness" (p. xxix). A perennial spectator, a poet not a lover, and a perfectionist in the smallest parameters of lyric poetry, he did not care very greatly for human relationships, nor for spiritual consolation, since neither loneliness nor anxiety were part of his experience. "Like Horace, he was not so much a man as a gentleman of letters. He was wise, he was easy, he was mellow" (p. xxxviii). Such a writer will not bear scholarly dissection, so Wolfe (at length; the Introduction is seventy-five pages long) promises merely to read a few poems in the vicarage garden, "not to beg souvenirs of Prudence Baldwin," and to allow Herrick to ramble off to the Dean Bourne with his spaniel, "freely whistl[ing] one of the airs to which his songs were set" (p. x).

All of us who read this will in the end be a fable, song, or fleeting shade. But Herrick is none of these things. It is early spring with him. The dew is on the grass. The larks are up, and, as we take our leave, we hear him, calling on a note of immortal laughter—
    Come my Corinna come, let's go a-Maying.
And they are going. (p. lxxxiv)

The *TLS* reviewer was not amused by either Wolfe's or Rutherston's effort. Although he understood that Herrick's "charm" presents a problem to a critic, he felt that the latter must not "forget the poet in the amiable eccentric."[58] He liked the volumes themselves, with their Fell types, octavo size, mould-made paper with deckle edges, and plain vellum binding more than either Wolfe's literary artifice or Rutherston's "exceedingly mannered pictures." Another reviewer, who also praised the presswork, paper, and format, criticized Rutherston for "ragging the subject."[59] If his frontispieces are too labored, it is understandable considering the complexity of his task. His decorations are a unique attempt to suggest the witty sensuality of some of the best-known of Herrick's poems, those which would entice the reader into perusing the entire volume. Furthermore, to place the drawings with their forebears, many nineteenth-century frontispieces (as we have seen) presented readers with the features of a gross and almost brutal sensuality which ignored both the allegorical background and the archness with which William Marshall depicted Herrick. Rutherston flaunts this convention by taking neither Herrick nor himself too seriously, and by gleefully acknowledging the poet's sensuality. He shows, as the nineteenth-century engravers do, a profane man, but his introduction is a vivacious welcome, full of Cavalier boldness and "harmless mirth," whereas theirs are cold warnings that the volumes are to be kept in the gentleman's library, so as not to offend drawing-room propriety.

    In the frontispiece of volume II of the Cresset Herrick, the poet is doing a "word-picture" of one of his mistresses. See Figure 6-3. He is intent on the

Fig. 6-3 Albert Rutherston, ils., *Poetical Works of Robert Herrick* (London: Cresset Press, 1928), vol. II, frontispiece. See #60.

poem he is writing, but is looking at the paper as if he were an artist, while the model seems coyly intent on getting him to concentrate on her. After all, why does he need a live model? His reason and hers may be different; perhaps she knows more about this than he is willing to admit. In any event, both motives involve passion: there is a spot of red in his cheek, mirroring that on his model's. Herrick's dress features ribbon pom-poms on the shoes, a waistcoat such as Charles II popularized, and knee-length breeches with scalloped edges peeking out beneath the coat. The elongated figures are well framed by the tree, leaves, and vine and also by the birds, bush, clouds, and sun-rays. The greens, yellows, and purples of the background contrast pointedly with the reds on gown and flesh. The fanciful effect is completed by the graceful calligraphic line with the strips of color running along it, and the cross-hatching to suggest texture and shadow. The mood Rutherston creates is just right for suggesting that, since the evidence of the poems is contradictory regarding clothing and nakedness ("Clothes do but cheat and cousen us,"

"Art above Nature: to Julia"), the illustrator will let the poet and his readers have it both ways. He manages to suggest several other poems as well: "Upon Julia's Clothes" (and their "liquefaction"), "Upon the Nipples of Julia's Breast," and "Upon Julia's Unlacing Herself." Rutherston suggests poetry's artful recreation of nature, and the problem of capturing beauty verbally. The poet himself did this in *Hesperides*, and his likeness is trying to do it in the illustration, despite the enticing obstacle. Above all, the artist enthusiastically invites us to share the sensuality of Herrick's world, somewhat as the 1648 frontispiece does, without Marshall's allegories, but with playful humor and garden background.

Rutherston's sketches are "cavalier" in the modern sense of the term: carefree, vivacious, self-assuredly indifferent to propriety. His work is immediately arresting, and calculated to amuse a general audience, as was Lovat Fraser's. This edition embodies the spirit in which Herrick's lyrics may still be read to women by the special men in their lives, be they schoolboys like Blades in Delderfield's *To Serve Them All My Days*, or undergraduates at Herrick's college, Trinity Hall, Cambridge, where in 1890 at least he was "still reckoned very pretty reading, even by boating men."[60] "There's not a poet in his teens," explains De la Mare's Henry Brocken to Electra, Julia, and Dianeme, "but warbles of you morn, noon, and night.... There's not a lover mad, young, true, and tender, but borrows your azure, and your rubies, and your roses, and your stars, to deck his sweetheart's name with."[61]

The Cresset Press format is at least equalled in attractiveness by the more austere classical style of Humphrey Milford's edition of 1935, which forms the first two volumes in his "Hesperides Series" (#63). The designer was the prestigious graphic artist, Bruce Rogers. The volumes were published in London, where Rogers brought out his lectern *Bible* the same year. After 1929, financial difficulties had forced most of the English private presses to close, and the lively experiments of 1920s book design gave way to conservative formats.[62] The style of the 1935 Herrick is an example. Rogers' goal here—as throughout his career—was to embody the spirit of the literature for the contemporary reader. He does not try to recreate the medieval Kelmscott aura, but is more in the spirit of Charles Ricketts, some of whose Vale Press books were aggressively advertised and distributed by John Lane, and who varied his style to fit the subject. But Ricketts' books often look like Renaissance Venetian works, while Rogers' are distinguished by what Wil Ransom called "subtle visual interpretation of the spirit of literary content as distinguished from detailed reproduction of historic or period style."[63] In the Herrick, Rogers suggests the elegant subtleties of "cleanly-wanton" lyric. He uses not Fell types but Centaur roman (with Arrighi italic), which he designed (in 1914) after Italian Renaissance models (and used in his 1935 *Bible*). The pages are very simply arranged, with no ornament of any kind (titles of poems and running titles are in italic), so that the dignified beauty of the typeface is emphasized. See Figure 6-4a. There are no shoulder-

356   *Hesperides*

The end of his worke.

Part of the worke remaines; one part is past:
And here my ship rides having Anchor cast.

To Crowne it.

My wearied Barke, O Let it now be Crown'd!
The Haven reacht to which I first was bound.

On Himselfe.

The worke is done: young men, and maidens set
Upon my curles the *Mirtle Coronet*,
Washt with sweet ointments; Thus at last I come
To suffer in the Muses *Martyrdome*:
But with this comfort, if my blood be shed,
The Muses will weare blackes, when I am dead.

The pillar of Fame.

Fames pillar here, at last, we set,
Out-during *Marble, Brasse*, or *Jet*,
   Charm'd and enchanted so,
  As to withstand the blow
      Of overthrow:
     Nor shall the seas,
     Or OUTRAGES
     Of storms orebear
     What we up-rear,
     ThoKingdomsfal,
This   pillar   never   shall
  Decline or waste at all;
But stand for ever by his owne
Firme and well fixt foundation.

To his Book's end this last line he'd have plac't,
Jocond his Muse was; but his Life was chast.

FINIS.

Fig. 6-4a *Poems of Robert Herrick*, The
Hesperides Series (London: Humphrey
Milford, 1935), II, 356. See #63.

*T*HE FLOURISH
OF MUSICK: THEN FOL-
LOWED THE SONG:

I

Tell us, thou cleere and heavenly
Tongue,
Where is the Babe but lately
sprung?
Lies He the Lillie-banks among?

2

Or say, if this new Birth of ours
Sleeps, laid within some Ark of
Flowers,

Fig. 6-4b *The Star Song A Caroll*
to the King (Mt. Vernon, N.Y.:
W.E. Rudge, 1924), p. 1. See #58.

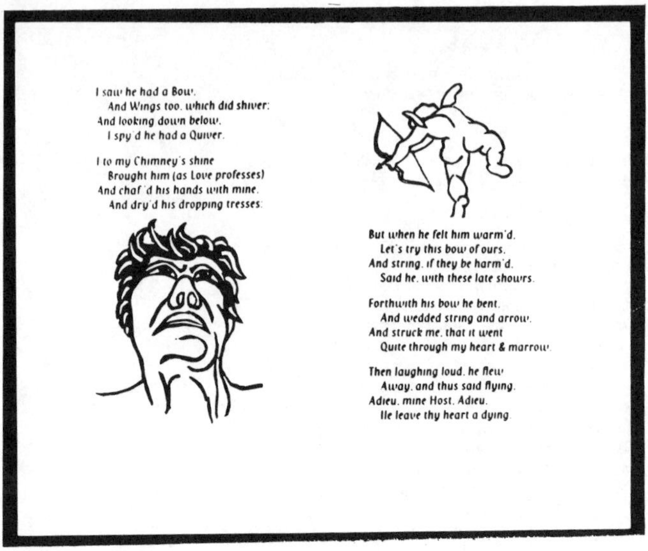
I saw he had a Bow.
And Wings too. which did shiver:
And looking down below.
I spy'd he had a Quiver.

I to my Chimney's shine
Brought him (as Love professes)
And chaf'd his hands with mine.
And dry'd his dropping tresses:

But when he felt him warm'd.
Let's try this bow of ours.
And string. if they be harm'd.
Said he. with these late showrs.

Forthwith his bow he bent.
And wedded string and arrow.
And struck me. that it went
Quite through my heart & marrow.

Then laughing loud. he flew
Away. and thus said flying.
Adieu. mine Host. Adieu.
Ile leave thy heart a dying.

Fig. 6-5 *The Cheat of Cupid: Or the Ungentle Guest* (Hexham, Northumberland: Septentrio Press, 1968), n.p. See #67.

notes, decorated covers or endpapers, art nouveau borders, or calligraphic text. The title page is extremely simple, again with no rules or flowers. Ornament appears only on the spine of the casing, in the form of tiny golden apples stamped on a background of red cloth. A gold-stamped border on the covers completes the elegant and severe effect.

In quite another mood is Rogers' design for W. E. Rudge's Christmas gift-book, consisting of Herrick's "The Star Song" (1924; see #58). For this he used italic type with Fournier ornaments. The title page is nearly identical in design to that Rogers used for Dowson's *The Pierrot of the Minute* the year before: type ornament in the form of roses, vines, and sunbursts strung together with fancy borders. Rogers whimsically termed his Dowson work "French millinery. . . . Rather over-decorated, but then the poem itself seems over-decorative."[64] The typographical artifice of the Herrick poem reinforces its conceits, as the speakers (or singers) inquire, in syllables rich with assonance and alliteration, of a noon-day star where the baby Jesus is to be found. See Figure 6-4b. Italics have often been found suitable for Herrick's verse, not only at Fanfrolico but, much more recently (1968), at the Septentrio Press. See Figure 6-5. The architectural sophistication of this *mise-en-page* includes the manner in which typeface and illustration are arranged on the facing pages and also the linear harmony of Klang italic with the lines of the drawing.

What Francis Meynell termed "allusive typography"[65] has accompanied the family reading habit in America and England since it was encouraged by drawing-room table books and well-printed cheap reprint series in the late nineteenth and early twentieth centuries. It has accommodated the varying tastes of the common reader for far longer than that. It reminds us of Meynell's reason for starting Nonesuch: he wanted to read his favorite authors in appropriate settings—not necessarily those which recreated the aura of a past period in the history of printing, but those which help the modern reader toward an impression of the tone or spirit of a work. Such impressions of course will vary greatly, and will uniformly annoy (or be ignored by) New Critics and scholars from Eliot's generation to our own day. As far as twentieth-century notions of how Herrick can best be set in "allusive typography" for the general reader is concerned, there are not only the representative volumes discussed above, but also those by the Medici Society (#57), the Peter Pauper Press (#64), New Directions ("The Poet of the Month," #87), Ernest Benn ("The Augustan Books of Poetry," #83), Chatto and Windus ("Zodiac Books," #86), Grey Walls Press ("Crown Classics," #90), and Rutgers University Press (#89). Whether the format of the volumes implies something specifically about Herrick's theme or style, or simply **affords an attractive background for lyric poetry, it imparts a luxury which** dignifies the reading experience, shaping one in which the individual can feel **comfortably at home.**

Most of us like a book in pleasant surroundings—sitting at an open window, by a river or on the rocks. A fact of life is that the mind likes to wander and absorb, even beyond the author's meaning. And if some persistent absorbent is there—the sea, a summer breeze—we like it, are comforted and it seems to help with the reading. Now, the argument for finely made books extends easily from there: the mind which needs absorption beyond the meaning of the printed page, will find it in the beauty and good sense of the overtones of the page. The river's function, the wind's job, is performed by the fitness of margin, the texture of paper. A fine binding is as good as a fine view. The whole slack of reading experience is taken up by the book.[66]

A Final Edition de Luxe: The Golden Cockerel Herrick, 1955

The Golden Cockerel Press had been serving for 35 years a clientele described by its third director, Christopher Sandford, as "small, very cultured, very sophisticated, very critical, but ultimately very appreciative"[67] when its Herrick volume appeared (#66). At that point, the press was only five years from closing, and had been forced by a shrinking market to take advantage of a temporary vogue for expensive gift-books sumptuously illustrated.[68] This meant relaxing its policies regarding woodcut decorations and editions of new and classical little-known writers who deserved to be better known among discriminating readers.[69] Its director accommodated the very popular William Russell Flint when the latter wished the press to publish his *One Hundred and Eleven Poems by Robert Herrick*, which project the artist financed himself. During the next five years hardy perennials such as Shelley, Dryden, Omar Khayyam, Ovid, and Shakespeare appeared. Flint planned a Keats,[70] and completed soon after the Herrick one of those pieces of erotic "curiosos" for which the Cockerel, and the Folio Society, were known:[71] "An Album of Caprices" entitled *Minx Admonished*. The advertisement for this volume featured a bare-breasted girl with her feet imprisoned in a pair of stocks. "Altogether different from the Herrick," the notice states, but a similar piece for the latter volume depicts a scowling nude, definitely a nubile minx, sitting in a richly carved, bedraped chair, her feet resting on a plush cushion. The copy reads in part:

The two water-colour paintings...and the forty chalk-drawings in sanguine which embellish the poems were a long-sustained labour of love—a great painter's tribute to a great poet...there is nothing robustious nor any straining after originality, but in all the drawings the melodies of Herrick's lyrics echo from a responsive heart.[72]

Although Flint was a very popular illustrator, writers of the stature of Colin Franklin, Harvey Darton, and David Bland have criticized his interpretations of literature as superficial.[73] Even the London *Times* obituary made a similar point, and went on to describe his female figures as "Alma-Tadema brought up to date."[74] This may, perhaps too-readily, be applied to *One Hundred and Eleven Poems*, most of the illustrations to which are of beautiful women, clothed or half-nude, idealistically posed. A closer look may be rewarded by a balanced judgement.

Flint, who everyone conceded was an accomplished draftsman, includes a portrait of Herrick, Prue, many "mistresses," and three goddesses: Diana, Venus, and Juno. Homely Prue is complaisantly smiling, and virtually swathed in clothing. The others, "stately goddesses," are statuesque and self-absorbed, nude or clothed, fascinating not only because of their beauty but because of their variety of poses and facial expressions. "Sapho" (the frontispiece, see Figure 6-6a) is inscrutable; Anthea stares over her shoulder, arms akimbo, seemingly in a fit of pique; Perilla pertly lifts her overskirt from the floor. Only Corinna smiles, and only Electra is sweetly unassuming. Julia is twice shown, in profile, and in the same elaborate, decollete gown embroidered with "airy silks": bows, ribbons, an "ascent of curious lace." She wears a jewelled necklace, and in one version an elaborate headdress. Her expression is severe and commanding. Several of the women are singing or dancing, therefore fully complementing the artfulness suggested by their carefully wrought costume and "tresses bound / Into an oval, square or round." The most persistent icons in the drawings are the lute (attribute of the muses and the lover) and the book (symbolizing the muses, learning, and perhaps the melancholy associated with the contemplation of love and beauty). The artist suggests that the women he has drawn—the kind Herrick finds irresistible—are quintessential examples of Cupid's power:

> And here we'l sit on Primrose-banks, and see
> Love's *chorus* led by *Cupid*; and we'l be
> Two loving followers too unto the Grove,
> Where Poets sing the stories of our love.
>   "The Apparition of His Mistresse calling him to Elizium"

Fig. 6-6a W.R. Flint, ils. *One Hundred and Eleven Poems*
(London: Golden Cockerel, 1955). Frontiespiece. See #66.

In one sense Flint's figures are truly like Abbey's or Alma-Tadema's.
Striking a balance for the viewer between distance and familiarity, they
suggest people who are his or her contemporaries masquerading as figures
from the romantic past. Their poses are formal and they wear period costume,
but the period is indeterminate rather than Caroline, and the clothing and
hair-style are those of a stage or film costume drama. There is no attempt to
reproduce period setting. The illustrations bear the names of the imperial
princesses of Herrick's imagination, but—as is true of Tadema's or Abbey's
"pretty people"—the women are recognizable as contemporaries of the artist.
They are like girls a male reader of *One Hundred and Eleven Poems* might
like to think he once knew. For female readers, they may be role-models who
put men in their power by their wit, the artfulness with which they adorn
their bodies, and the originality with which they recreate a variety of
irresistible female roles:

And each Ringlet of her haire,
and Enchantment, or a Snare,
For to catch the lookers on;
But her self held fast by none.
Let her *Lucrece* all day be,
Thais in the night, to me.
"What kind of Mistresse he would have"

Facing the opening "Argument" (Figure 6-6b) is a full-page drawing which sets Herrick's poetry and Flint's art in the imaginative pastoral universe which Llewelyn Powys describes as Herrick's proper milieu (see the epigraph to this chapter). It depicts an innocent, uninhibited "land of Shee" dominated by tall, graceful trees under which several women sit by the bank of a stream. One suns herself, another sings; two others, naked to the waist, dangle their feet in the water. The headpiece for the "Argument" shows a fifth. This fairy land of art and nature, and its eroticism, must be located very far from that delineated by E. A. Abbey, Reginald Savage, or Paul Woodroffe, but it is one, all the same—the one Havelock Ellis and William Jovanovich describe as satisfying twentieth-century's man's desire for vicarious romantic

Fig. 6-6b Headpiece, "The Argument Of His Book," p. 13.

experiences stimulated by an eroticism unimpeded by the *caveats* of "normality" and "respectability." Flint's illustrations, however superficially pretty, fill their audience's definite need for imaginative as opposed to visceral experiences. He thus focuses on one of Herrick's most basic appeals since his "rediscovery" early in the romantic period. Furthermore, Powys' praise of Herrick's own abilities to bridge the dichotomy between his mundane duties and his personal fantasies finds a parallel in Flint's complements to the poet's universal theme: the dual claims on the human psyche of sensual impulse and its artful refinement. The Golden Cockerel gift book, despite the advertisements which present it as sophisticated erotica, is one more example of the survival of nineteenth-century popular romanticism's emphasis on the vicarious pleasures of reading as enriching one's inner life. It is also evidence of the relevance of Herrick and his "cleanly-*wantonnesse*" to our own time.

Notes

[1]Jack Lindsay, *Fanfrolico and After* (London: Bodley Head, 1962), p. 52.

[2]*Fanfrolicana. June 1928. Being a Statement of the Aims of the Fanfrolico Press Both Typographical and Aesthetic...*(London: Fanfrolico Press, 1928), p. 8.

[3]See Urquhart trans., II, 23; John Hetherington, *Norman Lindsay: Embattled Olympian* (Melbourne: Oxford U. Press, 1973), p. 176; Jack Lindsay, *Life Rarely Tells* (London: Bodley Head, 1958), p. 176.

[4]Jack Lindsay, *A Retrospect of the Fanfrolico Press, With a List of Fanfrolico Books* (London: Simpkin, Marshall, 1931), n. p.

[5]Lindsay, *Fanfrolico and After*, p. 158; Anthony Adams, "The Fanfrolico Press: An Appreciation," *American Book Collector* 9 (1959), p. 11.

[6]Jack Lindsay, *Meeting With Poets* (New York: Ungar, 1969), p. 234.

[7]Jack Lindsay, "The Modern Consciousness," *The London Aphrodite*, no. 1, August 1928, p. 5.

[8]Lindsay, *Fanfrolico and After*, p. 182.

[9]Lindsay, *A Retrospect*, n.p.

[10]Roderick Cave, *The Private Presses* (N.Y.P: Watson-Guptill, 1971), p. 205.

[11]Edward Nehls, ed., *D. H. Lawrence: A Composite Biography* (Madison: University of Wisconsin Press, 1959), III, 301. Despite his revulsion, Lawrence was willing to let Fanfrolico publish the paintings. Lindsay quashed the project, he claims, not only because he felt Lawrence's views were antithetical to his own but also because the edition would have put the press in jeopardy of being closed down for obscenity. See *Fanfrolico and After*, pp. 149-51.

[12]*Fanfrolicana*, p. 7.

[13]*Fanfrolicana*, p. 9.

[14]*Times* (London) *Literary Supplement*, December 1, 1927, p. 911.

[15]One lapse in Lindsay's editorship—it may be simply a playful touch—is his treatment of "The Apparition of His Mistresse calling him to Elizium." Herrick wrote "Desunt nonulla" (the rest is missing") under the title, and broke off the poem after 1.66. Lindsay keeps the Latin, and breaks off the poem (with no ellipses) after 1.24.

In 1947, Lindsay edited a selection, *Poems of Robert Herrick*, for the Grey Walls Press (see #90). Little remains of the Fanfrolico ethic. The introduction, in lucid, unaffected prose, describes Herrick's life, reputation, and unique abilities as a song writer. It is an excellent introduction for the general reader.

[16]Lindsay, *Life Rarely Tells*, p. 129.

[17]Reported by Lindsay in *Fanfrolico and After*, p. 122.

[18]*Times* (London) *Literary Supplement*, December 19, 1927, p. 987. Identified by Lindsay as Edmund Gosse, who edited and introduced the Fanfrolico edition of Beddowes. Further evidence that Fanfrolico did not totally spurn the literary establishment when it could be of use is the introduction to the Theocritos by Edward Hutton.

[19]Frederick J. Hoffman, *Freudianism and the Literary Mind*, 2nd ed. (Baton Rouge: L.S.U. Press, 1957), p. 311.

[20]p. 5.

[21]Lindsay, *Meeting With Poets*, pp. 233-37.

[22]See *Life Rarely Tells*, p. 206; Jack Lindsay, *The Roaring Twenties: Literary Life in Sydney New South Wales in the Years 1921-26* (London: Bodley Head, 1960), p. 198.

[23]F. J. Harvey Darton, *Modern Book Illustration in Great Britain and America* (London: The Studio, 1931), p. 70.

[24]Lindsay, "The Modern Consciousness," p. 11.

[25]*London Aphrodite*, no. 3, back cover advertisement.

[26]Adams, p. 11.

[27]G. W. Ovink, *Legibility, Atmosphere Value, and Form of Printing Type* (Leiden: A. S. Sijthoff, 1938), p. 217.

[28]*Fanfrolico and After*, p. 121.

[29]*Fanfrolico and After*, p. 183.

[30]Robert Graves and Alan Hodge, *The Long Weekend. A Social History of Great Britain 1918-1939* (1940, rpt. New York: Norton, 1963), pp. 54, 199.

[31]Ifor Evans, *English Literature Between the Wars*, 3rd ed. (London: Methuen, 1951), pp. 8-12, 16.

[32]John Holloway, "The Literary Scene," in Boris Ford, ed., *The Modern Age*, A Guide to English Literature, Vol. 7 (London: Cassell, 1966), p. 63.

[33]J. B. Priestley, "Mr. J. C. Squire," *Figures in Modern Literature* (1924; rpt. St. Claire Shores, Mich.: Scholarly Press, 1970), pp. 190-215; John Betjemin, "Preface," *Collected Poems of J.C. Squire* (London: Macmillan, 1959), pp. vii-viii.

[34]John Gross, *The Rise and Fall of the Man of Letters*, p. 245.

[35]J. W. Saunders, *The Profession of English Letters*, p. 242.

[36]Evans, p. 20.

[37]Christopher Sanford, "Printing for Love," in *Cockalorum: Bibliography of the Golden Cockerel Press*, rpt. Paul A. Bennett, ed., *Books and Printing. A Treasury for Typophiles*, rev. ed. (Cleveland: World, 1963), p. 214.

[38]Frances Meynell, "Some Collectors Read," *The Colophon*, Part IV (1930), rpt. in Bennett, ed., p. 202.

[39]Francis Meynell, *My Lives* (New York: Random House, 1971), p. 189.

[40]Holloway, pp. 65-66.

[41]Nonesuch Prospectus for 1931, quoted in Holbrook Jackson, *The Printing of Books* (London: Cassell, 1938), p. 155. See also "Some Collectors Read," in Bennett, ed., pp. 191-211.

[42]Grayes and Hodge, pp. 198-99.

[43]Haldene McFall, *The Book of Lovat* (London: Dent, 1923), pp. 14-24; John Drinkwater and Albert Rutherston, *Claud Lovat Fraser* (London: Heineman, 1923), p. 12.

[44]"A Memoir by John Drinkwater," in Drinkwater and Rutherston, p. 12.

[45]William Gaunt, as quoted in *The Art of Claud Lovat Fraser* (Phila.: Rosenbach Foundation, 1972), p. 4.

[46]*The Art of Claud Lovat Fraser*, p. 47.

[47]William Jovanovich, *Now Barrabas* (New York: Harper and Row, 1949), pp. 91-96.

[48]Jovanovich, p. 100.

[49]Quoted in Holbrook Jackson, *The Fear of Books* (London: Soncino Press, 1932), p. 73.

[50]Donald Thomas, *A Long Time Burning: The History of Literary Censorship in England* (New York: Praeger, 1969), p. 304. See Noel Perrin, *Dr. Bowdler's Legacy: A History of Expurgated Books in England and America* (New York: Atheneum, 1969), pp. 252-53.

[51]Meynell, *My Lives*, pp. 163-64.

[52]"To Electra (I dare not ask a kisse)" in *The Lute of Love* (London: Selwyn and Blount, 1920), p. 46: with a headpiece of field and cloud, and a tailpiece of an evergreen tree. There may be one or more Herrick poems in the decorated broadsheets issued by the Poetry Workshop from 1914-1931. See Joy Grant, *H.H. Monro and the Poetry Workshop* (London: Routledge and Kegan Paul, 1967), pp. 111-12. Also, there is an impressionistic sketch in one of Fraser's unpublished notebooks entitled "The death of Herrick." The late Mr. Seymour Adelman, Canady Library, Bryn Mawr College, brought this to my attention.

[53]McFall, p. 177.

[54]Grant, pp. 112-14.

[55]John Russell Taylor, *The Art Nouveau Book in Britain* , p. 1148.

[56]"Claud Lovat Fraser, Illustrator," *The Printing of Books*, pp. 202-06.

[57]Rutherston and Wolfe worked well together; see the latter's *Cursory Rhymes* (London: E. Benn, 1927), illustrated by Rutherston.

[58]*The Times* (London) *Literary Supplement*, January 24, 1929, p. 18.

[59]Hamish Miles, "The Art of the Book—Recent Work of Some English Private Presses," *Creative Art*, May 1929, pp. 310-13.

[60]Augustine Birrell, *Obiter Dicta*, 2nd series (N.Y.: Scribners, 1890), p. 277.

[61]Walter de la Mare, *Henry Brocken* (N.Y.: Knopf, 1924), pp. 50-51.

[62]John Lewis, *Anatomy of Printing* (New York: Watson-Guptill, 1970), p. 215.

[63]Will Ransom, *Private Presses and Their Books*, p. 147.

[64]Paul A. Bennett, "B. R.: Adventurer with Type Ornament," in Bennett, ed., *Books and Printing*, p. 295-97.

[65]Francis Meynell, *English Printed Books*, 2nd ed., p. 44.

[66]Colin Franklin, *The Private Presses*, p. 15.

[67]Christopher Sandford, "Printing and Life," in *Bibliography of the Golden Cockerel Press* (San Francisco: Alan Wofsy Fine Arts, 1975), p. 105 (three volumes in one).

[68]David Bland, "Fine Books of 1954," *The Book Collector* 4 (Autumn 1955), p. 229.

[69]*Bibliography of the Golden Cockerel Press*, p. 50.

[70]William Ridler, *British Modern Press Books. A Check-List of Unrecorded Items* (London: Dawson, 1975), p. 133.

[71]Bland, "Fine Books of 1954," p. 133.

[72]In *American Book Collector*, June 1955, p. 5. The advertisement for *Minx Admonished* is in the January 1956 volume, p. 5. In the October 1955 number, the Press offered *Against Women*, concerning "the witchery and guile of woman undismayed in her captivity" (p. 9).

[73]Darton, p. 44; Franklin, p. 145; Bland, *A History of Book Illustration*, p. 375.

[74]London *Times*, December 30, 1969 (obituary)

Chapter 7

> This day Robin Herrick
> Was born in Cheapside.
> His father he laughed
> And his mother she cried,
> So to Sweet Robin Herrick
> 'Twas given to spy
> The tear in the marigold's
> Laughing eye.
> —Eleanor Farjeon, *The New Book of Days* (s.v. "August 20"), 1949.

The first editions of Herrick for young readers date from the late nineteenth-century "golden age of children's books," and the later ones from our own time, when one finds even more respect for the imagination and sensibility of the child. As one would expect from the popularity of *A Child's Garden of Verses, Peter Pan,* and Hawthorne's *Wonder Book,* by Edwardian and Gilded Age times moralistic treatises had given way to a literature of fancy and delight: a respect for "a very real and vital sense in which it is not true that the child is father to the man."[1] However, for all the turn-of-the-century emphasis on faerie, spontaneous gaiety, sprightly adventure, and ingenuous nonsense, children's literature was involved with nostalgia, sentimentality, and didacticism. This is true even of the best anthologies of great poetry suitable for children, edited by Coventry Patmore, W. E. Henley, J. G. Whittier. Further, children's writers and illustrators reflected adult fascination with their own childhood behavior; that is, with the romance of their own past. For instance, Kate Greenaway's little girls mimicked grown-up dress, hobbies, and manners in gardens, meadows, and country towns; Howard Pyle's stories and drawings recapture for adults the elan of carefree youth, as do C. D. Warner and T. B. Aldrich's fictionalizations of their own boyhoods.[2] Peter Coveney makes an interesting case for the romantics' notion of childhood being used by Carroll, Barrie, and Forrest Reid to regress into the security of mother-love and nursery-tale adventure.[3] This does not, of course, diminish the universal appeal of these artists' work. It does explain how adults and children's books tended to merge during the period.[4] Adults equally with children enjoyed gift books in which artists such as R. A. Bell and Paul Woodroffe delineated classical Greek youth and grace, in which Charles Brock and Hugh Thomson served up "merrie" England or in which Kate Douglas Wiggin collected folk and fairy tales. In the complex of motives

162

which forge adult attachments to security and repose, nostalgia certainly has a place, as Andrew Lang knew. In the introduction to his *Blue Poetry Book,* he notes that poetry written for children often appeals to a grown-up longing for "a distant fairy world," that its effect often depends on its writer's memory of experiences a child cannot have thought about, and that, consequently, it evokes "tears that do not come and should not come to the eyes of childhood."[5] Interestingly, his text itself is illustrated with lightly-clad, Arcadian lads and maidens, and the poets represented are those also included in the long-popular *Home Book of Verse.* It is a book for the drawing room, not the nursery.

Even works designed for the latter part of the house could have been "mother's helpers" rather than children's companions, their illustrations shown by the parent to the child as the story was being read. Although children were beginning to choose their own reading,[6] they could hardly be expected to do so in the case of classical poetry. Selections for reading aloud often included a moralistic slant, especially as regards praises of family life (the security that loving mother and prosperous father give). Bourgeois values attached to home, school, God and country—specifically loyalty, patriotism, humility, forbearance, and self-sacrificing gallantry—are recognizable in verses for the young as they are in adventure stories and fairy tales.[7] F. L. Lucas' *Another Book of Verses for Children* (1907), for example, begins with Robert Louis Stevenson's lyrics about good ("happy hearts") and bad ("unkind," "unruly") children; its sections include "Easy Lessons in Grammar and Geography," "Ballads of Battle," and "The Lesson Beautiful." Lucas contributes several of his own poems, including one about mother's visit to the playroom. The children need her tolerant guidance:

> . . . hasten to the shelf where hang
> The books of Mr. Andrew Lang.
> Then someone who has soft brown hair
> Comes singing up the nursery stair;
>
> . . . .
>
> We both pronounce her, then and there
> A prisoner in the rocking chair.
>
> . . . .
>
> To wit, our prisoner prized and proud
> Shall for an hour read aloud,
> With waving hand and lofty look,
> From any kind of fairy book.[8]

Moralistic and sentimental tendencies make Victorian and Edwardian children's literature a different mirror of the period's popular culture than is its less prescriptive counterpart at the present time. Today, critics and writers insist on principles which Edwardians were working toward (and often finding, in works by Stevenson and De la Mare), regarding the freedom of children to respond intuitively to reading for the simple joy in discovery, without having to abstract "early lessons." Edwin Muir's strictures, laid down in 1955, make the point with exceptional clarity. Poetry for children should not moralize (which kills imagination), should not be realistic (which is no substitute, to a child, for his own experience) should not deal with how to behave toward parents (which parents themselves must explain), and should not be an exemplar of how and why to be kind (for this results in sentimentality).[9] My treatment of *Hesperides* for children will show this shift in emphasis, as Herrick's lyrics are presented by various sensibilities as a garden of fancy and wonder in which boys and girls may find their own "sweet and civil verses."

"Sweet Robin Herrick"

The first children's book to illustrate poems by Herrick (1884; see #69) contains "His Grange, or Private Wealth," "A Tercentenary of Littles," and "A Thanksgiving to God for His House." Its title, *Herrick's Content,* and subtitle, "Verses Descriptive of the Poet's Simple Life," draw attention to that aspect of Herrick's personality which all subsequent treatments make paramount: his insouciant satisfaction with small resources. The illustrations, however, modelled after Caldecott, depict a nineteenth-century grotesque, more mad than contented. Possibly with antecedents in circus sideshow or theatrical pantomine,[10] he struts in frock coat, breeches and skullcap, beneath which blossom a remarkable pair of ears. A more likely illustration for "His Grange" is John Skelton's for H. E. Marshall's *The Child's English Literature* (1909; see Figure 8-3). It draws attention to the domestic pleasures afforded by pets, afternoon sunlight, a trim vicarage garden, and repartee with the housekeeper. De la Mare, in his notes to "A Thanksgiving to God for His House" for *Tom Tiddler's Ground* (1930), tells his readers that "this poem is about the parsonage, his 'cell' as he calls it. He thanks God for everything in it, though he lives a very simple life, 'void of state,' for that is his fortune in this world."[11] Herrick's simple piety does not strike us today as that quality most likely to attract children to him, but adults for a long time thought that it was. More likely, it was that aspect of his work they found most engagingly childlike. E. L. Darton, in his afterword to the "Children's Poets" Herrick (1915; #71), points out, once again in connection with "A Thanksgiving," the Christian moral: "Only a great heart is thankful, as Herrick was, who recognized in his smallest possession the unfailing bounty of God" (p. 100).

Darton points out much more, however, and this is where the emphases lie in later introductions for children to the man behind the poetry: conviviality, cheerfulness, kindness, and, above all, his ability to see a delicate beauty in small, and therefore overlooked, objects and experiences. Some sixty years after Darton wrote, the same qualities are thought just the right introduction: "he was a bachelor and a great celebrator of small occurrences. Any incident or creature might become a theme for a song: he wrote about his cat, his dog..., about country customs, fairies, his servants, and himself."[12] When more details are offered, in the Crowell and Bodley Head series of classical poets for older children (1967 and 1968; see #73 and 74), endearing details are added: young Herrick writing posies for rings, the chaplain on campaign with Buckingham, the vicar teaching peasants some Noble Numbers, throwing his sermon at his congregation, reading his poems to the local gentry, or defiantly reading "Dean Bourne Farewell" on his way back to London in 1648. One hears little about the epigrams (except that they are in bad taste), the more heated love poems, or the many mistresses. As for *carpe diem*, the closest any child's writer comes is Darton, and his interpretation not only insulates young readers from sexual connotations, but secures them with practical home truths: "Come, don't lie asleep in the sunny morning—jump out of bed—make haste! Every day is packed with pleasures for those who know how to enjoy life!"

Not many of these biographical sketches approach the suggestive connotations of Eleanor Farjeon's poem, which serves as an epigraph to this chapter, for only the childlike gaiety, the "laughing eye," but not the "tear," is presented. Eleanor Graham does suggest Herrick's weaker and darker moments. But only Geoffrey Grigson, in his anthology for children *The Cherry Tree*, approaches Farjeon's vision (not, of course, in a biographical context): "Spring turns into summer, flowers fall, young becomes not so young, and at the far end of these April and May poems this is exactly what you will find Virgil saying twenty centuries ago, Herrick saying three and a half centuries ago, and John Crow Ransom saying from modern America."[13]

"The Romance of Other days": Merrie England and Faerie

In turn-of-the-century gift books for lovers, artists such as Charles Brock, Ellen Forbes, and Florence Castle drew courting couples. Their postures and gestures may be indigenous to nineteenth-century drawing rooms, but could also be Elizabethan or Stuart in style, as the clothes, buildings, and artifacts certainly are. The artists suggest the purity of intention and romantic idealism associated with courtship in gallant, pre-industrial England. The book's reader could fancy his or her attentions toward a lady or beau to be similar to those in the costume-dramas depicted for them. *A Garland of Love* (1917; #72) adapts this kind of escapist fantasy as a bibelot for children, providing them with Cupids, fairies, and boys and girls in Cavalier dress. Its title page (Figure 7-1) shows a young man in Restoration costume (frock coat, buckled shoes, ruffled sleeves; his feathered hat, not worn in a lady's presence, lies by his side) reading to a maiden (with bare shoulders, stomacher, damasked underskirt) who works on a sampler. The couple, somewhat like Greenaway's younger children, are playing grown-up. The girl seems not yet a teenager, and the boy only slightly older than she. There

Fig. 7-1 Daphne Allen, ed. and ils., *A Garland of Love, from Herrick and Other Poets of the Seventeenth Century* (London: Headley Bros., [1917]), title page. See #72.

Fig. 7-2 Daphne Allen, "The Night Piece, to Julia," *A Garland of Love...*, p. 24.

are most practical reasons for depicting elegant royalists of this age. Children's book publishers had come by 1917 to categorize their potential market by age group and sex.[14] Young readers could, of course, choose some of their own books.[15] Quite common sensically, therefore, the illustrator, Daphne Allen, conceives her audience for love poetry to be composed of girls from about age 8 to 15. Her selection of poems, and the drawings which accompany them, reflect the tastes respectable, upper middle-class people would approve of in children that age.[16] The illustrator ought to know: she was 19 when the *Garland* appeared and had been publishing well-received drawings for several years.[17]

The Herrick poems Allen chooses are two playful pieces of Cupid-lore ("The Wounded Cupid" and "Bag of the Bee"), a romantic lyric ("The Night Piece To Julia"), and a song about transience ("To Blossoms"). Her Venus and Julia are posed by the same bare-shouldered, delicate-featured, flat-breasted girl depicted on the title page. "To Blossoms" is accompanied by a pastel watercolor of two girls in seventeenth-century gowns gathering apple blossoms from a tree. "A Quiet Conscience," by "King Charles the Martyr," shows him on his throne, with a little boy on his knee and his arm around a little girl. "Cherry Ripe," by Campion, shows a very pretty Cavalier boy—in boots and spurs, with gilt-handled sword, slashed sleeves, and purple cloak, seated bare-headed in a garden of Venus. An oval-shaped design for an excerpt from Marvell's "Nymph Complaining" ("The Girl and Her Fawn") shows a pale-skinned, pre-pubescent beauty feeding her white, pink-eared pet roses.

The notions of childhood which underlie Allen's *Garland* (and also Edwardian sketches for children of Herrick's life) are carefully analyzed in Gillian Avery's *Nineteenth Century Children* and *Childhood's Pattern*. First, poems about contentment are important because well-to-do middle-class children, who, by virtue of their social standing, are assumed to be naturally honest and sensitive, ought to be taught to be grateful and patient.[18] Poems about thanking God for one's house, or accepting one's lot, might teach "the minor joys which go to make social happiness" (to quote Kenneth Graham's praise of some of Eugene Field's verses).[19] Second, a child's prettiness, as a secular quality quite separate from saintliness, had become central in the late nineteenth-century adult's fascination with childhood (much as elfin grace in young men and women, as depicted by Woodroffe and Bell, had won the hearts of readers of lyric poets from Shakespeare to Keats). Thus S. R. Crockett's novel *Sweetheart Travellers* (1895): "To look into [my sweetheart's] eyes is to break a hole in the clouds and look into heaven, and the sunshine lies asleep upon her hair...."[20] Finally, such prettiness symbolizes innocence which should be preserved; the adult sees, in the child, himself or herself as s/he would wish again to be. Victorian and Edwardian imagination (as reflected in illustrated books of fiction and poetry) found escape not only to merrie England and ancient Greece, but to an ideal childhood of innocent play, trust, and a "cocoon" of protective mother love.[21] For these purposes

Allen's drawings complement "Robin" Herrick's Cupid stung by a bee and soothed by Venus, his gentle, dewy primroses and violets yielding to the soft hands of Cavalier maidens, and his Julia led by sprites through a moonlit garden (see Figure 7-2). This Julia is guided by the most chubby, chaste and good-natured of elves. The illustration, and the poem if read under its influence, meet Marie Corelli's criterion for the kind of fairy stories so enormously popular from 1900 to 1920:

Children should be encouraged to believe that there is nothing in this beautiful world, or beyond it, that can possibly do them harm. The boldness of perfect innocence is one of the most gracious and lovely attributes of childhood, and we should take the utmost pains to preserve that beautiful courage....[22]

Even more typical of such sentiments are Charles Robinson's angel-children, drawn for *A Posy of Verse from Herrick* (1903, #70) and a somewhat larger selection in "The Children's Poets" series (1915; #71). The poems illustrated in these tiny volumes are similar to those Allen chooses: four flower poems, "The Night Piece," "Upon a Child that Died," and "Ceremonies for Christmas." Robinson's popularity had been established with his illustrations for *A Child's Garden of Verses* and he continues in the Herrick to delineate the sweetest of fancies. The title-page epigraph to the 1915 volume sets the tone: "But listen to thee, walking in thy chamber/Melting melodious words, to lutes of amber." His children, who are either picking flowers or singing, seem to be either reciting the words of the poems, or otherwise responding to them in ways adults would find engaging. They appear surrounded with meadows, trees, thatched cottages, and mullioned windows. The *momento mori* implication is never absent from Herick's flower poems, but if Robinson's delicate children and rural surroundings suggest it, they do so only insofar as awareness of childhood's brevity makes his vision of childhood more ethereal and therefore more exquisite for adults to contemplate. Corelli's essay on fairy tales suggests another facet of Robinson's work—the platonic ideal underlying his children's prettiness and innocence:

I have often wondered if there might not be some remote recollection in [children's] minds of some far-away bright region...which they instinctively feel the memory of, and that this instinctive emotion impels them to drink in with delight dazzling descriptions of the glory, loveliness, joy of fairyland....[23]

See Figure 7-3; the title page onlay reproduces the frontispiece (illustrating "To Violets"), entitled "The maiden Posies." The tree and its absurdly crooked branches, the fleecy clouds meandering in strange directions, the billowy hills with their dark greens and purples all frame the little girl in her pink gown and red hair, and provide an "airy frivolity" at which children may laugh, and at which Edwardian adults would wistfully smile.

Fig. 7-3 Charles Robinson, ils., *Robert Herrick*, ed. E. L. Darton. "The Children's Poets." (London: Gardner, Darton and Co., 1915), front cover. The onlay reproduces the frontispiece, entitled "The Maiden Posies" ("To Violets"). See #71.

Hesperides for Children of Our Time

The contrast between Edwardian illustrators and "modern" ones such as Ellen Raskin and Lynton Lamb is a sharp one, and not because of the passage of several generations. The reason is that at the turn of the century, the image of childhood, its iconography, and the prevailing philosophy of how children's literature should work are, for all the talk of entertainment for child readers, quite opposed to ours. However attractive Robinson's and Allen's techniques, the feelings their style was intended to evoke seem somewhat unnatural to us. By the late sixties, children were much freer to use their imagination, even to confront the ugly or the tragic aspects of life. As the passage by Edwin Muir, summarized above, indicates, the idiosyncracies of a child's insights, and the fact that these insights should be unencumbered by conventional interpretations, are what make them important in the development of sensibility. In addition, adults want young readers to entertain themselves with the best art and literature, the writers of which face

Fig. 7-4 Ellen Raskin, ils., "Hesperides," *Poems of Robert Herrick*, ed. Winfield Townley Scott. "The Crowell Poets." (N.Y.: Crowell, 1967), pp. [12-13]. See #73.

life squarely and inform honestly.[24] In this sense, mid-century children's books in England and America do have an informative purpose surpressed in 1900. The full biographical introductions in the Herrick volumes in 1967 and 1968 are certainly serious and historically accurate. In addition, they put first importance on the child's freedom to interpret as he or she wishes. In doing so, they are representative of their time and genre.[25] In the 'fifties and 'sixties, the revolution which Harvey Darton felt had been effected fifty years previously seemed closer to becoming a fact, there being more evidence of the conviction that "children were their own spontaneous poets—the makers of their own world of imagination.... Experience is not [poetry's] essence, nor explanation to less perceptive persons a condition of its existence."[26]

With this in mind, we can contrast nature and faerie as Raskin describes it, and Lamb's recreations of seventeenth-century England, with the versions of Robinson and Allen, keeping in mind that Herrick's precise diction, sensual imagery, gay tone, pastoral setting, and inimitable humor provide the basis for all interpretations. Raskin's *mise-en-page* introducing *Hesperides* (Figure 7-4) outlines a winged swan, blooming flowers, and flowing water in lightly decorative manner, as does her title-page vignette of a flower-crowned girl with intensely reflective eyes. If this artist connotes innocence by her drawings, it is in a very different manner than Allen does, for there is no delicate prettiness, childish playfulness, or wistful humor at the

Two Graces

What God gives, and what we take,
'Tis a gift for Christ His sake:
Be the meal of Beans and Peas,
God be thanked for those, and these:
Have we flesh, or have we fish,
All are Fragments from His dish.
He His Church save, and the King,
And our Peace here, like a Spring,
Make it ever flourishing.

* * *

Here a little child I stand,
Heaving up my either hand;
Cold as Paddocks* though they be,
Here I lift them up to Thee,
For a Benison to fall
On our meat, and on us all. *Amen.*

OF HIS LOVE, REMEMBRANCES

Fig. 7-6 Lynton Lamb, ils., "Of His Love, Remembrances," *The Music of a Feast.* p. [57]. By permission of the Bodley Head.

Fig. 7-5 Lynton Lamb, ils., "Here a little child," *The Music of a Feast: Poems for Young Readers,* ed. Eleanor Graham (London: Bodley Head, 1968), p. 30. See #74. By permission of the Bodley Head.

expense of adolescents playing at being grown-up. Nor does Lynton Lamb exploit this vein. Although he draws several pretty young ladies, their postures and facial expressions are distinctly non-cherubic, and reflect minds and characters such as young readers can recognize. In one vignette Julia, by candle-light, reads Herrick's request to burn his poetry if he dies before it can be "perfected" by print. What she is feeling, and what she will do, must be inferred, clear-sightedly and without sentimentality, for this is how Lamb, an observer of character, not a caricaturist, has set the scene—as the speaker in the poem would wish.[27] "Anthea's Retraction" and "Here a Little Child I Stand" are graced with little girls whom adults would say were "cute." But the coy flirtatiousness the former practices, and the latter's smiling, somewhat tentative pose (Figure 7-5), create realistic pictures which children that age could put themselves into, if they were transported to the seventeenth century and had to play the roles the poems require. "Of His Love, Remembrances" (Figure 7-6) creates the seventeenth-century English countryside in precise detail: cottage, meadow, and stone bridge (over Dean Bourne?). The scene is not a myth of Arcadian merriment or rural contentment, nor is it nostalgic. The figure crossing the bridge may be Herrick himself. Banished from his living in 1648, he would have been in secular dress (but not have worn his 57 years so lightly), and he did recite those defiant verses to the rocky stream. Eleanor Graham reports the incident in her introduction. Lamb may have this in mind, or merely be making a telling suggestion about love clearly remembered. The poems in this section are about rural ceremonies, old friends, and merry feasts, not lovers. These kinds of reminiscences are as likely to be sad and lonely as tranquil and sunny (the "tear" in the "laughing eye"). Lamb's work allows young readers to think for themselves. He thus comes closest of all the children's book illustrators to doing for Herrick what Walter de la Mare hoped that the notes he appended to *Come Hither* would do: make young people see the value of comprehending literature passed down to them from a vanished place and time, "and so...cross again and again over the slender bridge between poetry and actuality, between the world of imagination and the world without. There will not be the less to be seen on either side by becoming familiar with both of them."[28]

One measure of the suitability of some of Herrick's poems for children may be the large number of English and American writers and artists for children who have involved themselves with *Hesperides* (as either editors, critics, or illustrators): William Allingham, Andrew Lang, John Masefield, Walter de la Mare, Lovat Fraser, Maurice Hewlitt, Louis Untermeyer and William J. Smith. Another criterion is Herrick's wide representation in many anthologies of children's poetry published in this century. The Brewtons' *Index To Children's Poetry*[29] and its supplements record approximately 150 items, which is less than have Shakespeare, Sandburg, or Frost, but almost as many as has Blake, and as many as are recorded for Rossetti, Keats, Milton, George Herbert, or Marvell. The most anthologized poem is "To Daffodils," with "A Grace for a Child" and "The Night Piece" second choices. Also popular are the ceremonies for seasonal holidays, the elegiac flower poems, the persuasions to love, and the praises of music. The fairy poems, because of their sexual connotations, are used in excerpted form, and the epigrams, notorious for their precise description of bodily infirmities and excretions, are sparingly used. *The Music of a Feast* does contain some; they, as the fairy verses, are curious enough to amuse young readers. However, modern editors seem interested in Herrick's musical rhythms, the engaging strangeness of his narratives, his sensual images, and the mythical aspect of the festive ceremonials: the "magical" qualities, which attract a reader before he can analyze the reason.[30] How well Herrick's poetry meets these criteria is best stated by Floyd Dell, who edited a selection for a "Little Blue Book" (see #80) in 1924:

Sooner or later every lover of poetry discovers, honors and delights in Herrick. Fortunate he who makes this discovery in early youth! This is when the mind is most eagerly open to poetic influences; and it is then that Herrick has most to offer.... There is a dewy freshness and fragrance.... In a certain kind of verbal music he is one of the greatest poets in the language. And he can make youth feel—what youth, troubled by many dreams, eternally needs to know, that life is beautiful and to be enjoyed (pp. 8-9).

Notes

[1]Percy Muir, *English Children's Books 1600-1900* (New York: Praeger, 1969), p. 226.

[2]William Feaver, *When We Were Young* (N.Y.: Holt, Rinehart, and Winston, 1977), p. 17; Cornelia Meigs, *A Critical History of Children's Literature*, rev. ed (London: Macmillan, 1969), pp. 244, 275-87.

[3]Peter Coveney, *The Image of Childhood*, rev. ed. (Baltimore: Penguin Books, 1967), Chapter 10.

[4]P. Muir, p. 291.

[5]Andrew Lang, *The Blue Poetry Book*, 3rd ed. (London: Longman's, Green, 1902), p. xi.

[6]Muir, p. 227.

[7]See Isabelle Jan, "Children's Literature and Bourgeois Values in France Since 1860," in Peter Brooks, ed., *The Child's Part* (Boston: Beacon Press, 1972), pp. 57-72; Cornelia Meigs, et al., pp. 288-89, 349-53; Roger L. Green, "The Golden Age of Children's Books," in Sheila Egoff, et al., *Only Connect: Readings on Children's Literature* (Toronto: Oxford U. Press, 1969), pp. 10-12.

[8]"Mr. Lang's Fairy Books," *Another Book of Verses for Children* (London: Wells, Garner and Darton, 1907), p. 378.

[9]Edwin Muir, "A Child's World is a Poet's," *N.Y. Times Book Review*, Nov. 13, 1955, in Virginia Haviland, ed., *Children's Literature Views and Reviews* (Glenview, Ill.: Scott, Foresman, 1973), p. 270. See also Judith Saltman, "Poetry," in Sheila Egoff, ed., *Thursday's Child: Trends and Patterns in Contemporary Children's Literature* (Chicago: American Library Association, 1981), pp. 222-26.

[10]Feaver, p. 8.

[11]*Tom Tiddler's Ground: A Book of Poetry for Children* (New York: Knopf, 1973), p. 239. First published 1930.

[12]Iona and Peter Opie, *The Oxford Book of Children's Verse* (New York: Oxford, 1973), p. 366.

[13]Geoffrey Grison, *The Cherry Tree* (New York: Vanguard Press, 1959), p. 38.

[14]Coveney, p. 282.

[15]P. Muir, p. 226.

[16]Gillian Avery, *Nineteenth Century Children: Heroes and Heroines in English Children's Stories, 1780-1900* (London: Hodder and Stoughten, 1965), p. 161.

[17]See her *The Birth of the Opal* (London: George Allen, 1913).

[18]*Nineteenth Century Children*, p. 162.

[19]Kenneth Graham, ed., *Lullaby Land: Songs of Childhood*, ils. Charles Robinson (New York: Scribner's, 1908), p. 10.

[20]Quoted in Avery, *Nineteenth Century Children*, p. 176.

[21]Gillian Avery, *Childhood's Pattern: A Study of Children's Fiction 1770-1950* (London: Hodder and Stoughton, 1975), pp. 48-55.

[22]Marie Corelli, "How To Tell A Fairy Story," *The Windsor*, 11 (December 1899), 17.

[23]Corelli, p. 20.

[24]Avery, *Childhood's Pattern*, p. 227.

[25]Frank Eyre, *British Children's Books in the Twentieth Century* (London: Longman, 1971),

pp. 17-18.

[26]Harvey Darton, *Children's Books in England: Five Centuries of Social Life*, 3rd ed., rev. by Brian Alderson (Cambridge: Cambridge U. Press, 1982), p. 314. First published, 1932.

[27]See John Lewis, *The Twentieth Century Book* (London: Studio Vista, 1967), p. 136: "Lamb seems to evoke naturally and thus successfully the true atmosphere of the author's *mise en scene*." See also Lynton Lamb, *Drawing for Illustration* (London: Oxford University Press, 1962), Chapter 5.

[28]3rd ed. (New York: Knopf, 1972), p. 478. First published 1923.

[29]John and Sarah Brewton, *Index to Children's Poetry* (New York: Wilson, 1942). There were supplements in 1954 and 1965. See also John Brewton and G. M. and L. A. Blackburn, *Index to Poetry for Children and Young People* (New York: Wilson, 1978).

[30]Edmund Blishen, ed., *The Oxford Book of Poetry for Children* (New York: Watts, 1963), pp. 17-18; C. Day-Lewis, ed., *The Echoing Green* (Oxford: B. Blackwell, 1957), pp. iii-iv; Louise Bogan and W.J. Smith, ed., "Introduction," *The Golden Journey* (Chicago: Reilly and Company, 1965).

Chapter 8

Pen and Pencil Portraits: The Eccentric-Wanton-Witty Gentleman-Poet-Priest

> "It is idle," cried Dianeme, "Herrick himself admired us most on paper."
>
> "And ink makes a cross even of a kiss, that is very well known," said Julia.
>
> "Ah!" said I, "all men have eyes; few see. Most men have tongues; there is but one Robin Herrick."
>
> "I will tell you a secret," said Dianeme. And as if a bird of the air had carried her voice, it seemed a hush fell on sky and greenery.
>
> "We are but fairy-money all," she said. "An envy to see, but take us!— 'tis all dry leaves in the hand. Herrick stole the honey, and the bees he killed. Blow never so softly, the tinder flames—and dies."
>
> "I heard once," said Electra, with but a thought of pride, "that had I lived but a little, little earlier, I might have been the Duchess of Malfi."
>
> "I too, Flatterer," cried Julia, ... "But, come to an end, what are we all? This man's eyes will tell ye! I would give white and red, nectar and snow and roses, and all the similes that ever were for—"
>
> "For what?" said I.
>
> "I think, for Robin Herrick," she said.
>
> —Walter de la Mare, *Henry Brocken. His Travels and Adventures in the Rich, Strange, Scarce-Imaginable Regions of Romance* (1904, rpt. 1924), Ch. 4.

The charm of *Hesperides* is so deeply involved with the personae in which its author appears that an impressive number of portraits exist, by both writers (Swinburne, De la Mare, James Branch Cabell, Rose Macaulay, Mark Van Doren) and artists (E.A. Abbey, Reginald Savage, Albert Rutherston, William Russell Flint). Many of their stories, poems, drawings, travel and biographical essays (with such titles as "Minister of Grace," "A Parsonage in the Hesperides," "A Universe in Filigree," and "Twilight in Devon") explore imprecise but irresistible questions for the general reader: what is the consequence to Herrick's psyche of engaging in poetic recreations of his fantasies, of submerging anxieties and disappointments beneath the golden surface of elegant songs, of finding outlets for his practical needs in the social persona of gentleman-priest: a role contradictory to others (lover, rake, detached observer of "love, liking and delight") which he assumes in his private, west-of-England Hesperides?

The Gentleman Priest

To start at the most domestic and comfortable level, the gentleman: many readers have found *Hesperides* to be a book "of that particularly delightful and attractive kind"[1] which makes the poet himself a congenial

and very accessible friend, ingenuous and self-revealing. Some poems are for
beloved relatives and friends (from peers to country squires), others about his
illnesses, his love of music and country holidays, his loss of motivation to
write poems (several on this), his "discontents in Devon," or his sleepy
congregations. The clothing, complexions, jewelry and hair styles which
most delight him about Julia, Anthea, Electra or Dianeme occasion quite a
few verses. "Few writers of that age appear more vividly in relief," says Gosse,[2]
a view echoed by Palgrave, Hazlitt, Mark Van Doren, and used by the
biographers F. W. Moorman and Marchette Chute as rationale for their work.
For certain evidence of this view, I present "A Dream of Herrick," a poem by
T. Bruce Dilks, set "in the vicarage garden at Dean Prior." The work describes Mr. Dilks sitting at Herrick's feet, and after luncheon served by
assorted mistresses of the vicar, engaging the latter in a singing match.
Taking the "lute from Julia's shapely hand," T. Bruce describes Phyllis
Dilks; Herrick, "with easy grace," throws Julia, Anthea, Diamene, Electra,
and Silvia into the fray, quite overpowering Phyllis.

> Willing I was to own the master-voice
>   Unwilling that my love should share my fall,
> When Herrick's whisper made my heart rejoice,—
>   "Thy Phyllis doth, I own, excell them all!"[3]

Once writers feel this intimacy, they conjure up nostalgic and
sentimental pictures (gleaned from the poems and such biographical sources
as are available) of a gentleman-poet of the old school at his snug West
Country seat. Walter de la Mare: "We see pottering Prue, the faithful ser-
vant of this fickle old bachelor; Tracey's tail wags; we hear his cock crow; his
geese gaggle."[4] John Moore sees the poet's early contempt for Devon's
cloddish rusticity mellowing after his return (after being "outed" from his
living in 1648 for royalism) in 1662. He watches, fascinated and aloof, as
youngsters frolic on May-day, an indulgent, wistful spectator.

Let the lasses and lads have their fun; old Herrick doesn't mind. . . . 'I too was young once!' And
he slowly turns over the pages of his book. Surely there were never so many kisses given and taken
within a few printed pages as there are here. Never so much sweet dalliance . . . Ah well, all that's
over now. . . .[5]

In a more active mood, the vicar recites poems to friends at dinner or reads
Horace at his fireside while Prue fetches sack (or, one night, dares him to write
her epitaph, which, out of gratitude or pique, he does, and includes in his
book).[6]

The effect of Devon on Herrick, then, is fancied to be positive, despite his
contempt for the peasants who snored while he sermonized—to whose
sweaty, gamey presence he preferred the company of a pet pig. Edith Sitwell
suggests that he even absorbed the faerie vitality of coombe and water-

meadow. She opens an appreciative essay with idiosyncratic conjectures on "the spirit of Herrick": it is like those of the fabulous tiny birds who, thriving on "the juyce of flowers and roses," revive from winter sleep in April, when the flowers are ready for them.[7] In a similar vein, Rose Macaulay envisions a martinet of a vicar, like "some sturdy sylvan god"[8] amongst the mean-spirited and superstitious natives, defiantly returning to London in 1648. Both Sitwell and Macauley were anticipated by Moorman, as the latter delineates Herrick's triumphant return after the Restoration. It was like "the reincarnation of some genial woodland divinity who...had come back...to restore [to the natives] their wakes and maypoles." At this routing of Puritan kill-joys, former resentments are mutually dismissed:

> We can imagine the smile of amusement that played on the faces of priest and parishoners, as the former crossed the waters of the once execrated Dean Burn [sic] and entered the village. But it was not a "rocky generation" which conducted the vicar along the half-mile of Devonshire lanes which led to the church and the vicarage, where the faithful Prudence Baldwin, reinstated like her master, was waiting to receive him. On both sides there was something to forget, but also much to remember that was tender and true.[9]

Finally, Rev. C. J. Perry-Keene, an incumbent at Dean Prior for even longer (1878-1926) than Herrick, and sponsor of a stained-glass window honoring the poet, sees his predecessor as not only joining the rustic ceremonies but as outgoing, always cheerful (even in the face of his biggest disappointment, the poor reception given his book), and much-loved about the district.[10]

The portrait of Herrick as gentleman-priest certainly relies upon an easily identified stereotype. However, a caricature, if it is one people have been fascinated by for two centuries, is highly revealing. For Victorians in general, with a yearning for pre-industrial rural simplicity and aristocratic gallantry, the image of a good-natured country parson indulging his idle hours in harmless recreations was irresistible. De la Mare remarks his lack of material wants, and his leisure to visit friends, to immortalize graceful ladies in occasional verses, and to observe at pleasure summer's greens and winter's crystalline frosts. Herrick's expulsion from his living was a "sheer twelve-year-long holiday," during which he allowed people to repay his own generosity and easy tolerances. Before one dismisses such impressions as trivial, he or she should consider two qualifications. First, the notion of Herrick as a happy man of almost childlike elan is shared by early readers and very recent ones: "abandonne...wholly gives himself up to his present feelings"[11] (1823); "unaffected candour and good will"[12] (1980). Second, there is an acknowledged obverse to this: a lack of depth, and an inability to deal with the tragic side of life; in fact, he is sometimes sentimental, melancholy, snobbish, and given to raging at people who annoy him.[13]

> Weepe for the dead, for they have lost this light:
> And weepe for me, lost in an endlesse night.

Or mourne, or make a Marble Verse for me,
Who writ for many. Beneditice.

("On Himselfe")

Geoffrey Grigson sees Herrick as an incomplete man compensating in occasional verses for inadequacies: "...a little irresolute and diffident, quizzical, fussy, rather on the verge of the maudlin, yet knowing more than one might expect, and ready to listen, and so every young body's safe uncle."[14] In his view (he is by no means alone) this poet does not even make his readers feel that the mistresses of his poems are anything more than shadows ("what might have been, if") upon which the poet's own mind projects whatever feminine charms (coyness, laughter, flowing hair, laces, silk gowns) enrapture him for a few hours at a time. He is a detached spectator at life's feast, self-sufficient and supremely egotistical in the sense of seeing his own work as very fine and critics of his own views of art, politics, and religion, rather than himself, as fallible.

Graphic artists have captured this witty, self-possessed seventeenth-century gentleman in several portraits resplendent with (to use a Cavalier term) "harmless mirth." By "portrait" in this sense I mean, of course, a representation of what purport to be the subject's actual features. The artist assumes that the kind of man the poet was and the kind of poetry he writes can be delineated in "the look of the man." The single contemporary drawing we have, by the skilled and popular engraver William Marshall, served as frontispiece for the 1648 *Hesperides*. See figure 8-1. It shows a classical bust of an odd-looking man, in profile. Double-chinned, thick-necked, curly-haired, and especially, hook-nosed, this very mundane fellow is surrounded by symbols of ideal beauty. He seems to be gazing at the winged horse, Pegasus, who is about to take flight from what might stand as both a pleasant Devon hill and the mount of Helicon. Cupids are about to crown Herrick with laurel, and roses fall from the wreathes. There are dancing muses, verdant hill and dale, and the stream of Hippocrene. The iconography, and the inscription on the bust, suggest the motifs of peace, song, innocence, which make profane love a proper subject for poetry. The all-too-mundane features profiled by Marshall make a wry contrast between the man and his book, between the realities of Herrick's life and the poetic fantasies he has chosen to surround himself with. The archness, very much a mark of a gentleman, tells us at the outset of his book a good deal more about the poet than would the usual syncophantic batch of commendatory verses.

All succeeding portraits depend, of course, on Marshall's delineation of Herrick's features. One pleasant example is Reginald Savage's (1903), illustrating "A Country Life: To His Brother, M. Tho: Herrick." The poem is a Horatian epistle in praise of bucolic contentment and stoic restraint. The drawing, like the poem, presents Herrick's love of relaxed agreeableness. See figure 8-2, and #16. A conversation piece, it shows Herrick and his brother strolling amidst the latter's "Rurall Sanctuary": a stream, flowers, trees, and shrubs, drawn with the same thick sinuous line used to represent the figures, and contrasting sharply with the white space used to denote field and sky in the upper left quarter of the picture. The pastoral setting thus provides a vigorous and congenial frame for the conversing men, alike in stature, comfortable girth, facial features, and even posture. The poet's head is turned toward his brother, so we may see the curly hair, nose and moustache as Marshall presented them. He wears the falling neck-band of the Anglican cleric. Thomas is decidedly secular; his moustache is waxed, his hair is shoulder-length, and he wears decorated petticoat breeches. In the distance one of his tenants works with a scythe; the illustrator lightly suggests (cf. "The Hock Cart") that gentry have a much more pleasant round of life.

A very similar representation, even down to the clothing, facial features, and pose, is John R. Skelton's luminous water-color of Herrick and his faithful maid Prue for H. E. Marshall's *The Child's English Literature* (1909). See figure 8-3. Of Herrick the author notes a "pleasure-loving nature," of his poetry the presence of flowers, sunlight, "the morning dews, the soft rains," and his concentration on "his own lovely garden and orchard meadow."[15] Skelton's portrait complements these statements not only with the figure of a portly, genial, introspective Anglican clergyman in accurate period dress, but especially with symbols of the kind of experience his collaborator describes: the shady garden corner, flowers, gateleg table (with writing paper, books, and wine), a cat, a spaniel ("Tracy"), even a Peacock, and Prue. She gazes ruefully at her employer, who seems vaguely aware of, and vaguely tolerant of, her presence. The figures occupy enough of the picture, and the viewer is close enough to them, to encourage intimacy. From the caption we see that the artist has in mind "His Grange, or Private Wealth," a Horatian poem of contentment with small resources.

Another excellent delineation of the gentleman-poet serves as frontispiece to the 1907 illustrated edition (#18). This is figure 8-4. Bulking large against a background of Devonshire hills, hedgerows, fields and trees, Herrick faces toward the title page with its drawing of his vicarage and church. He is dressed in a billowy white surplice trimmed in black, and wears an elegantly decorated neck-band. The roman nose, double chin, jutting jaw and thick neck are prominent, but so are the "veiled," introspective eyes and the thin lips enigmatically set in what may be a supercilious, confidential, or ironic smile. The artist suggests, as do Macaulay, Moorman, and Moore, that Herrick confidently knew his place in secular and ecclesiastical surroundings, and nonchalantly accepted his (however contradictory) attitudes and impulses. Mark Van Doren's judgment complements this portrait perfectly: "The vicar was a huge ugly man. . . . Who, then, seeing him every day, would have guessed the delicacy of his musician's touch, the cunning of his mind when he set out to carve the lyrics that will keep their shape forever?"[16] One senses a man of wit, wisdom, and equanimity, with an intense interior life confidently under control. A. S. Hartrick has drawn "a

A COUNTRY-LIFE: TO HIS BROTHER, M. THO: HERRICK

Fig. 8-2 A comfortable cleric and his brother. Source: Reginald Savage, ils. for *Hesperides, or Works...* (London: Newnes, 1903). I, facing p. 42. See #16.

Fig. 8-1 The only known contemporary portrait. William Marshall, front. engraving for *Hesperides* (1648). Source: L.C. Martin, ed., *Poetical Works* (Oxford: Clarendon Press, 1956).

Fig. 8-3 The poet in his vicarage garden. Source: Joseph R. Skelton, ils. for H.E. Marshall, *The Child's English Literature* (New York: Stokes, 1909), p. 372.

great man against a simple background" (to use Humbert Wolfe's praise of Marshall's engraving).[17]

The Buoyant Rake and The Aging Lover

Anyone who has heard of Herrick knows that he wrote a lot of sexually explicit poems to a whole team of pretty girls. Albert Rutherston's frontispiece portraits (see Figure 6-3) are delightful evidence of the poet as endearing rake. The Herrick of the Many Mistresses makes an irresistible selling point, as a paperback cover from 1962 (#93) shows: a cold-eyed, fiercely determined sensualist, with prominent lace collar, sash, and billowing sleeves, gazes almost cruelly at some very real object.[18] Here is an individual whose "wantonness" had to be glutted upon strong wine, lusty women, and hearty song. The impression, as many nineteenth-century frontispieces show (see Figure 1-2 and 1-3), is a long-standing one. Did not Anthea, Electra, and the rest have somewhere, at some point, an existence as real as Herrick's desire for them, and provide the most passionate, carnal experiences? Edmund Gosse conjectured that Julia was the poet's mistress at Cambridge, and bore him a daughter.[19] De la Mare agrees, and allows Anthea to have been vibrant flesh and blood also.[20] Rose Macaulay makes Julia a long-lost *femme fatale*;[21] Emily Easton sees her as fickle and hard-hearted, keeping Herrick a frustrated and abject suitor.[22]

Of another viewpoint are those men of letters who see in *Hesperides* not a

Robert Herrick.

Fig. 8-4 The gentleman-Poet-Priest. Source: A.S. Hartrick, front. ils. for Canon Beeching, ed., *Poems of Herrick*. The Golden Poets (Edinburgh: T.C. and E.C. Jack, 1907). By permission of the British Library. See #18.

poet's recollection in tranquillity of his experiences as a Cambridge and London rake, but a perceptive observer's fantasizing. For Humbert Wolfe Herrick was the most self-sufficient and "heart-free" of poets,[23] and for Austin Warren a reserved man who loved his freedom to observe more than physical possession, for "to possess is to be possessed."[24] Mark Van Doren's picture of a compulsive writer, whose great passion was his work (his book), is relevant here. So is the frequent conjecture—from the 1890s to the 1980s—that Herrick shared with Jonathan Swift not only a family tree and a benefice, but a chaste bachelorhood.[25]

The truth of these matters, being lost in "time's trans-shifting," is far less important than the vigor of the individual critic's conjecture about how the poet lived and wrote. In this regard the essays of Maurice Hewlitt and Llewelyn Powys must be highly respected. The former believed that to think a man could write so warmly of so many women without having delighted in their intimate presence is "to blink at the nature of man." Julia, therefore, must have been with Herrick in Devon. Although this "highly coloured, full-breasted, buxom lady" was married, she and the poet became progressively more familiar with each other; "that he really loved the handsome, flouncing, exuberant, hot-tempered girl, one of his most passionate poems, 'The night-piece to Julia,' is enough to prove."[26] Powys also acknowledges Herrick the sensualist, and, with the sensitvity of a writer for a kindred spirit, reconciles him with the poet. The sight of Julia, equally with that of Lettice Yard or Elizabeth Wheeler, would "make Herrick mad with mortal longings." But he could, if he willed it, escape the narrow bounds of carnality by translating the most desirable milkmaid or gentlewoman into a nymph indigenous to his *Hesperides,* which, as Powys describes it, reminds one of the *Delighted Earth* of Jack Lindsay and Lionel Ellis (see Chapter 6):

...where nothing had been mapped out but 'damaskt meadowes,' shining rivers, and pavillions of chivlary.... Herrick's sensuality is of a complexion so unabashed and generous that without effort he attains to that high state of heroical love passion when nothing that belongs to the body of the loved one can be anything but precious. This is a madness reserved for the true nurslings of Dionysus, fox children, whose blood moves like the tides every day of the week towards one central garden of Allah.[27]

One delineation of refined sensuality which draws some of the conclusions inherent in Powys' word-picture is *One Hundred and Eleven Poems by Robert Herrick* (#66), "selected, arranged, and illustrated" by William Russell Flint, who provides a carefully wrought personal interpretation of the poet's rude physiognomy. Herrick's portrait comes at the opposite end of his book from where one usually finds it: as headpiece of an afterword by the artist. See figure 8-5. Here, the poet is a mature, elegantly dressed restoration courtier, with high-heeled tongued shoes, petticoat breeches, silk stockings, and jacket and waistcoat to match the breeches. The books and lyre symbolize lyric poetry, and at the same time, the learning and

Fig. 8-5 An almost-young courtier. Source: William Russell Flint, collotype ils. for *One Hundred and Eleven Poems by Robert Herrick* (London: Golden Cockerel Press, 1955), p. 120. See #66.

art Cupid assimilates in his triumphs.

> The words we want, Love teacheth to endite;
> And what we blush to speake, she bids us write.
>
> ("Writing")

The pose is thoughtful, languid, even exhausted, as if the poet, despite his heroical passions, has been defeated by love, or has already seized his day, and the act of love-making, and/or the realization of time passing and vitality waning, have taken their toll. At the end of the book, the portrait subtly complements Flint's drawings *passim* of tree-lined brooks and slim, self-assured mistresses of Herrick. These figures, although determinedly erotic, have as their most outstanding features stateliness of bearing and elegant costume. The artist's exquisitely crafted drawings make the volume very much his own, but at the same time the poetry corroborates his visualizations of both the women's beauties and the poet's melancholy:

> Smooth *Anthea*, for a skin
> White, and Heaven-like Chrystalline:
> Sweet *Electra*, and the Choice
> *Myrha*, for the Lute, and Voice.
> Next, *Corinna*, for her wit,
> And the graceful use of it:
> With *Perilla*: All are gone;

Onely Herrick's left alone,
for to number sorrow by
Their departures hence, and die.

("Upon the losse of his Mistresses.")

One Hundred and Eleven Poems was an *edition de luxe,* with handmade paper, both watercolor and crayon drawings, and cream parchment quarter-binding. It was the kind of book in which preciousness might triumph over integration of type with design. But this doesn't happen. The same contrasts we have pointed out in Marshall's and Hartrick's portraits between "wanton" nature and "cleanly" refinement are in Flint's graphics, and he suggests even more: youth-age, loneliness-contentment, transience-permanence, and participation-observation. A passage from Macaulay's *The Shadow Flies* (British title: *They Were Defeated*) comes irresistibly to mind. After a long evening drinking with friends at Cambridge, Herrick thinks of his university days, Ben Jonson, and then only of Julia:

Robin's alone, alone for ever, since thou left him. What are the others to me? Toys, things of a dream and of an hour, the frail lusts of imagination, that I must toy with in my verses and in my fancy to save my heart from the cold grave thy going trod it into.[28]

Flint has met the spirit of his subject with a personal and highly imaginative empathy. His sophisticated delineation of the rake's experience comes to terms with the lurking and finally dominant nemesis of sensuality. A beautiful mood-piece by Agnes Repplier creates perfectly the ambience of *One Hundred and Eleven Poems.* She is describing Julia:

How kindly, how tranquil, how unmoved she is; listening with the same slow smile to her lover's fantastic wordplay, to the fervid conceits with which he beguiles the summer idleness, and to the frank and sudden passion with which he conjures her, "dearest of thousands," to close his eyes when death shall summon him.... How gently she would have fulfilled these last sad duties...; how sincere the temperate sorrow for a remediable loss! And then, out into the glowing sunlight, where life is sweet, and the world exults, and, underneath the scattered primrose blossoms, the frozen dead lie forgotten in their graves.[29]

Flint's portrait may be a bit too earnest to capture the nonchalance, wit, and sentimentality with which the Cavalier Herrick turns the moral of ephemerality. However, with a highly imaginative empathy, he recreates for our own century the consequences of gathering rosebuds as a brilliantly suggestive complement to the poet's "sweet and civil" verses.

This artist defends his illustrations as the work of one who shares the kind of creative impulses and temperament Herrick himself displays. "My wish," he concludes, "would be to please that fastidious jeweler's apprentice who became a Devonshire parson and one of England's great lyric poets. With good spirit and good care I have made the drawings and placed them with their poems, an affectionate tribute to Herrick and a consolation to myself during anxious years." (p. 121)

Flint was 75 when this book was published. The passage, the last phrase of which is not far from what Herrick might have said about his own book (which he published at 57), is yet another clue to explaining the pensive lassitude of the portrait figure. We must add Flint's name to those of Edward Newton[30] and Mark Van Doren (essayist-visitors to Dean Prior), William Allingham (poet of flowers and fairie, who speaks of and to Herrick in his lyrics),[31] Rev. Perry-Keene (nineteenth-century successor to Herrick at Dean Prior), Austin Dobson (who wrote a poem "For A Copy of Herrick"),[32] and Rose Macaulay (a descendant). For all, personal affinities induced idiosyncratic creative work.

The Pagan Bard

The ability of Herrick to enrapture the reader with a world of delicate, innocent beauty is praised *ad infinitum* during the late Victorian and Edwardian periods, that golden age of fine printing and a fashionable, upwardly mobile readership, for whom art and literature mattered, if only as part of the quality of life they cultivated. They did not forget his detached, playful approach, for this all the more suggested the kind of English gentleman-poet the age enjoyed: outrageous, but still with one eye on the frontiers beyond which it was not decent to step (thus the many praises of Herrick's lack of passion or heroic intensity). To wander in *Hesperides* was an occasional ramble to a recreative garden of pagan antiquity; thus the many *Selections,* which precluded prurience and indelicacies. The very secular imagination which created this pleasant place was seen as rising above mundane practicalities with the genial discretion one would expect in a gentleman of the old school.

One portrait which exemplifies this appraisal is E. A. Abbey's. In "To his Muse," the speaker wants his "mad maiden" to stay with him in the country. The illustration (see Figure 8-6 and #12) shows a chubby, gesticulating poet trying to control a slim Greek goddess of song who hears only her own music as she soars contentedly, only a little outside the poet's reach. Abbey captures the strange relationship between the two figures, a variation on the theme of innocence (the muse) and experience (Herrick): pleasant illusions and fat reality. The poet thus seems rooted in the shrubs (as he is by his age, position and social status) while the muse is young, ethereal and free. The former exudes a would-be fatherly benevolence and is a figure one might pity as well as laugh at, until one realizes that the wild, innocent muse is an incarnation of his own creative imagination. At this point, one rather admires him for his uniqueness. Abbey points out the two complementary facets of Herrick's life: his social persona, as gentleman-priest, with its responsibilities and restrictions, and his freedom, as a profane poet, to transcend this persona without obliterating the wit and temperament which make him so human and intriguing.

Fig. 8-6   The Poet and His Muse. Source: E.A. Abbey, ils. for *Selections from the Poetry of Robert Herrick* (New York: Harper's, 1882), p. [3]. See #12.

> In sober mornings, doe not thou reherse
> The holy incantation of a verse;
> But when that men have both well drunke, and fed,
> Let my Enchantments then be sung, or read.
> When Laurell spirts 'ith fire, and when the Hearth
> Smiles to it selfe, and guilds the roofe with mirth;...

> ("When he would have his verses read")

By the 1920s, consequences of Herrick's paganism were considered in a more daring light, especially by the Fanfrolico Press (#59). The illustrator Lionel Ellis recreates inimitably these consequences, by his contrasts between nature and art, nudity and clothing, and especially naturalistic as contrasted to mythological figures. The editor, Jack Lindsay, introducing a selection of Herrick some twenty years after his Fanfrolico adventure, was still forcefully stating the significance of these contrasts:

Fig. 8-7 Herrick in Arcadia. Source: Lionel Ellis, collotype ils.
for *Delighted Earth*, "Peter Meadows" [Jack Lindsay] (London:
Fanfrolico Press, 1928), p. [vii] See #59.

...it took his exile into Devon to bring out the full release of his art—the perfect union of the literary lyric with the sturdy life of the earth, the songs and customs and indominable renewals. Julia, the sweet ghost of scents and jewel-lights, strolls naturally among the youngsters of the May of the year; day-dream and folk tradition are successfully mated.[33]

Ellis' portrait shows Herrick playing a lute as six languid maidens in various stages of undress listen in various postures of rapture. See figure 8-7. They are all beautiful, very attentive, and much younger than the poet whom they surround. Herrick seems to be tonsured, and to be clothed in some fantastic version of a surplice and hose. His knee contrasts with the garment-draped thigh and bare foot of the reclining girl in the foreground—recumbent like Venus and tantalizing both in clothing and in nakedness, like Herrick's Julia. But let us call her and her sisters nymphs, for the mythological connotations are relevant: female spirits who inhabit sea and forest, and whom at times satyrs dandle on their knees (as Ellis' Herrick might have once done with his mistresses). This portrait lightly suggests the Hesperian garden by the general configuration of Marshall's pastoral horizon and the trees. Also, apples (golden or no) are in the right foreground, but these, like the bob of cherries and the winebottle, essentially complete a very intriguing picture of **various earthly delights: song, feminine beauty, wine, fruit, Arcadian hills** and dales. Herrick's own all-too-pedestrian features are all the more striking because their owner has managed to surround himself with universal icons of love, youth, and The Golden Age. This particular poet, as mundane-looking as he is, escapes his parsonage to become a mythical figure and to partake of delights we all might wish for. Ellis' drawing not only evokes sensuality; it invites fanciful, playful interpretations and thus forces the reader to consider the sensibility of the pagan bard.

> Honour to you who sit!
> Neere to the well of wit;
> And drink your fill of it.
>
> Glory and worship be!
> To you sweet Maids (thrice three)
> Who still inspire me.
>
> And teach me how to sing
> Unto the *Lyrick* string
> My measures ravishing.
>
> then while I sing your praise,
> My *Priest-hood* crown with bayes
> Green, to the end of dayes.

("An Hymne to the Muses")

A few portraits of Herrick as poet project him into a less benign context than flowers and meads. Mark Van Doren admires him for his dedication to his "perfect" craftsmanship in a time not given to lyric, and in a place where fit readers, or subjects, did not appear to be at hand. (p. 48) His striving for perfection, despite tragic realities of Civil War, is just as remarkable as his handling of classical and native English subject matter, and his metrical perfection. And then, there is a short story by James Branch Cabell, "Concerning Corinna,"[34] stranger than any of the fiction, poetry, essays, or artwork we have so far seen, and far different from them in its evaluation. But it must be dealt with, especially since, like so many others, it deals with the contrast between the man and the poet, and the effect on the personality of being a devoted poet. The story is about Herrick's death during a pagan ritual intended to lead him to communion with the spirits of the women he wrote about. The vicarage, 1674. Cabbalistic circles drawn on the floor. Herrick's personality dissected: an "unvenerable madman," indifferent to friend and foe, "the only poet in history who never demonstrably loved any woman," author of a MS on a preternatural world which may be contacted by arcane and forbidden ritual. These ceremonies being repeated by observers, the old poet appears in a cloud of smoke. Naked, in despair, muttering about hell, he stabs himself to death. Whether he has been devastated by the sight of this world beyond the veil, or whether he has failed to contact it and has been merely hiding, is not clear. Cabell's point, reiterated in the volume's nine other stories about literary figures, is that writing "perfectly of beautiful happenings" estranges one from human contact and commits one to the fate of a "changeling." What transpires is the swallowing up of the human personality by the demands of one's art, a dark pagan god on the order of Chronos. As Cabell explains in his "Auctorial Induction" (whatever muse he himself is possessed by would be wearing the cloak and hood of gothic romance), for the artist "no emotion...is endured without a side glance toward its capabilities of being written about." Thus the real world is a mine "wherein one quarries gingerly amidst an abiding loneliness...and wherein one often is allured into unsavory alleys in search of that raw material which loving labor will transhape into comliness." (p. 15)

If both historical evidence and the prevailing impression *Hesperides* gives of the man behind the poet run counter to "Concerning Corinna," it must be conceded that the first will always remain flimsy and the second subjective. What remains constant with all writers and artists is their interest in the temperament of the profane poet, and the contrasts between man and poet, the human realities of his existence and the visions his art brings to life.

Hesperides closes fittingly and paradoxically, with this couplet: "Jocund his lines were, but his life was chaste." What has fascinated commentators as diverse as Walter de la Mare, Lionel Ellis, Agnes Repplier, W. R. Flint, and Llewellyn Powys is Herrick's ability to accept the contradictions of his situation: priest and lyric poet, wanton yet cleanly, a lover of women—of ideal beauty and Latin names, a Christian leader in a community given to ancient rustic ceremonies but an aloof poetic shaper of these activities in the safe confines of his own imagination. The portraits these writers and artists have delineated are protean, deliberately paradoxical, and cannot be reduced to a composite. But a summary of the traits which make Herrick so attractive is possible. There stands a gentleman able to do his duty, please his friends, put up with private demons, and entertain his fancies through the medium of lyric poetry. Perhaps the most-abiding fascination he holds for imaginative readers involves the tension they sense between the Devon realities and the Hesperian myths. Some portraits (Hartrick, Van Doren, Macaulay, Flint) show a Herrick who has reconciled these opposites, or at least is secure in both worlds. In others (Cabell, Ellis) he emerges, for better or for worse, as a dreamer not much in touch with realities. Whatever the case, I think pen and pencil portraitists, whether serving or disdaining the cause of respectability, provide a heritage which should help us deal with what J. B. Broadbent called "Herrick's challenge... —to face his prurience, frailty, facetiousness as our own; and to face his genius along with those other qualities, as part of them...."[35] Such a man really once existed: Hampton Court, Cheapside, Westminster, Cambridge, and "Herrick's Walk": a copse of greenery bordering a high lawn at the back of the Old Parsonage near Dean Prior. Throughout most of the 19th and at least the first part of the 20th century, he was revived, vigorously, by a far-flung community of writers and artists whose work even the approach of the 21st century should not totally negate.

Notes

[1]F. T. Palgrave, ed., Introd., *Chrysomela, p. vi.*

[2]Edmund Gosse, "Robert Herrick," *Cornhill*, p. 179.

[3]*Temple Bar*, January 1896, p. 123.

[4]Walter de la Mare, "Robert Herrick," *The Bookman* (London), May 1908, p. 51.

[5]John Moore, "Twilight in Devon," *Country Men* (1935; rpt. Freeport, New York: Books for Libraries Press, 1969), pp. 50-51.

[6]Mark Van Doren, "A Visit to the Home of Robert Herrick," *Reporter*, March 26, 1955, p. 47.

[7]Edith Sitwell, "On Herrick," *A Poet's Notebook* (Boston: Little Brown, 1950), p. 254.

[8]*The Shadow Flies* (New York: Harper's 1932), p. 476. See also T.B. Swann, *Will o' The Wisp* (London: Corgi, 1976).

[9]F. W. Moorman, *Robert Herrick* (London: Nelson, 1910), p. 124.

[10]C. J. Perry Keene, *Herrick's Parish Dean Prior* (Plymouth: Brendon and Sons, 1927), p. 36.

[11]*Retrospective Review*, as quoted in W. C. Hazlitt, *Hesperides: The Poems and Other Remains...* (London: Smith, 1869), pp. clxx-xlxxvi.

[12]David Jesson-Dibley, ed., Introduction, *Robert Herrick Selected Poems* (Manchester, Eng.: Carkenet New Press, 1980), p. 17.

[13]Grosart, ed., *Complete Poems of Robert Herrick*, I, clxx-clxxvi.

[14]"A Note on Herrick," *Poems and Poets* (London: Macmillan, 1969), p. 3.

[15]Henrietta Marshall, *The Child's English Literature* (New York: Stokes, 1909), pp. 371-72.

[16]"A Visit to the Home of Robert Herrick," p. 48.

[17]Introduction, *The Poetical Works of Robert Herrick* (London: Cresset Press, 1928), I, xiii.

[18]*Herrick, The Laurel Poetry Series* (New York: Dell, 1962).

[19]Gosse, "Robert Herrick," p. 181.

[20]De la Mare, "Robert Herrick," p. 55.

[21]*The Shadow Flies*, p. 238.

[22]Emily Easton, *Youth Immortal, A Life of Robert Herrick* (Boston: Houghton-Mifflin, 1934). See especially pp. xi-xiv.

[23]Wolfe, Introduction, *Poetical Works*, I, lvi.

[24]Austin Warren, "Robert Herrick Revisited," *Michigan Quarterly Review* 15 (1976), 253.

[25]Jesson-Dibley, pp. 9-10.

[26]"Pretty Witchcrafts," *Wiltshire Essays* (1921; rpt. Freeport, New York Books for Libraries Press, 1969), pp. 110-13.

[27]"Robert Herrick: Minister of Grace," *Saturday Review of Literature*, February 8, 1936, p. 10.

[28]*The Shadow Flies*, p. 239.

[29]*Points of View* (Boston: Houghton-Mifflin, 1891), pp. 32-33.

[30]"In Dimpled Devonshire," *Yale Review*, 19 (1930), 762-72.

[31]*Poems* (London: Chapman and Hall, 1850), pp. 135, 266.

[32]In "Varia," *Collected Poems* (London: Kegan Paul, 1897), p. 433.

[33]*Poems by Robert Herrick*, p. 20.

[34]"Concerning Corinna," *The Certain Hour: Dizain Des Poetes* (London: Bodley Head, 1931), pp. 107-26. First published 1916.

[35]J.B. Broadbent, *Notes and Queries*, 221 (May-June, 1976), 272.

Appendix

Reprints of Herrick's Poetry, 1810 - 1980:
An Annotated Checklist

What follows is a listing of each 19th- and 20th-century edition of Herrick for which evidence of intended or actual publication is available. While I have not attempted a full-scale analytical bibliography, I do try to show parent editions in relation to their subsequent impressions and their varying issues and states. The quasi-facsimile title page transcriptions are intended to suggest the scope of the book and to give a brief notion of its design. The checklist is divided, in consonance with the discussion in chapters 2, 5, 6, and 7, into four major categories. In Part I, I give works listed in commercial (trade) editions between 1810 and 1920. These are divided into works (all but #1 complete and unexpurgated) for the gentleman's study (IA), Drawing Room Gift Books (IB), Bibelot (a subdivision of gift book—see IC), Cheap Series (ID), and School Texts (IE). Part II describes Private Press Editions, Part III Children's Books, and Part IV Commercial Editions from 1921 to 1980.

Many of the books listed below were in print for a long time. It is impossible to tell, without recourse to publishers' archives and a large number of copies, how many impressions were made in the latter years of the publication history of a book kept in print for as long as thirty years after the last recorded or reasonably inferrable impression. For example, the Routledge Photogravure and Colour Series volume (#17) carries no date on its title page. It was probably first published in 1906, and is listed in the firm's catalogue as late as 1938. Any copy in secondary binding may have been impressed (or "plated") in 1923, 1926, or 1907. Another example is Macmillan's well-received *Chrysomela* (#41). The latest title-page date is 1911, but a copy with or without that date could have been printed as early as 1911, or as late as 1932. Therefore, the listings under each title do not necessarily represent each impression or issue of any title. They do include each impression or issue I have seen and been able to identify as such.

In this compilation the national and trade bilbiographies of England and United States have been basic guides. In addition to the BM Catalogue, that of the London Library, and the National Union Catalogue (NUC: Library of Congress), I have consulted the *English Catalogue, The United States Catalogue, The Cumulative Book Index, The British National Bibliography, Publisher's Weekly, The Bookseller,* Lowndes' *Bibliographer's Manual of English Literature,* Roorbach's *Bibliotheca Americana, Books in Print,* and catalogues collected in *Reference Guide to Current Literature* and *Publisher's Trade List Annual.* The following contain significant lists of editions of Herrick's work; they are noted below in chronological order:

Alexander B. Grosart, ed., *The Complete Poems of Robert Herrick.* The Early English Poets (London: Chatto and Windus, 1876), I, viii-xi.

Floris Delattre, *Robert Herrick: Contribution A L'Etude de la Poesie Lyrique en Angleterre Au Dix-Septieme Siecle* (Paris: Alcan, 1910), pp. 543-47.

E. Marion Cox, "Notes on the Bibliography of Herrick," *The Library* 8, 3rd series (1917), 105-19. Rpt. London: Alex. Moring, 1917.

A. C. Judson, *Seventeenth-Century Lyrics* (Chicago: U. of Chicago Press, 1927), pp. 278-80.

Netty Roeckerath, *Der Nachruhm Herricks und Wallers* (1931, rpt. N.Y.: Johnson Reprint Corp, 1966), pp. 110-11.

Emily Easton, *Youth Immortal: A Life of Robert Herrick* (Boston and NY: Houghton, Mifflin, 1934), pp. 207-09.

Samuel and Dorothy Tannenbaum, *Robert Herrick: A Concise Bibliography* (Elizabethan Bibliographies No. 40) N.Y.: Eliz. Bibliographies, 1949. Supplement by George R. Guffey in *Elizabethan Bibliographies Supplements*, III (London: Nether Press, 1968).

New Cambridge Bibliography of English Literature, II, col. 1196.

Roger Rollin and J. Max Patrick, eds., *"Trust To Good Verses": Herrick Tercentenary Essays* (Pittsburgh: Univ. Press, 1978), pp. 240-43.

Ferruccio Ferrari, *L'Influence Classica Nell'Inghilterra Del Seicento E La Poesia Di Robert Herrick* (Messina-Firenze: G. D'Anan, 1979), pp. 163-66.

Elizabeth Hageman, *Robert Herrick: A Reference Guide* (Boston: G. K. Hall, 1983).

An asterisk (*) before an entry indicates that I have not seen the item. Some of these may indeed never have appeared (see especially 52). They must, however, be listed, because an announcement of appearance is in itself part of the record of the poet's reputation.

The table of publication dates prefixed to the checklist provides a chronological listing of first publication of each volume.

In attempting to describe cloth bindings, I have followed the system given in Philip Gaskell, *A New Introduction to Bibliography* (New York: Oxford U. Press, 1972), pp. 237ff.

Table 1

Editions of Herrick's Poetry: Publication Dates, 1810-1980

1. A few items, undateable, are not included—3e, 3f, 17a, 24, 43c, 43d, 43e.

2. Simultaneously released issues or states of a parent edition with only binding and / or imprint variants are not included. See checklist, nos. 7a, 8a, 12a, 15a, 16a, 16b, 18a, 23a, 27a, 30a, 47a, 47c, 59a, 87a, 92a.

3. ? = possible date of publication.

4. Some works may not have been published (as the checklist indicates).

1810	1	1893	10	1929	79a
1823	2	1895	51, 55	1930	82(?)
1825	2a	1897	6a, 8b, 15, 22	1932	62, 83
1939	37	1898	9	1933	84
1844	38	1899	12b, 23, 44	1935	44d, 63
1846	39	1900	10a, 45	1936	75a, 85
1848	49	1902	23b (?), 46	1938	86
1852	38a	1903	18, 25, 26, 44a	1941	64
1856	3		46a, 56, 70	1942	87
1859	4	1904	26a, 47	1946	64a, 88
1866	3a	1905	9a, 10b, 48	1947	75b
1869	5	1906	17, 27	1948	89, 90
1875	3b	1907	18, 26b, 27b	1951	75c, 84a
1876	7	1908	10c, 28, 29, 44b	1952	64b
1877	40, 41, 41a	1909	46b	1955	66, 66a
1879	3c	1910	12c, 19, 30, 31	1956	91
1880	3d, 41b	1911	33(?), 34(?), 32	1957	75d
1881	50(?)		41g	1960	84b
1882	12	1912	20, 25, 10d	1961	92
1883	3g	1913	21, 36, 48a	1962	93
1884	41c, 42, 69	1915	11, 71	1963	91a, 94, 94a
	69a, 69b	1917	72	1964	65
1885	42a	1918	35a	1965	95
1887	13, 42b, 43	1920	27c, 46c, 52(?)	1967	73
1888	41d, 43a	1921	75	1968	67, 74, 94b
	43b(?)	1922	57, 76, 77	1969	96
1890	3h, 6, 14	1923	44c, 78, 79	1971	68, 95a
1891	8, 41e, 53	1924	46d, 58, 80	1973	96a
		1927	47b 59, 81	1980	97, 98
1892	41f	1928	60, 61		

Table 2

Some Well-Known Editions and Their Places in the Checklist

1.	Abbey (E.A.), illus. (Harper's 1882)	12
2.	Aldrich (T.B.), intro. (Century Classics, 1900)	45
3.	'Canterbury Poets," ed. Horne (1887 et. seq.)	43
4.	Chrysomela (ed. Palgrave); Macmillan, 1877 et. seq.)	41
5.	Cresset Press, Rutherston fronts., ed. Wolfe	60
6.	Daniel Press eds (1891)	53, 54
7.	Elston Press (1903)	56
8.	Everyman ed. (Dent, 1908)	44b
9.	Fanfrolico Press (illus. Ellis, 1927)	59
10.	Golden Cockerel Press, illus. Flint (1955)	66
11.	Kelmscott Press (1895)	55
12.	Lamb (Lynton) illus., 1968	74
13.	Lindsay (Jack), introd. (1927, 1948)	59, 90
14.	Little Brown, 1856 (First American ed.)	3
15.	"Lovers' Library" (Lane, 1903)	26
16.	Maitland, ed. (first reprinted complete works, 1823)	2
17.	Martin (L.C.), editor (Oxford U. Press, 1956)	91
18.	Muses' Library (ed. Pollard, 1891 et. seq.)	8, 9
19.	Patrick, (J. Max) edition, 1963	94
20.	Pickering ed., 1846 (Caslon Old Style)	39
21.	Pickering Wreath ed. (1825)	2a
22.	"Red Letter Library" (designed T. Morris, 1904)	47
23.	Robinson (Charles), illus.	70, 71
24.	Rogers, Bruce, designer (1924, 1935)	58, 63
25.	Savage (Reginald), illus. 1902	16
26.	Woodroffe (Paul), illus., 1897	15
27.	"World's Classics," 1902 et. seq.	46, 84

I. *Commercial Editions, 1810-1920*

   A. Editions for the Gentleman's Library

      1. SELECT / POEMS / FROM THE / hESPERIDES / OR / WORKS BOTH HUMAN AND DIVINE, / OF / ROBERT HERRICK, ESQ. / WITH / *OCCASIONAL REMARKS* / BY / J.N. / *ACCOMPANIED ALSO WITH THE HEAD,* / *AUTOGRAPHE, AND SEAL OF* / THE POET. / [double rule] / *Effugient avidos carmina nostra rogos.* / OVID; / [double rule] / BRISTOL. / PRINTED AND PUBLISHED BY J.M. GUTCH, / 15, SMALL STREET. / SOLD ALSO BY MESSRS. LONGMAN, HURST, REES, AND / ORME, PATERNOSTER ROW, / AND I. MILLER, 72 CHANCERY LANE LONDON.

(8 x 5¼"): eng. front + A⁴B-P⁸ Q⁶ R⁸ S², 132 leaves; pp. [4], [i], ii-iv, [v-vi], [1], 2-253, [254]■

Front: profile head, after Marshall. Emphasizes Roman nose, arched eyebrow, fleshy neck. Oval shaped, signed "Schiavonetti." Probably Luigi, d. 1809. Possibly his younger brother. Steel engraving.
J.N. = John Nott, physician & antiquary. See Halkett and Laing, *Dist. of Anon. and Pseud. Lit.,* V, 216.
Price: 8s (E. Cat.); 9s 6d (Lowndes). In H.G. Bohn's 1841 cat. 35 (No. 17639).
Binding: issued in blue paper boards with paper label, "Robert Herrick's Poems, 1648" (Cox, p. 112).
Dating: Review by [Barron Field], *Quarterly Review,* 4 (Aug. 1810), 165-76.

Nott uses 280 poems from *Hesp,* and 4 from *Noble Numbers;* the latter acknowledged as inferior to the secular pieces. He uses footnotes for biographical and lexical glosses, critical appraisals, and occasionally to justify expurgations.
    Brandeis U., C.U.N.Y., U. No. Carolina, U. Texas Hum. Res. Ct. (all rebound).

2. THE WORKS OF / ROBERT HERRICK. / VOLUME FIRST. [VOLUME SECOND.] / [woodcut portrait in decorated borders; replica of poet's signature at bottom inscribed on scroll] / EDINBURGH: / REPRINTED FOR W. AND C. TAIT. / M. DCCC. XXIII.

(7 3/8 x 4 5/8"): vol. I: [a]⁸ b⁸, [A]⁸ B-S⁸, 160 leaves; pp. [i-v], vi-xxx, [2], [1-5], 6-288. vol. II: [A]⁸ B-X⁸, 168 leaves; pp. [2] [1-5], 6-296, [i], ii-xxxviii.
Price: 28s, 84s large paper (E. Cat); one guinea (Lowndes)
Port.: the woodcut vignettes depict a left-facing head, stressing nose, arched brow, thick neck and jowls, the latter two cast in shadow. Artist unknown.
Thomas Maitland, later Lord Dundrennan, states in his Biographical Notice that if Chaucer can be reprinted in full so may Herrick, whose works are "illustrative of the taste and manners of his time." Acknowledges that his edition is destined for "libraries of the curious," rather than for "drawing room[s]." Maitland, lawyer and antiquary, edited Marlowe, Carew and Drummond of Hawthornden, as well as Herrick.
Columbia, Yale, Cornell (all rebound); personal (large paper: in vol. II, pp. 10-15 out of sequence; 8 vo, pp. 13-14 vol. II lacking).

2a. (another issue or impression): THE / POETICAL WORKS / OF / ROBERT HERRICK. / VOL. I. [VOL. II] / PERENNIS / ET / FRANGANS. / LONDON: / WILLIAM PICKERING, CHANCERY LANE / [rule] / M. DCCC. XXV. [ll. 6-8 inside wreath]
Changes from the Edinburgh issue are 1) addition of front. port, vol. I. 2) new title

pages, both vols. 3) sig. b1, pp. xvii-xviii, vol. I, which is reset to excise Maitland's reference to the woodcut portraits on the title pages of the 1823 volumes. In copies examined this leaf is tipped in. In one copy the leaf on which is the t.p. bears a counter-watermark dated "1824" while all other such dates read "1817". There is however, no sign of a cancellandum stub (I have seen only rebound copies). There is also no sign of quarter--or half-sheet imposition, nor of any individual sheet of #2a being reset—all typeblocks seem identical to #2. Therefore, although the printer, Ballantyne of Edinburgh, may indeed have newly impressed sheets for Pickering—a possibility Keynes allows (*Wm. Pickering, Publisher,* p. 72)—it seems more likely that remaindered sheets were used, the Edinburgh title pages and sig. b1 of vol. 1 being cancelled.

Note that copies of the Pickering issue exist in both a thick laid paper, which both Keynes and Cox (*Notes on the Bibl. of Herrick,* p. 114) describe as used only for the Edinburgh edition, and in a ribbed, unwatermarked paper.

The Pickering "Wreath Ed." See also #39 below.

Port: front, vol. I Steel engrav. by [William] [Henry] Worthington, London engraver, 1795-1839. Below engr. is replica of poet's signature. Emphasizes curly hair, double chin, large nose, and introspective gaze.

Price: 21s (E. Cat, Lowndes).

Size of Ed: 250 copies (Keynes)

Binding: red cloth, paper labels (Keynes)

   Indiana U, Harvard, NY Public, personal (vol. I only, t.p. watermark "1824"), Texas (HRC).

3. HESPERIDES: / OR THE / WORKS BOTH HUMANE AND DIVINE / OF / ROBERT HERRICK, ESQ. / IN TWO VOLUMES. / VOLUME I. [VOLUME II.] / [rule] / BOSTON: / LITTLE, BROWN AND COMPANY. / SHEPARD, CLARK AND CO. / NEW YORK: JAMES S. DICKERSON. / CINCINNATI: MOORE, WILSTACH, KEYS AND CO. / M.DCCC.LVI.

(6 3/8 x 4"): vol. I: tipped-in front. +[a]⁸, b⁴, 1-21⁸, 22²; 182 leaves; pp. [4], [i-v], vi-xxii, [xxiii-xxiv], [1], 2-340.

vol. II: a⁸, b⁶, 1-18⁸, 19⁶; 144 leaves; pp. [i-iii], iv-xxv, [xxvi-xxviii], [1], 2-298, [299-300].

Portrait: Front. steel engraving, oval-shaped. Similar to Worthington's.*North Am. Rev.,* April 1857: "...the nose very prominent and deeply curved, the cheeks heavy with flesh, the lips sensuous, the eyes eager, — altogether a face which, though all may not be struck pleasantly by it, few will find it easy to forget." (p. 501)

Price: cloth, 75¢ per vol.

Binding: Black diaper-grain cloth. Front and back boards blindstamped with 4 borders around edges; diamond-shaped floral device in center. Spine divided by blind-stamped rules into 6 sections. Gold-stamped in top section: The / British / Poets. In second section: HERRICK / 1 [2]. Bottom section: press emblem.
   Variant: half-calf (probably publisher's), marbled paper boards, edges and endpapers to match boards. Gold-tooled spine in six sections.

Note: "Advertisement," by [F.C.] C[hild], Brown's editor for the British Poets (Herrick vols. #51 and 52) states, "...we have followed, in most respects, the Edition published by Pickering in 1846 [see #39 below]... We have, however, endeavoured to render these volumes easier reading by rectifying the absurd punctuation; and by modernizing the print in respect to capital and italic letters...." Singer's Biographical Notice (termed Preface by Pickering) is used.

   Printed by H. O. Houghton, who was favored with much work by James Brown.

Copies examined in half-calf lack in each vol. the last, blank, leaf of the preliminaries present in the cloth issue.

Indiana U, Gettysburg Coll, Univ. So. Carolina, Columbia, Cornell (all cloth); Free Lib. of Phila, personal (half-calf)

3a. (2nd impression): *THE* / POETICAL WORKS / OF / ROBERT HERRICK. / *WITH A MEMOIR.* / VOL. I [Vol. II.] / [wreath enclosing Perennis / et / Fragrans.] / BOSTON: / LITTLE, BROWN, AND COMPANY / 1866.
Preliminary gatherings not signed. One issue limited to 100 copies, with 11.2 and 7 of t.p. in red.

NYPL (limited to 100 copies), Harvard: both in half-calf

3b. (3rd impression): HESPERIDES: / OR THE / WORKS BOTH HUMANE AND DIVINE / OF / ROBERT HERRICK, Esq. / VOL. I [VOL. II] / [monogram of press: JRO worked together, and CO. in cartouche] / BOSTON: / JAMES R. OSGOOD AND COMPANY, / LATE TICKNOR & FIELDS, AND FIELDS, OSGOOD & CO. / 1875.

Ticknor and Fields bought the rights to the British Poets series from Little, Brown in 1866. The former published Milton (1868-74), and Keats (1867, 70), but a Herrick did not appear under this company's imprint. Osgood joined the firm in 1871, and his reimpression of the Herrick set in 1875 may have been occasioned by the need to have the entire series for display at the Centennial Exhibit in Phila. in 1876.
Price: the set in cloth, $2.00; half-calf, $4.50 (Am. Cat., 1876).
Binding: both cloth and half-calf, same as #3.

Harvard (cloth), U. of Penna. (half-calf)

3c. (fourth impression): HESPERIDES: / OR THE / WORKS BOTH HUMANE AND DIVINE / OF / ROBERT HERRICK, ESQ. / TWO VOLUMES IN ONE / [monogram of press: H and O worked together on shield] / BOSTON: / HOUGHTON, OSGOOD, AND COMPANY. / The Riverside Press, CAMBRIDGE, / 1879.

The preliminaries differ from #3, as does the size of the sheets: 7½ x 4 5/8″: [a]⁸, b¹⁴. An unpaginated sheet after p. 340 (sig. χ 1) carries on recto a section title for volume II.
Front: same as #3.
Price: $1.75 in cloth; $3.50 in half-calf. Offered in the Houghton-Mifflin *Portrait Catalog* (1905), and in *U.S. Cat*, 1928 ($2.00)
Binding: purple sand-grain cloth. Gold-stamped in rectangle at top of spine: BRITISH / POETS / HERRICK. Directly below bottom of rectangle: RIVERSIDE EDITION. On front cover, centered: gold-stamped shield with lion rampant. Top edge gilt. Houghton may have been indulging his preference for a binding "...as plain and simple as the dress of a Quaker maiden." (Comparato, *Books for the Millions*, p. 101).
Note: Houghton bought the rights to publish and the plates from Osgood in 1877. From then until 1880 they were partners (after that the firm was Houghton, Mifflin): the series was announced as completed with a new ed. of Chaucer in late 1879 (see "Boston Letter," *PW*, Jan. 31, 1880, p. 420).

Bridgeport Public, Brooklyn Public, SIU Carbondale, Drury Coll. (Missouri).

Title-page imprint variants for subsequent impressions:

3d. BOSTON: / HOUGHTON, MIFFLIN AND COMPANY. / The
Riverside Press Cambridge (1880. (personal)   • • •

3e. BOSTON AND NEW YORK / HOUGHTON, MIFFLIN AND COMPANY /
The Riverside Press / 1800. (personal)

3f. BOSTON / HOUGHTON, MIFFLIN AND COMPANY. / New York: 11 East
Seventeenth Street. / The Riverside Press Cambridge (this office opened 1881. personal,
Penn State.

3g. BOSTON..., 1883 (Lehman Branch, CUNY)
*3h. BOSTON..., 1890 (St. Joseph's [Pa.]; reported in NUC)

4. THE / POETICAL WORKS / OF / ROBERT HERRICK, / CONTAINING
HIS / "HESPERIDES," AND "NOBLE NUMBERS." / [rule] / WITH A
BIOGRAPHICAL MEMOIR / BY E. WALFORD, M. A. / LATE SCHOLAR OF
BALIOL COLL., OXFORD. / [rule] / LONDON: / REEVES & TURNER, 238,
STRAND / [rule] / 1859.

(7 3/8 x 5"): tipped-in front. + [A]⁶, [B]⁸, C—2Q⁸, 310 leaves; pp. [i-iii], iv-xi, [xii],
[1-5], 6-608.
Note: p. 273 (sig. T1r) reads "27".

frontispiece: Lithograph by [Richard] [James] Lane, a great-nephew of
Gainsborough and lithographer to the Queen. Head without background. Neck,
nose, arched brow and fixed eye prominent; mouth bears hint of a smile. In *Notes
and Queries,* 6, 8th ser. (Nov. 3, 1894), Walford stated that "...the expression of the
poet is sensual and ugly in the extreme." (p. 359) He seems to be referring to
Marshall's version, which of course Lane copied.
Price: 6s (Eng. Cat)
Binding: brown cloth, diaper grain. Paper label on spine: THE /POETICAL /
WORKS / OF / ROBERT HERRICK.
    Lib. Co. of Phila, Newberry, Brit. Lib.

5. HESPERIDES / THE POEMS AND OTHER REMAINS / OF ROBERT
HERRICK NOW / FIRST COLLECTED. / EDITED BY / W. CAREW
HAZLITT. / [press monogram: scroll and shield] / *VOLUME THE FIRST.*
[VOLUME THE SECOND.] / LONDON / JOHN RUSSELL SMITH / SOHO
SQUARE / 1869.

(6¾ x 4"): vol. I: tipped-in front. + [a]⁸, b⁸, c¹, B-R⁸, S¹; 146 leaves; pp. [i-v], vi-xxx, [4][1], 2-
256, 255*, [256*].
vol. II: χ¹⁰, T-2K⁸, 2L; 2 ⁶, 137 leaves; pp. [4], [257], 258-526.
Coll. Note:
    In vol. I, sig. SI paginated as "255*"; asterisk distinguishes it from 255. The originally
conjugate leaf to SI may be the leaf signed "c" tipped in between facsimile of 1648 t.p. (b8)
and the first leaf of text, B1. The tipped-in—leaf contains the introductory poem "To...
Charles, Prince of Wales." The poem is not listed in the index, vol. II; the poems contained
on p. 255* are listed.
    In vol. II, the leaf signed "LL" (pp. 513-14) seems to be tipped in preceeding a (final)
6-leaf sheet.
Front: replica of Marshall.

Price: 8s

Binding: variants as follows:

a) purplish red diagonal-wave cloth, paper label on spine, fore-edge untrimmed.

b) green sand-grain cloth, spine divided into 5 sections by gold-stamped rules with title and vol. number also gold-stamped on spine. Blind-stamped rules and diamond-shaped floral device, upper and lower cover.

c) purplish red cloth, same as b) above, except that blind-stamped design on covers composed of a more elaborate floral design than b).

half-title (both vols.): "Library of Old Authors"

Note: James Russell Lowell, in *My Study Windows,* (Boston: Houghton, Mifflin, 1885), in the course of an attack on "the way in which old books are edited in England by the job" (p. 337), berates Hazlitt's revision of Singer's Biographical Notice (see #39 below), and his editing (pp. 350-51).

  Cornell (paper labels), Newberry, personal [binder's ticket ("Bone and Sons")].

6. (revised, reset edition of #5): HESPERIDES / *THE POEMS AND OTHER REMAINS* / OF / ROBERT HERRICK. / EDITED BY / W. CAREW HAZLITT. / Second Edition, Revised / *IN TWO VOLUMES* / VOL. I [VOL. II] / LONDON: REEVES AND TURNER 196 STRAND / 1890.

6¾ x 4¼"): vol. I: tipped-in-front. + [a]⁸, b-d⁸, 3², A-O⁸; 146 leaves; pp. [i-v], vi-lxiv, [4], [1], 2-223, [224].

Vol. II: [a]⁸, b⁶, A-S⁸, 158 leaves; pp. [2], [i-v], vi-xxvi, [1], 2-286, [(1)] (2).

Coll. Note: last leaf in vol. II (sig. S8) lists Hazlitt's works published by Reeves and Turner.

Front: replica of Marshall.

Price: Scribner's "Catalog of Importations: lists at $3.20 (from 1897 to 1907).

Binding: See b) and c), #5 above.

  Cornell, Harvard, C.U.N.Y (Lehmann)

6a. (another issue or impression of revised ed. with floral decorations on t.p.): HES-PERIDES, THE POEMS AND OTHER / REMAINS OF ROBERT HERRICK: / EDITED BY W. CAREW HAZLITT: / LONDON, GIBBINGS AND COMPANY, / LIMITED: IN TWO VOLUMES: VOLUME / ONE: [VOLUME / TWO:] MDCCCXCVII

Produced from either remaindered sheets or stereotype plates by arrangements with Reeves, Turner. New half-title and title page in each volume.

Price: 5s (Gibbings' 1910 catalog)

Binding: green sand-grain cloth (identified as "buckram" in catalog). On front cover: three gold-stamped stylized flowers with stems, in a two-dimensional art nouveau design. They occupy the upper quarter of the board. The lower eighth is decorated with similarly designed flowers, seen edge-on. This design is identical to the one on the t.p. On spine, gold stamped: HERRICK'S / POETICAL / WORKS / [flower decoration, as on upper part of cover, slightly reduced] / VOL. I [VOL. II]. Top edge gilt. Fore and lower edges untrimmed.

  Lake Forest (Ill.) College

7. Early English Poets. / [rule] THE / COMPLETE POEMS / OF / ROBERT HERRICK. / EDITED, / WITH / Memorial-Introduction and Notes, / BY THE / REV. ALEX-ANDER GROSART. / [decoration: urn, snake, flowers in circular medalion design]/ IN *THREE VOLUMES-Vol. I [Vol. II] [Vol. III.]* / LONDON: / *CHATTO AND WINDUS PICCADILLY.* / 1876.

(7½ x 5"): vol. I: tipped-in front. + [a]⁸, b-s⁸, [A]², B-M⁸, 234 leaves; pp. [iv], v-cclxxxv, [cclxxxvi], [1-7], 8-182.

vol. II:ᴛ⁸, aa⁶, B-U⁸, 166 leaves; pp. [i-iv] v-xxvii, [xxviii], [1], 2-304.

vol. III: a⁸, aa⁴, B-F⁸, G⁸ (±G5), H-U⁸, X⁶, 170 leaves; pp. [i-v], vi-xxiv, [1], 2-316.

Front: Steel engraving by W. J. Alais, after Marshall. A head of the poet, which Grosart (I, cclxx) compares very favorably to previous fronts. by Worthington. Schiavonetti, Lane, and that used on t.p. of Maitland's edition; he asserts that it delineates "much of the voluptuous force of the best type among the Roman emperors," and "interprets to us Herrick's book." The phrasing is copied from Ed. Gosse, "Robert Herrick," *Cornhill,* Aug. 1875, p. 179.

Price: 18s in 1891: reduced to 10s in 1897 (E. Cat) in Scribner's "Cat. of Importations" from 1897 to 1903 at $4.00.

Binding: fine sand grain dark blue cloth. Paper label on spine, bordered and printed in red: Early English / Poets / VOL. I [VOL. II] [VOL. III] / *EDITED BY* / REV. A.B. GROSART.

Lib. Co. of Phila. Brit. Lib., Cornell (half-calf), Lib. Cong.

personal (sig. [A]2 vol. I, lacking, tipped in after sig᙮6 in vol. III)

*7a. Also issued in large paper, 50 cc [Temple Scott], *Book Sales of 1895* (London: Cockram, 1896), item 3448.

8. ROBERT HERRICK / THE HESPERIDES AND NOBLE / NUMBERS: EDITED BY / ALFRED POLLARD / WITH A PREFACE BY / A.C. SWINBURNE. / Vol. I. [Vol. II.] / [device of press: "L" and "B" framing greek maiden and ox] /

LONDON:	NEW YORK:
LAWRENCE & BULLEN,	CHARLES SCRIBNER'S SONS
169 New Bond Street, W.	743 & 745 Broadway,
1891	1891

(5¼ x 3¾): vol. I: tipped-in front. + [a]⁸, b⁴, c², [1]⁸, 2-16⁸, [19]⁸, 18-20⁸, 18-20⁸, 174 leaves; pp. [i-xiii], ix-xxvi, [2], [1-3], 4-318, [2]. Vol. II:ᴛ⁴, I-22⁸, 23², 82 leaves; pp. [8], [1], 2-356. "Appendix of Epigrams": [24]⁸, 25-26⁸, 24 leaves; pp. [357-59], 360-404.

Grant Richards, *Author Hunting,* p. 82: a "separately printed appendix which has neither title on its wrapper, nor title page, nor printer's nor publisher's name."

Front: replica of Marshall

Price: 10s, $3.50, for both 1891 and 1898 eds.

Binding: Fine net grained cloth, elaborately gold-stamped. Standing female in greek robe placing laurel wreath on head of seated male, writing with quill, in greek outdoor dress, with buskins. Background of leaves and tree. Scrollwork below leaves bears lettering "The Muses' Library." On spine: gold-stamped tree and leaves, gold blocked scrollwork with lettering HERRICK'S / WORKS / A.W. POLLARD. Vol. number and publisher's name also gold-stamped. Top edge gilt. Fore and bottom edges untrimmed. Bound in blue or brown cloth.

Reviews: The Speaker, Jan. 16, 1892, p. 82: "...the sort of book one handles affectionately and feels a certain pleasure merely in holding it, long after one has cased to read."

Athenaeum, July 23, 1892: "And yet if the edition appeals to scholars, why should it be tricked out in daintiness and elegance?"

U. of Illinois, Lib Cong., Harvard, Penn State, Texas HRC (all in blue cloth, lack appendix), personal (brown cloth; appendix bound separately). Syracuse U., Rosenbach Mus (Blue cloth, App. present).

8a. Another issue (200 copies), on large paper (6⅞ x 4⅜). Green linen-covered boards, quarter vellum, gilt. T.e.g., others untrimmed. T.p. imprint variant: only Lawrence and Bullen mentioned. Appendix bound in vol. II.

personal, Syracuse U.

8b. (another issue, imprint variant):

LONDON	NEW YORK:
LAWRENCE & BULLEN, Ltd	CHARLES SCRIBNER'S SONS
16 HENRIETTA STREET, W.C.	153-157 FIFTH AVENUE
1897	1897

(names of publishers in red)
    Univ. of Penna. (lacks appendix)

9. (revised subedition of #8): ROBERT HERRICK / THE HESPERIDES & NOBLE / NUMBERS: EDITED BY / ALFRED POLLARD / WITH A PREFACE BY / A.C. SWINBURNE / Vol. I [Vol. II] / *REVISED EDITION* / [device of press, as in #8 above]

LONDON	NEW YORK
LAWRENCE AND BULLEN, Ltd.	CHARLES SCRIBNER'S SONS
16 Henrietta Street, W.C.	153-57 Fifth Avenue
1898	1898

[I. 1, and names of publishers (1.11) in red]

In vol. I, text (except for a "Note to the Second Edition") is basically the same as 1891. Some sententia are italicized and footnotes changed. There is a renumbering of the poems, starting with #402, p. 193, to correct an error in the first edition. Signatures are unchanged, so plates for the first edition could have served. The "Notes" for Vol. I (as for Vol. II) were completely revised, and these leaves show a complete resetting of type. Collation is [17]^8 18-20^8, 21^2, ending on p. 322. Changes in the text of Vol. II are similar, pagination and signatures being the same through sig. 17, p. 272. From that point, collation runs 18-23^8 24^2; pp. [273-75], 276-372. The "Appendix of Epigrams" is as follows: [24]^8 25-26^8 (p. [373] is sig. 24); pp. [373-75], 376-420. In three copies seen, these are printed on a rougher paper than the rest of the book. They are found in the back of vol. II, without wrappers (in all copies seen).

    The Appendix with its notes is unchanged from 1891 except for pagination and signatures. The Rev. C.P. Phinn, the "veteran student" (I, xxvii) responsible for the enlarged notes in both vols, has not commented upon the "coarser" epigrams. See L.C. Martin (#91 below), pp. v-vi.

    personal, Temple Univ.; Penn. St. (Appendix on same paper as rest of book) U.N. Car., Syracuse.

9a. (second impression of the revised sub. ed): The Muses' Library / [rule] ROBERT HERRICK / THE HESPERIDES AND NOBLE NUMBERS / EDITED BY / ALFRED POLLARD / WITH A PREFACE BY / A.C. SWINBURNE / VOL. 1 [VOL. II.] / *REVISED EDITION* / [monogram of Routledge] / LONDON: / GEORGE ROUTLEDGE & SONS, LIMITED / NEW YORK: E.P. DUTTON & CO.
As in #9, above there is a renumbering of the poems starting with #402, p. 193 of vol. I. There is no front., and no appendix of epigrams at the end of vol. II, although the "Editor's Note" in vol. I, stating the presence of the "detachable appendix," is in this impression. On p. [323], vol. I: "Printed at the Edinburgh Press, 9 and 11 Young St." Verso t.p. vol. I, rubber-stamped: "Made in Great Britain."
Price: 2s; $1.00. Still listed at 2s in Routledge 1940 cat.
Dating: E. Cat: "Jan. 1905"
Binding: blue-calico-grain cloth. Gold-stamped on spine, in cartouche: HERRICK / I [II] / The / MUSES LIBRARY / ROUTLEDGE. Background of vines and buds, running from bottom to top. Upper and lower covers undecorated. Also available in leather and lambskin.
Size: 5⅞ x 3½".

CUNY (Cohen lib), Columbia, U. No. Carolina

10. THE POETICAL WORKS OF / ROBERT HERRICK / EDITED BY / GEORGE SAINTSBURY / IN TWO VOLUMES / [device of press: bell and anchor] / VOL. I [VOL. II.] / LONDON / GEORGE BELL & SONS, YORK ST., COVENT GARDEN / NEW YORK: 112 FOURTH AVENUE / 1893.

(6¾ x 4"): vol. I: tipped-in-front.+a-c⁸, d⁴, B– ·T⁸, U, 176 leaves; pp. [2], [i-v],. vi-liii, [liv], [1-5], 6-293, [294], [2].

     Vol. II: [a]⁸, b⁴, B-U⁸, X², 166 leaves; pp. [i-v], vi-xxiv, [1-3], 4-308.

Front: replica of Marshall

Price: 2s 6d each vol.: 75¢ per vol (so listed Macmillan's cat, through 1910).

Binding: red dotted-line cloth. On spine, gold-stamped: HERRICK'S / POETICAL / WORKS / I. [II.] / G. SAINTSBURY / [press device; bell and anchor] / ALDINE EDITION

Note: In 1855 Bell and Daldy purchased the rights to many of the Pickering-Chiswick Press works, including the Aldine Poets (the 1846 Herrick was not a part of this series); the Bell ed. was printed at Chiswick.

    Duke, Bryn Mawr

*10a. Second impression, 1900.

*10b. Third impression, 1905.

10c. Fourth impression, 1908. Verso t.p.: "First issue...1893. Reprinted 1900, 1905, 1908."

    personal

*10d Fifth impression, 1912. (reported in NUC, vol. 243, p. 12).

11. THE POETICAL WORKS / OF / ROBERT HERRICK /EDITED BY / F.W. MOORMAN / OXFORD / AT THE CLARENDON PRESS / 1915

(8¾ x 5½"): tipped-in front. + a⁸, b⁴, B-Hh⁸, Ii⁶, 258 leaves; pp. [i-v], vi-xxiii, [xxiv], 1-5, 6-492.

Front: replica of Marshall, but with his name removed from lower left corner of pedestal of bust.

Price: 12s 6d; $4.20 (US Cat, 1928); British price holds through 1940.

Binding: Dark blue cloth. Blind-stamped border, upper and lower cover. Monogram of press blind stamped, center of upper board. Gold stamped on spine border top and bottom. HERRICK'S / POEMS / EDITED BY / F.W. MOORMAN / OXFORD D.j. (eggshell; blue lettering) states on back that Oxford Eng. Texts available in "cloth with paper labels" and in "blue cloth, gilt lettering."

Note: the revised, expurgated ed., published in the "Oxford Poets" series and provided with an introduction by Percy Simpson (1921; see #75 below), states (p. 7) that the 1915 volume was part of the "Oxford English Texts" series.

    Saturday Review (London), June 5, 1915, p. 583 commends typography (Fell types) and scholarship, and notes that the book design eschews the decorated endpapers and "catchy" illustrations of other reprints.

    Lib. Cong., Harvard, U. of Penna. (all blue cloth)

I. B. Drawing-Room Gift Books (1882-1913).

12. (in red, on scroll work ; ll. 1-5 in upper-right fo ground of drawing of woman posed before steps of country house): Selections from / ·'\· Poetry of / Robert Herrick / with Drawings by / Edwin A. Abb‹ HARPER AND BROTHERS PUBLISHERS / FRANKLIN SQUARE - NEW YORK 1882 [ll. 6-8 at bottom of page]
Wood-engraved illustrated title page with calligraphic lettering, numerous full-page illustrations after Abbey, with some floral vignettes, headpieces, and tailpieces by Alfred Parsons (to whom the book is dedicated). Line drawings, reproduced by wood engraving.
(11¾ x 9⅜"): engraved title page and 45 full-page illus. (for which pagination is inferred) tipped in + [A]⁶, B⁴, [1]⁴, 2-12⁴, 13¹; pp. [12], i-vi, 1-188.
Introduction: Austin Dobson
Portrait: p. [3], as illus. for "To his Muse"
Price: $7.50 (Am. Cat.); 42s (released simultaneously with Am. publication by Low, Marston, Seale and Rivington).
Binding: "Beige cloth, probably designed by Abbey with radiating sun blocked in gold, floating flowers in light olive-green extending around spine and lower cover, lettered in red and black." (Eleanor Garvey, *The Turn of a Century* [Cambridge, MA: Houghton Lib, 1970], p. 108). Title on front cover, in calligraphic lettering. On spine in red, running top to bottom: HERRICK. Blue endp. with binder's blank leaves; a.e. gilt. Issued in decorative box: Title, illustrator, publisher, and date within elaborate Renaissance Arabesque border on front of box.
Printed in modern face with decorated fancy italics used for titles of individual poems. Verso title page: TYPE FROM "YE LEADENHALLE PRESS" (FIELD AND TUER), LONDON.
CUNY, Harvard, U of Penna., Yale U (Bienecke Lib.; Austin Dobson's copy); personal (boxed)

12a. (another issue, imprint variant): "S. Low" Brit. Lib.
12b. (second impression, 1899 [so stated on t.p.]): Variant bindings: (a): green cloth, blind-stamped upper cover with small floral designs and EAP / AP enclosed in two ornaments resembling interlocked quill pens. Decorated border. HERRICK'S POEMS in upper center, above decorated rule. Similar design on lower cover, no lettering. Spine gilt. (b): similar design, upper and lower covers, stamped in dark green on light brown, coarse net-grained cloth. Spine gilt. T. e. g., others untrimmed. Plain white endpapers.
Price: $4.00.
CUNY (Var. a), personal (Var. b)
12c. (third impression, 1910): "Copyright 1910" verso tp. (no t.p. date). Same binding as 1899, variant (a), but AP not present on upper cover, and with gilt lettering on spine arranged differently (pub. name not present).
Harvard, U. So. Carolina

*13. *Christmas Greeting: A Selection of Christmas Poems.* New York: Stokes, 1887. $2.50 (Am. Cat). Illus. by W. Schmediger.

*14. *Let's Go AMaying.* London: R. Tuck, [1890]. 2s 6d. Illus. by Bessie Nichol (who exhibited in London in the 90s).
Dating E. Cat: Nov. 1890. (at Harvard)

15. A / COVNTRY GARLAND / OF TEN SONGS / GATHERED FROM / THE / HESPERIDES / OF / ROBERT HERRICK / SET INTO MUSIC BY / JOSEPH S. MOORAT / WITH A COVER & / XV DRAWINGS BY / PAUL WOODROFFE /

LONDON - GEORGE ALLEN / PUBLISHER-RUSKIN HOUSE / 156 CHARING CROSS RD.

Decorated half-title, title page, and contents page, with 11 full-page line drawings (inc. front) illustrating the ten poems.
(11½ x 8½"): [A]⁴, B - G⁴; pp. [1-6], 7-53, [3]
Price: 5 sh
Dating: verso t.p.: "All Rights Reserved / 1897." See review in *The Studio,* June 1898, p. 70.
Binding: Paper covered boards, quarter bound in deep brown morocco-grain cloth. Front and back covers designed with sinuously-curving vines and flowers, with two *putti* playing pan-pipes and fiddle. Orange on white, with HESPERIDES at top center. On spine: HESPERIDES, from bottom to top, framed by two bees with wings spread. Front and back endpapers decorated with rose-tinted vines, flowers, and birds; two androgynous youths with wings hold up rose-chain at either edge of drawing. Top edge gilt, others trimmed.
    personal

15a. *Imprint variant:* added after Allen imprint: NEW YORK / FREDERICK A. STOKES COMPANY PUBLISHERS; typeface different from rest of page (fancy, with swash letters).
    Texas Woman's Univ.

16. (in square compartment on upper half of engraved design, framed with columns and flowers): HESPERIDES / *OR WORKS* / *BOTH* HUMAN / *AND* DIVINE / *BY* / *ROBERT HERRICK* / *TOGETHER WITH* / *HIS* NOBLE NUMBERS OR / *HIS* PIOUS PIECES / (in cartouche): *VOL. 1 [Vol. 2]* / (at bottom of design, in compartment framed with putti): LONDON / *GEORGE NEWNES LTD* / NEW YORK / *CHARLES SCRIBNER'S SONS*

Vol. 1: tipped in front and 12 plates by Reginald Savage. Line drawings, each illustrating one poem on a facing page; listed, p. xxiii. Reproduced by photo-lithography, except for front., in photogravure. Decorated t.p., and endpapers signed "Garth Jones." Vol. 2: Front. and 12 plates by Savage, as in vol. 1. Listed, p. xxvii. T.p. as in vol. 1.
(6¼ x 4"): vol. 1: tipped in front. and t.p., +a⁸, b⁶, A-T⁸; pp. [2], [i-ii], iii-xxiii, [xxiv], [2], [1], 2-304.

vol. 2: tipped in front and t.p., +a⁸, b⁶, A-T⁸; pp. [2], [i-ii], iii-xxvii, [xxvii], [2], [1], 2-303, [304].
half-title, both vols: "The Caxton Series". Not a complete works. Many epigrams and sexually frank poems excluded: some bowdlerization.
Fronts. are illustrations of individual poems.
Portraits: conversation pieces. I, facing p. 42: "A Country Life, to his Brother..."; I, fac. p. 130: "Upon a Physician"; II, fac. p. 62: The Invitation."
Price: 5s 6d in leather; $2.50. $2.25 in 1928 (US Cat).
Dating: Front, vol. 1, dated 1902. E. Cat, as part of Caxton Series, 1902. London Library cat, 1902. BM cat, 1903.
Binding: deep red calico cloth. Upper cover: HERRICK'S / HESPERIDES gold-stamped above blind-stamped floral dec. Spine gold-stamped. T.e.g.

16a. Limited to 30 copies (on Jap. vellum)
16b. 106 copies (o.w. paper).

Bindings: 1) quarter-bound blue cloth, light grey paper boards, leather labels on spine. T.e.g.

2) quarter-bound in vellum, gold stamping on spine; decorated endpapers by A. G[arth] J[ones]. T.e.g., lower edge untrimmed. Bindings seen on issue limited to 106 copies.

   LSU (rebound), personal (trade and limited issues), U. No. Carolina, (vellum quarter-binding)

   See also #20 and 48 below.

17. FLOWER POEMS / BY / ROBERT HERRICK / With a Note on Herrick by / ALGERNON CHARLES SWINBURNE / Illustrated with Twelve Coloured Plates by / FLORENCE CASTLE / [device of Routledge: profile of crowned man, roman arch, with "R" worked into design] / LONDON / GEORGE ROUTLEDGE & SONS, LIMITED / NEW YORK: E.P. DUTTON & CO. (lines 1, 3, 7 and 10 in red)
Tipped-in front. and 11 other illustrations in water-color, reproduced on clay paper by half-tone process, each plate illustrating a single poem. Tissue guards. Listed, p. 21. Castle (b. 1867) exhibited at London galleries, including R.A. and New English Art Club. Poem titles (usually one poem per page) shoulder-noted against fore-edge. Typeface similar to Morris' Golden (Plantin?).
(8¼ x 5½): [A]⁸, B-F⁸; pp. [1-6], 7-96.

Preface by Swinburne as in #8 above.
Half-title: "The Photogravure and Colour Series"; printed on Japanese vellum.
Dating: appears in Dutton's catalogue for first time in 1906, with 12 other titles. In 1905, only five titles in the series were listed. In cat. of London Library (1928-50 supplement) as 1905.
Price: 3s 6d (E. Cat.); $1.50 ($2.50 in leather) Routledge's 1910 catalogue lists only 2 titles in this series, not including *Flower Poems.* But listed in the 1936 and 1938 *Ref Cat. of Current Lit.* at 5s.
Binding: Green calico-grain cloth, bordered in black on upper cover and spine, the colors being divided by an undulating gold-stamped line.
On upper cover: gold-stamped reproduction of the illustration facing p. 24—three maidens with bent heads and clasped hands, weeping over flowers. Oval frame. Above this, also gold-stamped: HERRICK'S [floral device] / FLOWER-POEMS / with Coloured Plates / by Florence Castle. Gold-stamped on spine (on green cloth bordered in black): HERRICK FLOWER POEMS (running top to bottom). Lower cover in green, no border. Top edge gilt.
Binding variant, later issue (?): blue calico-grain cloth, no decoration. On spine, gold stamped: HERRICK FLOWER POEMS (top to bottom). Probably a secondary (remainder?) binding—other series titles exist in similar variant. Top edge plain. No tissue guards.

   Indiana U., Newbury, Syracuse U., personal (secondary binding)

18. POEMS OF / HERRICK / *Selected & with an / Introduction by* / The Rev. Canon Beeching D. D. / [line and wash drawing of "The Vicarage and Church / Dean Prior (today) / Devon." Rectangular, bordered with stylized roses and thorny vines] / EDINBURGH / T. C. AND E. C. JACK
Engraved front. and t.p. (line drawings reproduced in photogravure), and 8 plates, water colors reproduced full-page by half-tone process on clay paper. Listed, p. xv. The plates by Eliz. Stanhope Forbes, who with her husband founded the Newlyn School of Art, 1899; both were active in New English Art Club. Front. and title vignette by A.S. Hartrick, experienced at line drawings of famous people for *The Daily Graphic.*
Half-title: "The Golden Poets / EDITED BY OLIPHANT SMEATON"
(6½ x 4 3/8"): *⁴, b-c⁸, A-R⁸; pp. [i-viii], ix-xliv, [1], 2-256.

Front: Profile of Herrick, wearing surplice and neck-band, with folded arms against a background of Devon hills and hedgerows. Emphasizes jutting jaw, and adds introspective eyes and lips set in what might be a supercilious, confidential, or ironic smile.

Dating: B.M. gives 1907. Review in *Bookman,* 31 (March 1907), pp. 253-54.

Price: 2s 6d

Binding: Dark purple cloth, elaborately gold-stamped: double rules in knotted design on left edge of upper cover, progressing three-quarters of way across the board, ending in bud-like design, and interested by vertical rules, POEMS OF HERRICK on upper right, near center. Lower cover carries similar design. On spine: gold-stamped rules (4 sets of 4 lines), title, editor, and illustrator named. T.e.g; others untrimmed.

    Brit. Lib.

18a. (another issue or impression; imprint variant): reads LONDON: CAXTON PUBLISHING CO. Design and position identical to above; no date. Caxton—as Jack—had both Edinburgh and London addresses; perhaps in this case the former firm acted as London distributor for Jack.

Binding variants for the Caxton issue:

1.) brown sand-grain cloth, decorated on upper cover with orange design; stylized elongated stems, leaves and petals similar to work in the art nouveau style by the Glasgow School (dominant vertical rhythms, parallelism, slightly curved lines). Part of this design is adapted for spine decoration. Lower cover undecorated.

2.) Purple sand-grain cloth. Two borders in white on upper cover, with gold-stamped harp inside wreath, and THE / GOLDEN / POETS / in purple inside wreath, on gold background. Author, editor and distributor gold-stamped on spine.

    personal

19. (abridged ed. of #18): POEMS OF / HERRICK / ILLUSTRATED BY / E. STANHOPE FORBES / [rule] / [harp; tendrils and flowers entwined in its strings] / LONDON / T.C. AND E. C. JACK / AND EDINBURGH

Four full-page illus. on clay paper, as in #18: "Bright tulips..." (front.), "A sweet disorder in the dress" (facing p. 10), "Cherry-ripe..." (facing p. 16), "Gather ye rosebuds" (facing p. 20).

(5 3/4 x 4½"): A⁸ B⁸, pp. [1-4] 5-25, [26], [4].

Dating: E. Cat.: "Oct. 1910"

Price: 1s (not in Jack's 1910 cat).

Binding: red linen-grain cloth, elaborate gold stamped design on upper cover involving Bird of Paradise intertwined with stems, tendrils, and vines. Gold-stamped lettering in border.

    Brit. Lib.

*20. (abridged ed. of #16): *Poems and Songs of Robert Herrick.* London: Simpkin, Marshall, Hamilton, Kent and Co.: 1912. "Gravure Series"; 6d (E. Cat).

    Advertised as "entirely new series" (i.e., for this publisher), "illus. by R. Savage" with "three-coloured cover, bound in cream parchment and frontis-piece in photogravure." 64 p. Size 7" x 4½"...also bound in velvet Persian, gilt top, tastefully boxed" (Simpkin's 1913 cat.). Apparently Newnes sold plates of the illustrations to Simpkin, Marshall; the latter put the book together using Savage's front. and some other of his plates.

21. *HERRICK / SOME OF HIS / LYRICS / WITH DECORATIONS BY / T.R.R. RYDER / LONDON / GAY & HANCOCK / MCMXII* (bordered by irregularly curving vines with thorns; in three corners of border are a set of roses, seen from above).

(8½ x 6½): [1-6]⁴; pp. [1-48]

Calligraphic representations of 11 poems, a *mise-en-page* for each. Thick asymmetrically-arranged borders, black background with white decorations.

Price: 3s 6d. In Gay and Hancock 1920 cat, "by Mrs. Ryder."

Binding: linen-grain light green cloth; upper cover: gold-stamped flowers and vines at the left of HERRICK / Decorated by / T.R.R. RYDER. On spine: HERRICK. Swash initials. White laid paper endpapers.

Colophon: "Printed by Geo. W. Jones, at *The Sign of the Dolphin*, Gough Sq., Fleet St., London E.C."

Brit. Lib.

I. C. Bibelots (I use this term to designate a group of small volumes meant for display in drawing-room or boudoir and in most cases serving as inexpensive but intimate gifts).

22. (in floral border, with Cupid in upper right, strewing petals; seated Venus, playing lyre, in lower left): THE LYRIC / POEMS OF / ROBERT / HERRICK. / EDITED BY ERNEST / RHYS / J.M. DENT & CO ALDINE HOUSE / 69 GREAT EASTERN ST LONDON E C (calligraphic lettering; lines 1, 2, 3, 4, 7 and 8 in red)

Decorated t.p., vignettes; poems asymmetrically set on page, with titles against left margins; notes set opposite titles on right half of text block.

(6 x 3 3/4"): [a]⁸, b⁴, A-L⁸, M⁴; pp. [i-iv], v-xxiv, 1-182, [2].

Price: 2s 6d; 5s in leather; $1.00, $1.50 parchment (Macmillan cat. for 1897).

Dating: E. Cat: "Nov. 1896", BM cat, 1897. *Front:* replica of Marshall

Binding: greenish-blue sand-grain cloth, elaborately gold-stamped; upper cover: outer border of stylized leaves and vines, superimposed on pattern of gold dots. Inner panel formed by rectangular border surrounded by undulating rectangle of vines and stems, some of which float freely above and below the panel, in which is inscribed The / LYRICAL / POEMS / OF / ROBERT / HERRICK. On spine is design as on outer border of upper cover, statement of series (THE / LYRIC / POETS), author and publisher. Lower cover undecorated. T.e.g. Fore- and bottom edges untrimmed.

Note: This was Rhys' first association with Dent. See Rhys, *Everyman Remembers*, p. 232: "Now when I look over the lyric volumes they appear almost too pretty-pretty in their pale blue and gold, and too small of print for my notion of a viable poetry book." Rhys' introduction for the Everyman Library Herrick makes its first appearance in #22. See #44b., below.

Brit. Lib., Harvard, Penn State, U. Texas (HRC)

23. (in decorated border of vines and roses, with *putti* holding cameo head of girl in Stuart dress at center of top horizontal panel and flaming heart at center of bottom panel): *HERRICK'S / WOMEN, LOVE / & FLOWERS* [emblem of press: androgynous near-naked figure reading book] / *LONDON / GAY and BIRD / 1899* (calligraphic lettering)

Half-title: "The Bibelots"

Front. by W. L. Colls, decorated title page and vignettes (floral designs, Venus and Cupids, languid maidens posing before mirrors or with heads resting on hands) by H[erbert] C[ole].

(5 x 2 3/4"): a⁶, A-H⁸, I⁴; pp. [i-v], vi-x, [xi-xii], 1-135.

Frontispiece: after Worthington's for Pickering (see #2a and 39), with Herrick's signature below. Signed "W.L. Colls, Ph. Sc."

Price: 2s 6d in leather (E. Cat. 1899). So listed in Gay and Hancock (successor to Gay and Bird) cat. of 1913 (p. 6), as well as in Gay and Bird ad. in *Bookseller*, Nov. 3, 1899, p. 1077.

Binding: I have not seen an original cloth binding.

23a. A variant issue in vellum with thongs. Stamped in gold on right half of upper cover: HERR... / RICK'S.. WOMEN / LOVE & .. / FLOWERS. On spine: WOMEN. / LOVE. / FLOWERS. / 1899. This issue has colophon, p. [iv]: "This edition on Japanese Vellum is limited to Sixty Copies, of which this is no..."
    Brit. Lib.

23b. (a latter issue, with imprint variant on t.p.): [press device: books, hand holding lamp, IN LIBRIS FELICITAS in scrollwork] / *New York* / *Truslove, Hanson & Comba* / *67 Fifth Avenue.*
    Probably issued in US in 1902. Listed for that year in John Lane's American catalogue, at $1.00. Index of *Publisher's Trade List Annual* for that year refers to Lane for listings of Truslove, Hanson and Comba.
    Harvard (rebound)

*24. *Poems.* The Miniature Series. Edinburgh: Nimmo, Hay, and Mitchell, 19--.
    Probably issued between 1903 and 1908, in Nimmo's Mineature Series, no. 27. Not in Nimmo's 1902 catalogue. The 1910 cat. lists as the new entries in this series nos. 40 and 41, and in 1908, the publishers list only the new volumes in the series, which bear numbers greater than 27. In Sampson, Low catalogues for 1928 and 1932.
1s in "yapped velvet cloth"; 6d in cloth.
Advertised as a substitute for a greeting card.

25. (in compartment decorated with sinuous vines, leaves, and stylized flowers): LOVE POEMS / OF HERRICK / JOHN LANE / LONDON & NEW YORK / MDCCCIII

Violet borders and decorated running titles on each page. Printed in violet on tinted paper. Designed by Phillip Connard.
(5⅛ x 2¾"): π⁸, A-L⁶; pp. [i-iv], v-xii, 1-127, [128], [4].
"The Lover's Library", #8
Price: 1s 6d (2s in leather; 3s in vellum); 50¢ (75¢ in leather, $1.00 in vellum). First listed in Lane's American cat. 1902. Offered in Lane's 1924 cat. in paper-covered boards, leather, cloth, and parchment.
Binding: (2 states reported, violet and green): copies seen in green cloth, with gold-stamped design on spine and upper cover: intertwined vegitation possibly suggesting roots, trunk and branches of tree. Upper cover, framed by stylized vegitation, gold-stamped: LOVE POEMS / OF / HERRICK. On spine: LOVE / POEMS / OF / HERRICK / THE / LOVER'S / LIBRARY. Decorated endpapers: sinuously curving stylized flowers and stems, in violet on white background. A. e.g.
    Brit. Lib., Lib. Cong., Harvard

*26. *Songs From the Hesperides of Robert Herrick.* Guildford, Surrey: The Astolat Press, 1903. 78 pp.
    See Wm. Ridler, *British Modern Press Books: A Descriptive Check List of Unrecorded Items,* p. 12, #4. He records owner of the Astolat Press as A.C. Curtis.

26a. (second impression): Songs / From / The Hesperidies [sic] / by / ROBERT HERRICK / [device of press: copse of trees with path in background] / THE ASTOLAT PRESS / Great Castle St. W. / MDCCCCIV
3¾ x 2½: pp. [i-iv], v-viii, 9-77.

Price: 1s (E. Cat.) This and subsequent impressions published in London by H. Siegle and Assoc.

Binding: light brown cloth. Upper cover red-stamped with design of leaves and vines, rising from bottom to arborial design at top. Centered in border, surrounded by leaves: "Songs From / The Hesperides / R. Herrick." On spine, running from top to bottom: "Songs: Herrick."

    Brit. Lib.

*26b. (third impression): *Songs from Robert Herrick*. London: Siegle, 1907. "Songs of Our Islands" series. 1s (E. Cat.)

Catalog of Siegle, Hill & Co., Langham Place, W., 1910, p. 3: "...dainty design in gold and two colours, enclosed in envelope." Size stated as 4½ x 2 3/4"; printed on Japanese vellum.

See #30 and 32 below.

27. THE POEMS OF / ROBERT HERRICK / Edited, with a Biographical Introduction by / JOHN MASEFIELD / [vine leaf] / LONDON / E. GRANT RICHARDS / 1906 (4 7/8 x 3 1/8"): [a]⁸, b⁸, c¹, A-T⁸, U⁶; pp. [i-iv], v-xxxiv, 1-313, [314]. (sig. c1, last leaf of preliminaries, tipped in).

Price: 3s 6d (stated in some copies on p. [ii]), $1.00 (U.S. Cat.)

Binding: a) white vellum, with interwoven kid thongs used as ties. On spine, in black: THE POEMS / OF / HERRICK / [arabesque design] / THE / CHAP-BOOKS. U.S. Cat. reports a slipcase. Fore- and bottom edges untrimmed. T.e.g.

b) brown calico-grain cloth; paper label on spine. Bottom edge untrimmed. Top edge stained green.

    U. No. Carolina, Harvard (both cloth)

27a. American issue, with imprint variant: NEW YORK / FREDERICK A. STOKES COMPANY / PUBLISHERS

    personal (vellum)

*27b. (second impression): reported in *Eng. Cat.*, 1907

*27c (third impression): reported in E. Cat., 1920

28. *Herrick / Calendar / for / 1908 /* [flowers and stems on either side of date] / O. Anacker / London (t.p. printed in green; calligraphic script)

Floral tailpieces and decorated initials. Poems printed in italics; entire book printed in green. Colophon: "Printed and published by O. Anacker at 22, New Yard, Great Queen Street, London: W. C."

(5 3/8 x 3 7/8"): no sigs, no pagination. 14 leaves.

Price: 6d

Binding: Beige paper covers, foreedges of wrappers yapped. On upper cover: A HERRICK CALENDAR / FOR / 1908 [swash Rs]

    Brit. Lib.

29. THE LOVE POEMS / OF / ROBERT HERRICK / [vine leaf] / LONDON / GRANT RICHARDS / 7 CARLTON ST. S.W.

(5x3¼"): front, tipped in, + [A]⁸ B-F⁸; pp. [1-7] 8-93, [94].

Front: a complete bust standing on a shelf against a dark background. It shows, in profile, a youngish, reflective individual, with prominent nose and curls, a slightly arched eyebrow, a downward turning mouth, and the hint of a smile. The face is sensual, the expression reflective. After a print inscribed "London. May 1, 1822. Published by W. Walker...Grays Inn Square." "Drawn by G. Clint A.R.A. Engraved by E. Smith." The Omar Series, No. 8.

Price: 6d. In *Ref. Cat. of Current Lit.*, 1940, 2s. in leather.

Dating: BM Cat.: 1908. Verso t.p. "1908"

Calico-grain light red cloth. Blind stamped floral dec. and title on upper cover. Title gold-stamped on spine.

Brit. Lib.

30. Songs from the / hesperides / BY / ROBERT HERRICK / [vine leaf] / SIEGLE, HILL AND CO. / 2 Langham Place, W.

(3 5/16x2 1/8"): [A]⁸, B-H⁸; pp. [1-4], 5-127, [128], [2].

Price: 1s (Siegle, Hill 1910 cat.) In 1938 *Ref. Cat. of Current Lit.* (1s 6d) distributed by Leopold Hill.

Dating: E. Cat. date is Sept. '09 Listed in Siegle 1910 catalog, as #25 in the Langam Booklets series (p. 5).

Binding: purple suede; black-stamped rule running in continuous line from foreedge of upper cover, across top and bottom of spine, to foreedge of lower cover. The quarter-inch of suede outside this rule, not reinforced by endpaper, extends downward over pages (i.e., "yapped"). Pale purple, marbled, endpapers. All edges gilt. Gold-stamped on spine, running from top to bottom: "Songs: Herrick."

Brit. Lib.

30a. American issue, imprint variant: LONDON / THE ASTOLAT PRESS / DAVID McKAY / PHILADELPHIA Rubber-stamped: "Printed in England," verso free front endpaper. In McKay catalog for 1909 (50¢)

personal

See #26, above, and #32, below.

31. (in compartment formed of greek columns, base, and keystone of arch): THE / LAUREL WREATH / SERIES / LOVE / POEMS / BY / ROBERT HERRICK / Illustrated by / C. E. BROCK / LONDON: ERNEST NISTER / NEW YORK: E.P. DUTTON & CO. (below base): No. 2803 (rubber-stamped at foot of page): "Printed in Bavaria."

Four full-page watercolor illus. by Brock, titled with lines from Herrick, reproduced by half-tone on clay paper, and tipped in: Front: "The Night-Piece, to Julia."

Also black and white vignettes, floral and landscape designs, many signed E.A.P. (Alfred Parsons [?]) (5 3/16 x 4"): no sig. three 8 leaf gatherings; pp. [1-5], 6-47, [48].

Contents Note: there are 30 poems reprinted. "A Sweet Disorder in the Dress", p. 17 is entitled "The Poetry of Dress" as it is in Palgrave's *Golden Treasury.*

Dating: two of the illustrations are signed "1909" Announced as addition to the Laurel Wreath Series in *Bookseller*, Oct. 14, 1910, p. 1360, s.v. Special Autumn Announcements (subheading: Fine Art Publications).

Price: 6d (see *Bookseller* announcement above); 25¢ (50¢ in vellum); advertised in Dutton's 1910 catalog: "Little Treasures of Classic Literature. Daintily bound and beautifully illustrated in color." (p. 17).

Binding: in addition to the vellum stated above (not seen), clay paper wrappers. Upper cover: color reproduction (half-tone) of man and woman holding hands on bench in arbor. In contrast to the "Jacobethan" style of dress Brock uses, these figures are in Regency costume. Under the drawing: LOVE POEMS BY / ROBERT / HERRICK. On lower quadrant of upper cover: "Let me / ever dwell / in thy remembrance."

Penn St. Univ. Capitol Campus, N.Y. Public (rebound; wrappers preserved)

*32. *Selections from Herrick*. London: Siegle, 1911. (E. Cat. "May 1911") 12 mos. 1s 6d (in leather). boxed.
See nos. 26 and 30 above. In 1928 and 1938 cat. of Leopold Hill, earlier a partner of Siegle, s.v. "Selected Series."

33. (in decorated compartment with pastel coloring, rose border: girl in medieval costume sitting on garden bench, writing. Background of flowers, birds, trees, drawn with two-dimensional effect, suggesting a stained-glass window): ROBERT HERRICK / LONDON AND GLASGOW / COLLINS' CLEAR-TYPE PRESS

Illustrated front., title page (clay paper, tipped in) and two illustrations on clay paper each tipped by one horiz. side onto a leaf of gray uncalendered paper with gold border. Front. titled "Sweet, be not proud of those two eyes." Dated "1910," as is the first illus. All three (possibly by J.E. Sutcliffe) are representational drawings of men and women in Stuart (or "Jacobethan") dress. Title page design signed "A. [?] A.D." (possibly A.A. Dixon) and dated "1910."
(5½ x 3½"): [A]¹⁶, B-D¹⁶, 64 leaves; pp. [1-2], 3-127, [128].
Binding: sand-grained pale-green paper-covered boards. Upper cover and spine bear design of sinuous green vines, with blue flowers, on background of gold dots; pastel shades predominate. In gold-bordered rectangle, yellow background, upper half of upper cover: HERRICK. In larger rectangle into which vines and flowers intrude, on lower half of upper cover: POEMS. On spine, in similar rectangular space, running from bottom to top: HERRICK. Lower cover undecorated. A.e.g. Illustrated endpapers on clay paper. Front.: milkmaid, shepherdboy piping to her, on hillside; village with church [with Norman Tower] in background. Rear: same girl and boy, walking down hill.
personal.
NOTE: Collins' Clear-Type Press' catalogues and advertisements from 1910 to 1924 list 6 series of "Booklets" with a format like that of the book described here. It is impossible to tell in which of these series this volume takes its place, and in fact it might have been used interchangeably in each of these series. These booklets—like those of Simpkin (see #20) and Siegle (#26, 30, 32)—were meant as inexpensive novelty gifts (6d to 1s). In this case, the books not being available in the BM, the LC, or other libraries (the one described is a personal copy), and not having been listed in the *English Catalogue*, it is impossible to tell which, if any, are impressions from a parent edition or are separate resettings of type. Therefore I list below all possible "Series" of which the volume described under #33 might be a part.

a. The Gem Booklets: Fifty of these were boxed and sold as a set, with "a specially designed Greeting Card," at 2s the box. *Bookseller*, Oct. 6, 1911, p. 1286. Entitled "Gems from Herrick."

b. The Silver Echo Series: also "a greeting card with each volume." The Herrick first advertised in *Bookseller*, Oct. 14, 1910, p. 1322. 6d, 2s boxed. Entitled "Rose-buds from Herrick."

c. The Cameo Poets: "The culture of the age very rightly insists on a dainty format for the poets..." 1s. Entitled "Herrick. Lyrical Pieces." See *Bookseller*, Oct. 6, 1911, p. 285.

d. The Queen Books: entitled "Lyrics from Herrick," 1s 6d: 2s 6d "velvet calf boxed." *Bookseller*, Oct. 6, 1911, p. 1286. Not listed in Collins' 1910 catalogue.

e. The Poets' Realm Booklets: "With coloured illustrations, end papers, and designed title page." Also a Christmas card with the volume. 1s 6d. Entitled "Herrick. From the Hesperides." In Collins' catalogue for 1913, p. 5.

f. added in 1926 cat. "Magic Lute Series. "Art cover, gilt edges."

34. (In decorated compartment above black-and-white line drawing of woman being distracted from writing on scroll by *putti* showing her a mirror): GEMS / FROM / HERRICK / LONDON AND GLASGOW / COLLINS' CLEAR-TYPE PRESS (11.4 and 5 below drawing).

(4 1/6x2¼"): Illus. front. and t.p. on clay paper, tipped in +[A]¹⁶ B-D¹⁶, 48 leaves; Front. identical to that of #33 above, but entitled "O how that glittering taketh me!" ("Upon Julia's Clothes," however, is not included in this selection.) Vignettes on each text page. Poem titles in Gothic. Paper self-wrappers. In decorated border on upper cover: *Gems from Herrick*. Below title, also in border, is color drawing of man and woman in medieval costume, reading scroll. Signed "Maclarid." Title on spine. Pale pink marbled endpapers. Fifty "Gem Booklets" were boxed and sold as a set, "with a specially designed Greeting Card, at 2s the box. See *Bookseller*, Oct. 6, 1911, p. 1296. Not listed in Collns' 1910 cat.
    personal.

35. HESPERIDES / BY ROBERT HERRICK / A SELECTION / LONDON THE ST. CATHERINE'S PRESS / OSWALDESTRE HOUSE / NORFOLK STREET STRAND (5⅜ x 4⅜):⚓⁸, a-b⁸, pp. [1-8], 9-48. Printed paper boards, floral designs (yellowish brown, white, gray), paper label on upper cover. Halftitle: The Arden Books. Dating: 1912 (B.L. cat).
    Brit. Lib.

*35a. 2nd impression, 1918.

*36. *Selected Poems of Herrick*. Oxford: Oxford U. Press, [1913]. "Oxford Moment Series." In O.U.P. Cat. 1913, '20, and '24, & in *U.S. Cat*. 1912-18, 1s, cloth; 2s, leather, 50¢.

I. D. Cheap Series (1839-1913)

37. SELECTIONS / FROM / THE HESPERIDES AND WORKS / OF THE / REV ROBERT HERRICK, / (ANTIENT) VICAR OF DEAN-PRIOR, DEVON. / BY THE LATE / CHARLES SHORT, ESQ. / F.P.S. AND F.S.A. / LONDON: / JOHN MURRAY, ALBEMARLE STREET. / MDCCCXXIX.
(6½ x 3 7/8"): [A]⁸, B-O⁸, P⁴; pp. [i-vii], viii-xiv, [2], [1], 2-216.

Notes: Short is aware that his text is similar to Nott's (#1 above) and that Herrick's "contemptible couplets" present a problem. As to the latter, "it is not true, in fact, that no other English poet ever produced as much filth." A table, p. [130], is intended to show that Short exercises greater selectiveness than Nott in printing 95, not 284, "Amatory Odes." Both anthologists change titles and lines when this is considered "prudent or decorous."
    Divided into sections: Invocations, Epitalimia, Amatory Odes, Fairy-land, Pastorals, Anacreontic and Bacchanalian, and Moral and Pathetic. Each poem numbered in small caps Roman.
Price: 5s 6d
    New York Pub., Harvard (both rebound)

38. HESPERIDES, / OR / WORKS BOTH HUMAN AND DIVINE, / OF / *ROBERT HEARICK*. [sic.; facsimile of his signature] / EDITED BY / HENRY G. CLARKE. / VOL. 1 [Vol. 2.] / LONDON: / H.G. CLARKE AND CO., 66, OLD BAILEY. / [rule] / 1844.

(5¼ x 3¼"): vol. 1: A⁸, [B]⁸, C-O⁸; pp. [i-v], vi-xv, [xvi], [17], 18-213, [214], [ccxv], ccxxiv, [4]. vol. 2.◢², [A-B]⁸, C-Q⁸, pp. [2],[i], ii-xvi, [17-18], 19-238, [ccxxxix], ccxl-ccliv, [8].

Note: Divided into sections: Invocations, Amatory Odes, Anacreontic and Baccanalian, Epithalamium, Pastoral and Descriptive, Fairy Land, Charms and Ceremonies, Epitaphs, Aphorisms, Ecomiastic Verses, Moral and Pathetic. Numbered in small cap. Roman. Thus, arrangement very similar to #37.

"Clarke's Cabinet Series."

Price: 4s

Binding: paper wrappers. Upper cover, in 5-color lithograthed compartment after medieval MSS decoration: HESPERIDES / OR / THE WORKS BOTH / HUMAN AND DIVINE / OF / ROBERT HERRICK / VOL. I [VOL. II.] / London. / H. G. CLARKE & Co. / 66, Old Bailey. Below compartment: W. SMART LITHO. NO. 10, LEATHER LANE. Lower cover, both vols.: CLARKE'S ENGLISH HELICON (in blue and green).

   Brit. Lib. (lacks vol. 1), Columbia (first sig. of vol. 1 lacking), Harvard (paper wrappers preserved), U. Tulsa (rebound 2 vols. in one.)

38a. (2nd impression): HESPERIDES: / OR, / WORKS BOTH HUMAN AND DIVINE, / OF / ROBERT HERRICK / LONDON: / H.G. BOHN, YORK STREET, COVENT GARDEN. / 1852.

Front: woman, eyes downcast, in Stuart costume but Victorian hairstyle, reclining on sofa before open window disclosing night sky, mountain, lake, and sail. At her feet: lute, footrest, open locket, jewel box. Entitled "The Pleasure Tired"; signed [George] Cattermole. Steel engraving in the style of the Keepsakes.

5½ x 3". Red, morocco-grain decorated cloth binding. 3s (3s 6d with gilt edges). Two vols. in one, probably produced from plates of Clarke's 1844 ed, with fresh title page, & with front. added. Gathered in 12's. The two page advert of Bohn's "Mineature Library," bound in back of the vol., lists the Herrick as "complete," but Clarke's text eschews many epigrams and several erotic love poems. There are no *Noble Numbers.*

   Harvard

39. HESPERIDES / OR THE WORKS BOTH HUMANE / AND DIVINE OF ROBERT / HERRICK ESQ. / VOL. I [Vol. II] / [motto of press: ALDI DISCIP. ANGLVS with vignette of Dolphin and Anchor] / LONDON / WILLIAM PICKERING / 1846.

(6⅛ x 3¾"): vol. I.: [a]⁸, b⁸, B-T⁸; pp. [i-v], vi-xxvii, [xxviii-xxxii], [1], 2-288. vol. II.◢², B-X⁸, Y⁴; pp. [4], [1], 2-325, [326].

Caslon old style typeface. Its revival pioneered by Pickering and Whittingham, his printer. Pickering's experience as a used book dealer might have first attracted him to Renaissance writers.

Front: same as #2a above.

Price: 12s

Binding: "issued in brown or blue cloth, with paper labels" (Keynes, p. 72). Label: HERRICK'S / HESPERIDES / AND / NOBLE / NUMBERS / VOL. I [VOL. II] / [rule] / PICKERING / 1846

   Free Lib. of Phila, Morgan Lib (both rebound), Harvard (brown cloth; in vol. II, after Y3 is a 2-leaf sheet with adverts)

40. FAVORITE POEMS / BY ROBERT HERRICK. / ILLUSTRATED. / [device of harp and wreath] / BOSTON: / JAMES R. OSGOOD AND COMPANY, / LATE TICKNOR AND FIELDS, AND FIELDS, OSGOOD AND CO. / 1877.

Vignettes, decorated capitals, and four full-page wood engravings (listed, p. [vii]), inscribed with couplets from the poems. Two of these, "And underneath thy cooling shade," and "Go, happy rose," are copied from engravings by John Gilbert which first appeared in *Shakespeare's Songs and Sonnets* (London: Sampson, Low, 1863), pp. 30, 29. The first of these is after Francis Danby's oil, "Disappointed Love."

(5 x 3⅛"): no sigs.; pp. [i-x], [11], 12-96.

Price: 50¢

I have not seen a copy in original binding.

"The Vest Pocket Series"

Another impression, see #50 below, s.v. School Texts.

New York Pub. (rebound)

41. Chrysomela / *A SELECTION FROM THE LYRICAL POEMS OF* / ROBERT HERRICK / ARRANGED WITH NOTES BY / FRANCIS TURNER PALGRAVE / LATE FELLOW OF EXETER COLLEGE, OXFORD / [Steel engraved vignette signed "C.H. Jeens": cupid with brand, vase, with shaft of wheat and skeleton protruding from vase. Oval border] / Hoc nullus labor est, ruborque nullus / Hoc iuvit, iuvat, et diu iuvabit / London / MACMILLAN AND CO. / 1877

(6¼ x 4"): [a]², b⁸, c⁴, B-N⁸, O⁴; pp. [i-v], vi-xxviii, [iv], vi-xxviii, [1], 2-199, [200].

Price: 4s 6d; $1.25

Note: Printed in a modern version of Old Face, with some bracketed serifs and letterforms of equal weight. The letterpress leaves plenty of white space, and is lightly inked, affecting a plain elegance.

Binding: green sand-grain cloth with gold-stamped border and medallion of Golden Treasury Series on upper cover. Spine contains this device at foot and title at top, both gold-stamped. Brown coated endpaper; half-title with medallion of series. T.e.g.

The volume, as Palgrave states in his dedication to the 19-year old Lady Beatrix Maud Cecil, is for "women's quiet hours." Divided into sections: Prefatory, Idyllica, Amores, Epigrams, Nature and Life, Graviores.

Harvard, personal

*41a. (Second impression): Oct. 1877.

*41b. (Third impression): 1880.

41c. (Fourth impression): 1884. Dark blue cloth, goldstamped border and reproduction of t.p. vignette on upper cover. Black coated endpapers.

Harvard

41d. (Fifth impression): 1888. "New and cheaper ed.": 2s 6d, $1.25. Binding same as 1st impression. Title page reads: London / MACMILLAN / AND NEW YORK / 1888. See *Bibliographical Cat. of Macmillan and Co.'s Publications from 1843 to 1889:* "...reprinted Oct. 1877, 1880, 1884, 1888."

Harvard

41e. (Sixth impression): T.p. as in 40c, dated 1891.

Harvard, Texas HRC

41f. (Seventh impression): 1892. T.p. dated. Blue cloth, medallion of series in gold cartouche on upper cover.

personal

41g. (Eighth impression, 1911): T.p. imprinted: MACMILLAN AND CO., LIMITED /

ST. MARTIN'S STREET, LONDON / 1911. Dark blue cloth, medallion of series goldstamped on upper cover, blind-stamped borders. In print 1928 ($1.40); 1932 (3s 6d).

42. HESPERIDES / OR / Works both Human and Divine / OF / ROBERT HERRICK / *WITH AN INTRODUCTION BY HENRY MORLEY* / LL.D., PROFESSOR OF ENGLISH LITERATURE AT / UNIVERSITY COLLEGE, LONDON / LONDON / GEORGE ROUTLEDGE AND SONS / BROADWAY, LUDGATE HILL / NEW YORK: 9 LAFAYETTE PLACE / 1884.
(7½ x 5"): [A]¹⁶, B-K¹⁶; pp. [1-5], 6-319, [320]. 1s—40¢; Distributed in U.S. by Dutton. Blue decorated cloth, black stamped flowers and stems, with HERRICK'S / HESPERIDES in cartouche and MORLEY'S / UNIVERSAL / LIBRARY / 13 in circular border, upper cover. Triple border, middle one decorated.
Expurgated; some bowdlerization.
L. Cong, Texas HRC (2 copies, marginalia by A.E. Coppard and C. Mackenzie).

42a. (Second impression): with SECOND EDITION above imprint, dated 1885. Undecorated grey cloth, paper label on spine. Edges Trimmed. Pub.'s adverts on endpapers. Binding variant: Blue-green cloth, quarter-bound vellum with author and title gold-stamped on spine. T.e.g., others trimmed. No pub. adverts on e.p.'s
     Harvard, Columbia (rebound), personal (binding var.), Suny, Buffalo

42b. (Third impression): THIRD EDITION above imprint, dated 1887. 2s in Routledge's 1920 cat.; 35¢ in Dutton's 1910 cat. Binding: undec. grey cloth as in 42a. Top edge trimmed; others untrimmed. Pub. adverts on endpapers.
     U. of Penna (rebound), personal

43. (in red border): HESPERIDES: POEMS / BY ROBERT HERRICK. / EDITED WITH NOTES / BY HERBERT P. HORNE, AND / WITH AND INTRODUCTION BY / ERNEST RHYS. / LONDON: / WALTER SCOTT, 24, WARWICK LANE, / AND NEWCASTLE-ON-TYNE. / 1887. [initial "H" in l. 1 in red]
(5½ x 4"): [a]⁸, b⁸, c⁴, 244 [sic]-262⁸; pp. [i-iii], iv-xxxviii, [2], [1], 2-301, [302]. Adverts on final leaf.

"IN SHILLING *Monthly Volumes."* Price varies with binding style: roan, morocco, parchment offered. Scott 1906 cat. offers a "superior edition bound in Art Linen, with Photogravure Frontispiece. 2s." In 1920 cat. at same price. The Canterbury Poets. The Herrick first advertised on slip tipped into the Poe vol. in the series, 1885.
Red borders each page, poems printed one to a page, creative use of white space.
Binding variants: (1): brown sand-grain cloth. Upper cover: HERRICK outlined by gold-stamped cartouche. Black stamped: birds in flight, The Canterbury Poets (at top). On spine: Herrick's / Poems outlined in gold-stamped cartouche. Black stamped: leaves, branches of tree. At tail of spine: WALTER / SCOTT. Edges in red. (2): undecorated sand-grain deep blue cloth. Red-bordered paper label on spine: POEMS / ROBERT / HERRICK / With notes by / H.P. HORNE. Fore and bottom edges untrimmed.
     U. of Penna. (var. 2); Harvard (two copies, both binding states represented)

43a. (Another issue or impression): imprint variant: W. J. Gage & Co., / TORONTO: 54 FRONT STREET WEST. / LONDON: 24 BOUVERIE STREET. / 1888.
     Toledo OH Public Lib.

43b. (Another issue or impression): imprint variant: NEW YORK AND LONDON / WHITE AND ALLEN.

Advertised in *Publisher's Weekly*, Sept. 22, 1888, p. 368 as "Westminister Edition" at 50¢ ("imitation calf"), 75¢ ("full white vegetable parchment"), $1.00 (half turkey morocco"), $2.00 ("full turkey morocco, padded, round corners, gilt edges"). ". . . the handiest of all editions, . . ."
C.U.N.Y.

43c. (Another impression): imprint variant: EYRE & SPOTTISWOODE, / *Her Majesty's Printers.* / *LONDON:* / *GREAT NEW STREET, E.C.* / *EDINBURGH, GLASGOW, MELBOURNE, SYDNEY, AND NEW YORK. Title page reset, as in 43d below. Half-title:* The Canterbury Poets / EDITED BY WILLIAM SHARP / HERRICK.
Binding: Black leatherette, inner dentelles. Upper cover: "Herrick," in calligraphic lettering. Repeated, reduced, on spine. Smooth black endpapers. All edges gilt, corners rounded. Text reproduced without red (borders or titlepage initial).
Harvard.

43d. (Another impression): imprint variant: THE WALTER SCOTT PUBLISHING CO., LTD., / LONDON AND FELLING-ON-TYNE / NEW YORK: 3 EAST 14th STREET.
(5¼ x 3½"): t.p., tipped in, ✠❡² 1⁶, 2-21⁸, 22⁴. Pagination as in the first impression. Text reproduced without red borders or red initial on t.p. No half-title, no series statement. Bound in red suede; blind-stamped stylized floral design and swirling lines on upper cover, re-produced in part on spine. Gold-stamped on upper cover: HERRICK. On spine, in blind-stamped cartouche: POEMS / OF / hERRICK [swash P and h]. T.e.g.
Under rule, p. 301: printer's statement and "2-07" [1907?].
Possibly the impression advertised in Parker J. Simmons' 1905 and 1906 catalogues at 40¢.
personal (2 copies; one rebound, another in red suede, poss. pub. in U.S. from British plates, lacks half-title with series statement, & pub. "catalogue" noted on verso of half-title).

43e. (another issue of 43d): imprint variant; Scott's address given as 24 Warwick Lane. The "superior edition"; the front. reproduces the Clint engraving (see #29 above). White linen-grain cloth, with gold-stamped floral decoration running from upper cover to spine and lower cover. On spine, gold-stamped in circle: HERRICK'S / POEMS [swash P.]
U. Texas, HRC.

44. (in asymmetrical decorated floral border): HESPERIDES: or / THE WORKS / BOTH HUMAN / & DIVINE / of [swash f] ROBERT / HERRICK / VOLUME I [VOLUME II]. [first word in l. 1, second word in 1.5, and 1.6 in red]. (below border, in red): MDCCCXCIX PUBLISHED BY J.M. DENT. / AND CO: ALDINE HOUSE LONDON E.C.
(6 x 3 ¾"): vol. I: tipped-in front. ❡, A-S⁸, T⁶; pp. [4], 1-299, [300]. vol. II: tipped-in front. ❡², A-N⁸, O⁴; pp. [4], 1-214, [215-16].
Front: vol. I: replica of Marshall. vol. II: "Memorial Tablet in Dean Prior Church Devon."
2s; 50¢ per vol. (MacMillan cat. for 1906; 75¢ in limp leather. Dutton cat. for 1910 lists for 45¢ per vol). Still for sale by Dent in 1940, 2s.
"The Temple Classics"
Binding: dark blue morocco-grain cloth, blind stamped publisher's device (owl in border) on upper cover. On spine: gold stamped decoration of tree of knowledge (?) at top and lamp of wisdom (?) at tail. Worked into design: HESPERIDES / OR THE / WORKS / BOTH HUMAN / AND DIVINE / OF / ROBERT / HERRICK / VOL. ONE [VOL. TWO]. J.M. DENT / AND / CO.
U. of Va. Charlottesville, Case Western Reserve, Harvard

44a. (Second impression): 1903 (on title page: MDCCCCIII).

St. Bonaventure Coll. (Friedsam Lib), Texas HRC (E.A. Parsons' copy)

44b. (third impression; 1st issue of Everyman Lib. subedition): (in decorated border, part of *mise-en-page* title opening after Kelmscott Press designs): HERRICK'S / HESPERIDES & / NOBLE NUMBERS / [vignette of Good Deeds, in border into which is worked motto of Everyman's Library] / LONDON: PUBLISHED / by J. M. DENT. & Co / AND IN NEW YORK / BY E. P. DUTTON & CO.

(6 3/4 x 4"):𝛑⁸, A-Q¹⁶; pp. [i-vi], vii-xvi, 1-512.

Dating: verso t.p., 1923 impression; E. Cat.: Feb. 1908.

1s, 2s in leather; 35¢, 70¢ in leather.

Everyman's Library, #310.

olive rib-grain cloth; blind-stamped border, emblem of press at center, upper cover. On spine: gold-stamped floral design and HERRICK'S / HESPERI / -DES AND / NOBLE / NUMBERS / J.M. Dent / E.P. DUTTON / & CO. Top edge stained green. Decorated endpapers: swirling leaves and vines, motto of press in scrollwork, woman in medieval robe carrying parchment and fruit (Good Deeds?).

Introd. by Rhys same as in #22 above.

U. of Penna., Harvard, U. of Pitts, U. So. Carolina (rebound)

44c. (fourth impression 2nd issue of Everyman subed.): 1923. Dating: verso t.p. 80¢ in 1928.

U. of Penna., Cornell

44d. (fifth impression, 3rd issue of Everyman subed.): 1935. Title page reset and redesigned: POEMS / [vignette: abstract design] / ROBERT HERRICK / LONDON: J.M. DENT & SONS LTD. / NEW YORK: E.P. DUTTON & CO. INC.

Endpapers in pale orange, with abstract design by Eric Ravillous. Binding: green calico-grain cloth, blind-stamped pattern on upper cover. On spine, gold-stamped: POEMS / HERRICK / EVERYMANS / LIBRARY.

(dust jacket: green, version of t.p. vignette on front, adverts on flaps and back panel)

Dating: verso title page.

personal

45. (in red rectangular border) The Century Classics / [rule] / POEMS OF / ROBERT HERRICK / A SELECTION FROM / HESPERIDES AND NOBLE NUMBERS / WITH AN INTRODUCTION BY / THOMAS BAILEY ALDRICH / [vignette: book, circular design printed in red, wreath] / NEW YORK / The Century Co. / MCM

(7 5/8 x 5"): guarded front. ⁴𝛑⁴, 2-3𝛑⁸, 4𝛑⁶, 1-13⁸, 14², 15⁸; pp. [i-iv], v-1, [2], 1-227, [228].

Front: replica of Marshall

$1.00 ($1.25; $2.00 in sheepskin; 1905 Cat.).

Printed and designed by T. L. DeVinne. One of the first six books issued in the series. "... the publishers have had in view the high standing and intrinsic merit of the works to be reprinted, purity of text, elegance of typography, and beauty of external form.... The type has been cut with particular care, and will be used only in these volumes." [Advert. in *The Century Illustrated Monthly*, 60, no. 5 (Sept. 1900), 9]. In *Bib. Am. Lit.*, I, item #387. Green calico-grain cloth with blind-stamped arabesque design on both covers and spine, reproduced on endpapers. Gold-stamped border running from fore-edge of upper to fore-edge of lower cover. Gold stamping: CENTURY CLASSICS (on upper and lower covers), CENTURY CLASSICS / [2 rules] / POEMS OF / ROBERT / HERRICK / [rules] / THE / CENTURY / CO. (on spine). T.e.g.; others untrimmed.

personal, Princeton, Harvard.

46. THE POEMS OF / ROBERT HERRICK / [rectangular device: "G" and "R" entangled in vines] / LONDON / GRANT RICHARDS / LEICESTER SQUARE / 1902. (5 3/4 x 2 3/8"): [a]⁸, b⁶, A-2b⁸, 2C²; pp. [i-iv], v-xxvii, [xxviii], [1], 2-402, [2]. "The World's Classics," #16.
1s; 2s in leather; 75¢, $1.00 limp leather (in cat. of Herbert B. Turner, Boston, for 1904). Binding: Copy in original cloth not located.
    Harvard (rebound)

46a. (second impression imprint variant): THE POEMS OF / ROBERT HERRICK / [device of press] / HENRY FROWDE / LONDON, EDINBURGH, GLASGOW / NEW YORK AND TORONTO
Dating: verso t. p. "In the World's Classics [Herrick's poems] were first published in 1902, and reprinted 1903." front (after Clint engr.) and suppl. t.p., tipped in.
    In Oxford. U. Press 1907 U.S. catalogue, offered at 40¢, and $1.00 in limp lambskin.
    Hunter College (rebound), personal

*46b. (third impression). ". . .reprinted 1909."
*46c. (fourth impression). ". . .reprinted 1920."

46d. (fifth impression, imprint variant): HUMPHREY MILFORD / OXFORD UNIVERSITY PRESS / London Edinburgh Glasgow Copenhagen. . .Shanghai. ". . .reprinted 1924"
Binding: olive calico-grain cloth, three borders blindstamped, upper and lower cover. On spine, gold stamped: floral design emphasizing vertical rhythms (first advertised in O.U.P. 1907 cat) and POEMS / OF / ROBERT / HERRICK / OXFORD. Paper dust jacket has replica of Marshall portrait and first 6 lines of "Argument of his Book" on front panel. 80¢ (US Cat 1928)
See #84, below.
    Hunter Coll (no D.J.), personal

47. (asymmetrically set in decorated border with arabesque floral design, part of mise-en-page title opening with front. on facing page): POEMS / BY / ROBERT HERRICK / [floral vignette] / WITH AN INTRODUCTION BY / ALICE MEYNELL / BLACKIE & SONS LTD EDINBURGH
(5 3/4 x 3 7/16"): front. and title page, on clay paper, tipped in + [A]⁸, B-2A⁸, 2B⁴; pp. [i-ii], iii-xvi, I, [2], 3-374, [2].
"The Red Letter Library" (half-title)
Front: after Schiavonetti's for Nott ed (see #1 above).
Dating: 1904 (BM cat [this copy now lost]), *Am. Cat.; Eng. Cat* ("Jul. '04")
1s 6d, 2s 6d in leather; $1.00 in limp leather (dist. Boston: Caldwell). Offered in Nimmo of Edinburgh 1913 cat. at 3s 6d in "velvet calf."
Note on Design: red running titles for each poem more than one page long, 2 red vine leaves after each poem title, half-title in red and black.
Binding: designed, as was title page opening, by Talwin Morris, Scottish art nouveau designer. See Taylor, *Art Nouveau Book in Britain*, pp. 127-30 (illus. of series bindings).
New York Pub. (rebound; lacks front.)

47a. (another issue): t.p. variant: BLACKIE & SON LTD LONDON"
    Texas HRC

47b. (second impression): (in double border): *Herrick* / [2 rules] / POEMS / INTRODUCTION BY / ALICE MEYNELL / [2 rules] / BLACKIE AND SON LIMITED / LONDON GLASGOW AND BOMBAY

(5½ x 3¼"): tipped-in front. + [A]¹⁶, B-M¹⁶, N⁴; pp. [i-ii], iii-xvi, [1-2], 3-374, [2]. $1, 4 signed "B147)". $4 signed "2".

"The Wallet Library." Price: 1s 6d; in *Ref. Guide to Current Lit.*, 1940, same price

Dating: BM cat. (April 1927)

Front: replica of Marshall.

Binding: blue cloth, blind stamped border both covers.

On spine: gold-stamped: POEMS / [vignette] BY [vignette] / ROBERT / HERRICK / BLACKIE. "Coloured wrappers" (i.e., d.j.) (1932 cat.) Cream brown endpapers.

Harvard (lacking t.p.), Hunter Coll., Brit. Lib., Indiana U (none in d.j.)

*47c. (another issue): t.p. variant: London: Gresham Pub. Co.

*48 (in square compartment on upper half of engraved design, framed with columns and flowers): HESPERIDES / OR *WORKS* / *BOTH* HUMAN *AND* / DIVINE / *BY ROBERT HERRICK* / *TOGETHER WITH* / HIS NOBLE NUMBERS OR / *HIS PIOUS PIECES* / [centered, at bottom of design, in compartment framed with putti]: LONDON / *GEORGE NEWNES LTD.* /NEW YORK / *CHARLES SCRIBNER'S SONS*

Dating: E. Cat, 1905. Newnes' Thin Paper Classics. This is apparently a one-vol. unillustrated ed. with the same title page and frontispiece used in the Caxton Series: see #16 above. 3s; $1.25 (Scribner's 1905-07 catalogues).

*48a. (another issue)?: advertised in Simkin, Marshall, Hamilton, Kent and Co. catalogue for 1913. See also #20, above. Simpkin's 1920-28 cats. list this ("Simpkin's Thin Paper Classics"), specifying a photogravure front. and t.p.

I.E. School Texts

49. SELECTIONS FROM HERRICK, / FOR / TRANSLATION INTO LATIN VERSE. / With a Short Preface. / BY / THE REV. A.J. MACLEANE, M.A. / TRINITY COLLEGE, CAMBRIDGE: / PRINCIPAL OF BRIGHTON COLLEGE. / [rule] / LONDON: / GEORGE BELL, 186 FLEET STREET. / [rule] / MDCCCXLVIII.

(6½ x 4"): [a]⁴, b², B-E⁸, F⁴, G², pp. [i-iii], iv-xii, [1], 2-76.

Price: 2s 6d

4-page catalogue sewn in at end offers, with the Herrick, "Selections from English Poetry for the use of Classical Schools."

Fine diaper-grain brown cloth, paper label on upper cover with title. Paper label on spine: bottom to top: HERRICK. Smooth yellow endpapers.

Harvard, personal.

50. Modern Classics. / [rule] / FAVORITE POEMS / BY / GEORGE HERBERT, WILLIAM COLLINS, JOHN / DRYDEN, ANDREW MARVELL, AND / ROBERT HERRICK. / *ILLUSTRATED.* / [vignette] / BOSTON: / HOUGHTON, MIFFLIN AND COMPANY. / NEW YORK: 11 EAST SEVENTEENTH STREET. / The Riverside Press, Cambridge.

(5 5/16x3½"): no sig.; pp. [2], [1-11], 12-112 (p. [8] numbered "vi"), ²[5-11], 12-95, [96] (p. [6] numbered "vi"), ³[3-11], 12-95, [95] (p.[6] numbered "vi").

Pages ³[3]-96 contain the text of *Favorite Poems* [of Herrick] in the 1877 "Vest Pocket Series": see #40 above. On Dec. 29, 1879, during the partnership of Osgood and Houghton, the stock of the series was damaged in a warehouse fire. In 1881 Houghton-Mifflin, who now owned the plates, bound the remainder of the stock three-volumes-in-one and reissued as "Modern Classics." Whether or not a reimpression was made from the plates, the Herrick portion of this text is a subedition ~~&~~ #40. The series was marketed as "hav[ing] been put into a cheap form for school use" (*The Firm of Houghton, Mifflin, and Company*, Publishers... [Cambridge, Mass.: Riverside Press, 1887], p. 40). On front paste-down endpaper of the Modern Classics volume: "...the illustrations...in these volumes make them particularly suitable for use in schools for supplementary reading..."

Dating: Listed in Houghton's 1881 catalogue at 50¢. Reduced to 40¢ in 1887.

Green bubble-grain cloth. Upper cover elaborately blind-stamped with tree leaves and stems, birds in flight, and cartouche containing MODERN CLASSICS. Gold-stamped on spine: FAVORITE POEMS / BY / HERBERT, COLLINS / DRYDEN / ETC. Blind stamped floral design and press emblem.

Washington and Lee Univ. Lib.

51. Athenaeum Press Series / [rule] / SELECTIONS / FROM THE POETRY OF / ROBERT HERRICK / EDITED BY / EDWARD EVERETT HALE, JR., PH.D. (HALLE) / PROFESSOR OF ENGLISH IN THE STATE UNIVERSITY OF IOWA / [French rule] / BOSTON, U.S.A. / GINN & COMPANY, PUBLISHERS / 1895.
(7¼ x 4¾"): no. sig.; pp. [i-xi], xii-lxx, [1-3], 4-200, [2].
Front.: steel engr. of wide-eyed, reflective poet, mouth curled in slight sneer, signed "O. Grosch."
60¢; 4s 6d. In print at 80¢ in 1928, and at 3s 6d in 1940.
Green sand-grain cloth, blind-stamped floral border on upper cover, with THE ATHENAEUM / PRESS SERIES gold-stamped at top left (tied letters, swash R, bracketted serifs). On spine: gold-stamped floral border and lettering: POEMS / OF / HERRICK / [rule] / HALE / [2 leaves] / GINN & COMPANY.

U. of Penna. personal.

*52. *Herrick and his Poetry* (London: Harrap, [1920?]) In Harrap's 1920 cat., as #31 ("Shortly [ready]"), s.v. the "Poetry and Life" series, gen. ed. Prof. Wm H. Hudson of Cornell Univ. This vol, ed. by T. Bruce Dilks, probably did not appear. It is not in either the Eng. Cat. or Am. Cat., not in BM (under Herrick or Dilks), nor in any subsequent Harrap Cat. The volume would have had a frontispiece, and have been 55% biography and 45% poetry, the latter illustrating the former. The series is advertised as suitable for use in schools, and designed to introduce young readers to the poetry.

II. Private Press and Limited Editions, 1891 - 1971.
53. HERRICK / HIS / FLOWERS / [rule] / PRINTED BY H. DANIEL: OXFORD: / CHRISTMAS: 1891.
(6¾ x 4¼"): no sig, two 8-leaf gatherings; pp. [1], 2-30, [2].
100 copies printed for a sale at St. Thomas Orphanage, Oxford. Sold at 2s 6d. Twenty-three poems are included, printed with Fell typeface and ornaments. See [Falconer Madan], *Memorials of C.H.O. Daniel with a Bibliography of the Press, 1845-1919* (Oxford: Bodleian Library, 1921), pp. 105-06 (item 22).
Binding: Madan: "...paper projecting covers, [i.e., "yapped"] bearing on the front the title within a border of ornaments, and on the back, very prettily, 'H' between ornaments, two of which are [Alfred] Parsons' flower devices." It was fairly common to bind small, privately printed vols. of poetry in "yapped" covers.

Harvard, Br. Mus.

54. CHRISTMAS / *from the* / NOBLE NUMBERS / *of* / ROBERT HERRICK / [rule] / PRINTED BY H. DANIEL: OXFORD: / CHRISTMAS: 1891.
(6¾ x 4¼"): no sig, two 8-leaf gatherings; pp. [16], 1-16.

60 copies were printed as Christmas gifts for 36 friends of Dr. Daniel's daughters. There are six poems in the volume. Fell typeface.
Binding: cream paper wrappers. Upper cover, inside border of Fell type ornaments: HERRICK / HIS / CHRISTMAS. Lower cover: two floral vignettes, as in no. 53 above. Madan, item 23: "The book is like no. 22, and similarly bound in paper projecting covers, with similar printing on them.... (p. 107).
   Harvard, Br. Lib.

55. (on verso of *mise-en-page* title opening in decorated woodcut border, facing "The Argument of his Book," which is also in decorated border with the title printed in red): POEMS / CHOSEN / OUT OF / THE / WORKS OF / ROBERT / HERRICK
(8⅛ x 5⅝"): [a]⁸, b-t⁸, u⁴; pp. [i], ii-xiv, [2], [1], 2-296.
Woodcut borders and decorated initials by Wm. Morris; printed in black and red, golden type. Colophon: "Edited by F.S. Ellis from the text... of 1648. Printed by William Morris, at the Kelmscott Press,...and finished on the 21st day of November, 1895...."
260 copies printed, sold at 30s (8 vellum copies at 8 guineas). Issued Feb. 6, 1896 (The 37th book published by Morris). Bound in limp vellum with silk ties: HERRICK in gold on spine.
   See G.S. Tompkinson, *A Select Bibliography of the Principal Modern Presses Public and Private*...(London: First Editions Club, 1928), pp. 117; S.C. Cockerell, "An Annotated List of All the Books..." (1898), reprinted: H. Sparling, *The Kelmscott Press and Wm. Morris Master Craftsman* (London: Macmillan, 1924), p. 161 (Item #37); Marsden J. Perry, *Chronological List of the Books Printed at the Kelmscott Press* (Boston: n.p., 1928), pp. 19-20 (Item #170); John Walsdorf, *William Morris in Private Press and Limited Editions* (Phoenix, Az.: Oryx Press, 1983), pp. 72-73.
   Br. Lib., Lib. of Cong., Harvard, Texas HRC, Rosenbach Mus.

56. (centered 1¼" from top of otherwise blank page): POEMS SELECTED FROM THE / HESPERIDES / OF / ROBERT HERRICK (lines 1 and 3 in red)
(8 ⅞ x 6⅝"): no signatures; pp. [1-2], 3-154, [155-58].
Printed in a Caslon Old Roman, with decorated initials in red, and running titles on the shoulder of the page; titles of each poem given as shoulder notes to the side of the text. Shoulder titles printed in red. Rectangular woodcut vignette after Ricketts or Burne-Jones above opening poem; circular vignette with colophon, which is printed in red and black and reads "...Two hundred and sixty copies have been printed with initial letters and decorations cut on wood by H.M. O'Kane...Printed and sold at the Elston Press New Rochelle New York. Finished this May-Day MDCCCCIII." The 17th book issued by Elston. An entry in the *Eng. Cat.* dated Aug. 1903 indicates that arrangements might have been made for David Nutt to distribute this book for 30s. Price in US: $7.00.
Bound in grey paper-covered boards with white linen quarter-binding. Paper labels on spine with title. Copies also reported in cloth with top edge gilt. See Colin Franklin, *The Private Presses* (Chester Springs, Pa.: Dufour, 1969), p. 159.
   L. of Cong., Harvard, personal

57. (in border of two rules): *SELECTIONS FROM* / ROBERT HERRICK / [2 rules] / [drawing, by Lovat Fraser, of house and cloud] / [2 rules] / THE MEDICI SOCIETY LTD. / London: 7 Grafton Street, W.1 / Liverpool: 63 Bold Street / Boston, U.S.A.: 755 Boylston Street.
(5⅛ x 3¾"): no sigs; pp. [1-6], 7-29, [30-32]. First leaf of first gathering, and last leaf of final gathering, laid down on front and back boards respectively.
Printed at the Curwen Press. Listed in the Medici Society cat. 1924 and 1928, s.v. Shyllynge Garland Series, #3. Wm. Ridler (*British Modern Press Books,* Folkstone: Dawson, 1975)

reports this as uniform with the series' Donne, 1922. The Fraser design was prepared (as no. 24) for *A Shropshire Lad.*

Purplish-pink laid paper-covered boards with paper label on upper cover; in border: SELECTIONS FROM / ROBERT HERRICK.

U. Texas, HRC (J.R. Abbey's copy)

58. (In elaborate border printed in red, composed of type ornaments some of which are arranged to form stars, and others to form roses, the whole ruled in red): THE / STAR SONG / *A Carroll to* / *the King* / BY / R. HERRICK / [ornament] / (at bottom, in circular border of ornaments, in red): 1924

(7⅞ x 4¾): one octavo signature, with the poem printed on recto of four leaves numbered 1 through 4.

Half-title: *A CAROL* / *Printed by William Edwin Rudge* / *for his Friends* / CHRISTMAS 1924.

Designed by Bruce Rogers. The title page design is adapted from that of Dowson's *Pierrot of the Minute,* done by Rogers for the Grolier Club in 1923. The poem is printed in Wren italic type with Fournier ornaments, with each page bordered in red, and with a sunburst vignette as tailpiece. See Walter Klinefelter, *A Bibliographical Check-List of Christmas Books* (Portland, ME: Southworth-Anthoensen Press, 1937), p. 81; Frederic Warde, *Bruce Rogers Designer of Books* (Cambridge: Harvard U. Press, 1926), p. 70 (item #187).

Bound in pale red paper-covered boards with paper label on upper cover: *A Christmas Carol* in circular border of type ornaments in green, with double rectangular outer border.

Columbia U, Texas HRC

59. *DELIGHTED EARTH* / *A SELECTION BY PETER MEADOWS FROM* / *HERRICK'S 'HESPERIDES'* / *WITH ILLUSTRATIONS BY LIONEL ELLIS* / *PUBLISHED BY* / *THE FANFROLICO PRESS* / *Five Bloomsbury Square* / *London, W.C.* / [small ornament] (lines 2-8 in blue; lines 1, 3, and 6 in Koch Kursive capitals; lines 2, 4, 5 in small capitals of same typeface).

(9x5¾"): [A]⁶, B-L⁸, M⁶7⁴ (final gathering on a different paper: note regarding separate printing of illus. recto first leaf, and 4th leaf laid down as endpaper to board of lower cover). pp. [12], [1-2], 3-120, [10]. 10 line-and-wash drawings, the first on [A]5r (first leaf after title) and inscribed DELIGHTED EARTH, next eight introducing sections of the text and inscribed with section titles, the 10th a headpiece for colophon. Reproduced by collotype. All but the 10th are full-page.

Portrait: 1st illus. shows the poet, recognizable in profile, wearing a surplice and playing a lute, attended by nymphs.

Colophon, sig. M6r: ". . . . The book set up by hand in Rudolph Koch Kursiv type and printed at the Curwen Press, now published by the Fanfrolico Press. . ., November Nineteen-twenty-seven."

Sig. [A]2r: "This edition is limited to 550 numbered copies. . . ." Edited by founder of press, Jack Lindsay, under the pseudonym of "Peter Meadows." His introd. entitled "Robin Herrick," on pp. 3-10. See Jack Lindsay, *A Retrospect of the Fanfrolico Press, with a List of Fanfrolico Books* (London: Simpkin, Marshall, 1931), n.p. The first use of the typeface in a complete book in England. Laid Vidalon paper. See also *Fanfrolicana, Being a Statement of Aims...* (London: Fanfrolico Press, 1928), p. 12: "This is the 'prettiest' book yet issued. . . ." 30s; 25 copies on Japanese vellum, 5 guineas. Distributed in U.S. by McKee at $12.00. In 1930, Lindsay sold rights to the books to Simpkin; the Herrick is offered in their 1932 cat. (30s).

Bound in blue balloon cloth. Stamped in black on upper cover: DELIGHTED EARTH / FANFROLICO PRESS. On spine, running from bottom to top: DELIGHTED EARTH. Slipcase, covered in dark blue cloth.

Personal, Penn State (no slipcase), Texas HRC (Hugh McCrea's copy)

59a. (Another issue): 25 copies signed by Ellis: bound in white vellum. A.e.g. Printed on Japanese vellum. Preliminaries arranged differently. Final 4-sheet leaf not present.
  Penn State

60. The Poetical Works / of / ROBERT / HERRICK / With a *Preface* by / HUMBERT WOLFE / and *Decorations* by / ALBERT RUTHERSTON / Volume I [Volume II] [Volume III] / HESPERIDES [Volume IV / NOBLE NUMBERS / and / ADDITIONAL POEMS] / LONDON / *The Cresset Press Ltd.* / 1928

(7½ x 6″): vol. I: [a]⁸, b-e⁸, f⁶, B-F⁸, G⁶; pp. [i-viii], ix-lxxxix, [xc], [2], [i-viii], ix-xiv, [1-2], 3-174, [175-76].
vol. II: [A]⁸, B-M⁸, pp. [2], [i-vii], ix-xiv, [1-2], 3-174, [175-76].
vol. III: [A]⁸, B-L⁸, M¹⁰; pp. [i-viii], ix-xv, [xvi]; pp. [1-2], 3-178, [179-80].
vol. IV: [A]¹², B-I⁸; pp. [i-viii], ix-xii, [1-2], 3-144.
In-text vignettes and 4 front. drawings in water-color (reproduced by lithography).
Portraits: vol. II front.: the poet measuring with his eye a posing half-naked girl (and holding a sheet on which he is writing a poem rather than drawing a picture). vol. IV front: Herrick kneeling on a cushion in prayer, far beneath which are thorns of repentance.
vol. I, p. [4]: "This edition is limited to 750 sets handset and printed in Fell type on mould-made paper at the University Press, Oxford. 475 sets are for sale in the United Kingdom and 250 sets in the United States of America." 84s; $34 (distributed in U.S. by Inman).
  See Will Ransom, *Private Presses and their Books* (N.Y.: Bowker, 1929, p. 238 [item 7 s.v. Cresset Press]).
  Vellum-covered boards, with gold-stamping on spine: POETICAL / WORKS OF / *Robert / Herrick* / VOLUME / I[II][III][IV] / *The Cresset Press.* Top edge gilt, fore-and bottom edges ˌuntrimmed.
  Brit. Lib. (fronts. not in color), NYU, Texas HRC

61. Three Poems / for / Christmas / by / *Robert Herrick* / *With Decorations by* / *C. Lovat Fraser* / [vignette, in red, of girl with basket, back turned against the wind, which catches her skirt and hair] / Printed, not published for / the friends of / EARL AND FLORENCE FISK / CHRISTMAS / 1928
Printed and designed by Earl Fiske, the 8th and last Christmas volume he worked on, and issued in the largest number of copies: 75. The poems are "A New yeares gift sent to Sir Simeon Steward," "Ceremonies for Candlemasse daye," and "Ceremonies for Christmas." The drawings are of a snow-covered house, a man smoking a pipe, and a wind-blown girl carrying a basket (which appears as a decoration for "Ceremonies for Christmas" as well as on the title page). Fraser's decorations appeared first in *Poems of Charles Cotton* (London: Poetry Shop Press, 1922), as headpieces or tailpieces to "Winter," on pages 49, 47, and 44 respectively. See Klinefelter, p. 41.
  L. of Cong, Texas HRC.

62. VERSES FROM THE / [in red] HESPERIDES / OF ROBERT HERRICK. Title on paper wrapper in which is loosely laid 2 folded sheets, 9¼ x 11¾″. A Christmas Booklet of 5 poems. "Printed... / At the Alcuin Press... / ... MCMXXXII"
  Brit. Lib.

63. **THE POEMS** / OF / ROBERT HERRICK / IN TWO VOLUMES / I [II] / LONDON / HUMPHREY MILFORD / 1935
(7⅜ x 4 9/16″): Vol. I: [A-B]⁴, C-2G⁴, 2H⁶; pp. [8], [1-5], 6-242.

Vol. II: [A]⁴, B-2G⁴, 2H⁶; pp. [8], [243], 244-486.

Sig. [A] lv (both vols): "500 copies printed at the University Press, Oxford by John Johnson printer to the university."

15s.; $5.00

"The Hesperides Series," consisting of six titles of which this is the first. Designed by Bruce Rogers, at the time of his association with Milford in the production of a lectern bible for Oxford Univ. Press. Rogers' "thistle", in red, on Sig. [A]lr both volumes, under The Hesperides Series and an ornament in the shape of an apple (see binding). Baskerville type. Phrasing verso t.p., vol. I, identical with that of World's Classics revised edition of 1933 (see #84 below), suggests (as does pagination) that this ed. was used as Rogers' copytext. unexpurgated.

Binding: red cloth. Gold-stamped horizontal rule top and bottom, upper and lower covers. At top of spine, gold-stamped: POEMS / ROBERT / HERRICK / I [2], and 17 small golden apples (same shape as on sig. [A]lr). Top edge gilt, fore-and bottom edges untrimmed. Dust jacket: white patterned paper, with lettering and decoration on spine identical to that on cloth binding, but in green.

See Irwin Haas, *Bruce Rogers: A Bibliography* (Mt. Vernon, NY: Peter Pauper Press, 1936), item 166.

Beineke Lib (Yale U), Brooklyn Public, personal (DJ), Suny Buffalo.

64. (in triple border in pink, with l. 1 in elaborate border of type ornaments): *Robert Herrick / SONGS AND / LYRICS /* LOVE POEMS / NATURE WINE. MIRTH / MORALITIES / HIMSELF & HIS BOOK / EPITAPHS / PETER PAUPER PRESS / MOUNT VERNON

(9¼ x 5½"): no signatures; pp. [2], [1-4], 5-108, [2].

Divided into sections, as indicated on title page.

Colophon: THIS TEXT HAS BEENE / SETTE IN THE ESTIENNE TYPES, / & PRYNTED ON PAPER / MADE ESPECIALLIE FOR / THE PETER PAUPER PRESSE.

Published 1941, at $2.00; 1450 copies. See Will Ransom, *Selective Check Lists of Press Books, A Compilation...,* Part I (NY: Duschnes, 1945), p. 29 (item 66).

Binding: 2 states: boards covered either with white paper decorated by diamond-shaped floral designs in red or with light green paper decorated with red roses and green leaves and stems. The latter quarter-bound in white patterned cloth. Both states with paper label on spine (HERRICK [floral device] SONGS & LYRICS) running from top to bottom and slipcase with paper label on front.

Cohen Lib. SUNY, Univ. of Pa., U. So. Carolina (all white paper boards), Cornell (green paper boards)

*64a Second impression, 1946

*64b. Third impression, 1952

In 1956, distributed in England by Mayflower & Vision at 18s. Reported as in print in "Collected Ed." in 1968 ($2.95): W.F. Courtney, *Reader's Advisory,* (NY: Bowker, 1978), p. 109.

·65. (in double border of typographical ornaments, outer border in olive green): THE POET AND / HIS MISTRESS / *Twenty-two Poems* / BY ROBERT / HERRICK / [vignette: *putti* within wreath] / PRIVATELY PRINTED AT THE / MAIDSTONE COLLEGE OF ART [ll.1, 2, and vignette in olive green]

(5 x 2½"): no sigs; pp. [1-2], 3-23, [24].

Colophon: "This edition of poems by Herrick designed and produced by Anthony D.

Estill...March 1954...."
Poems set in italics with titles in Monotype Bembo. Wood-engraved vignettes in olive-green.
Printed wrappers (stiff card): eggshell with design of printer's ornaments in olive green.
On spine, bottom to top: ROBERT HERRICK
    personal

66. ONE HUNDRED AND ELEVEN / POEMS / BY / ROBERT HERRICK [watercolor of woman in period gown with bows and frilled sleeves, jewels in hair, facing toward frontispiece] / SELECTED ARRANGED AND ILLUSTRATED / BY / SIR WILLIAM / RUSSELL FLINT / P.R.W.S. / R.A. / 1955 / THE GOLDEN COCKEREL PRESS (1.2 in blue.)

(10⅞ x 7¼"): no signatures; pp. [1-8], 9-127, [128].
2 watercolor drawings, and numerous chalk-drawings reproduced in collotype.
Vignettes, headpieces, tailpieces, and 18 full-page: many of women clothed in period dress, or half-naked; 10 are inscribed with names of Herrick's mistresses (all of these full-page).
Front: watercolor of woman in period gown, standing before curtain looking directly at reader; holding lute which is resting on a book near her feet. Inscribed "Sapho."
Portrait: headpiece, showing Herrick, recognizable by his profile but at about age 35, in Restoration dress, resting his left foot on a pile of books, face in shadows and downcast (p. 120).
Colophon: "...produced for subscribers by the Golden Cockerel Press.... This edition is limited to 550 numbered copies.... Numbers 106-550 are bound in cream parchment with blue cloth boards...." 10 guineas; $31.25 U.S.
Reported as for sale in 1968 (W.F. Courtney, ed. *The Reader's Advisor..*, p. 109).
Christopher Sandford, in *Cok-A-Hoop...A Bibliography of the Golden Cockerel Press Sept. 1949-Dec. 1961*, says that the book was "printed for the artist at his request and expense. Indeed the type was already set when he asked me to make it a Cockerel" (p. 33). As Flint himself writes in his "Note on Herrick," p. 121, "Every detail of this book's design is my own.... With good spirit and good care I have made the drawings..., an affectionate tribute to Herrick and a consolation to myself during anxious years."
    U. of Louisville, L. of Cong. New York Pub.

66a. (another issue): As colophon of cloth-bound issue (and *Cock-A-Hoop*, p. 33) reports, copies 1-105, signed by Flint, were "bound in white alum-tanned sheepskin and...accompanied by eight extra plates." 20 guineas.
    personal

67. (printed in red, in decorated border in blue, made of type ornaments): THE CHEAT / OF CUPID: / OR THE / UNGENTLE / GUEST / HERRICK
One 4-sheet sig., n.p. Contains single poem as stated on t.p., and 3 lino-cuts by E.D. Jordan, of Septentrio Press, Northumberland. Colophon: "...Printed on 21 lb. White Wove paper and 3 sheet card as cover by a foolscap folio treadle platen. An edition of one hundred copies for the Publishing Group of the British Printing Society. September MCMLVIII." 6s.
    L. of Cong.

68. [in green]: *A Thanksgiving To God / For His Little House / Robert Herrick / 1591-1674.*
Verso title page-leaf: St. Teresa's Press / Carmelite Monastery / Flemington, N.J. U.S.A. / 1971

(7" x 5"): 8 leaves, [2], [1-2], 3-10, [4] (one sig.)

Eight hand-tinted vignettes (lithographs)

Colophon (recto second unnumbered leaf after p. 10):

"Handset in Garamond / sixteen point italic. Printed on / Curtis Tweedweave paper / with original handtinted / cuts. / Bound in Strathmore Beau / Brilliant. / Two hundred copies were made / of which this is the ['51st']".

Binding: Green stiff card, textured, folded double.

Flyleaves wrapped-around the signature; gathering sewn with eight-stich. Paper label on front cover: A Thanksgiving To God / For His Little House / Robert Herrick No pastedown endpapers.

   Bailey Library, Univ. of Vt. (boxed)

III. Children's Books, 1884-1968

69. HERRICK'S CONTENT - / HIS GRANGE AND HIS BOOK OF LITTLES / [colored line-drawing of house, domestic animals, birdhouse, and man at doorway] / Verses by Robert Herrick [vignette] Illustrated by Ellen Houghton

(6½ x 10¼" [oblong]): two 8-leaf gatherings, with title-page leaf and its conjugate wrapped-around 1st gathering; 18 leaves—no sigs. or pagination.

Two poems, "His Grange, or Private Health," and "A Ternarie of Littles...." are printed with decorations on each recto or verso p. The colored drawings feature children, animals, a maid and an old man in a skullcap, knickers and hose, and frock coat. The figures, and the line and coloring, recall Caldecott, and the designs themselves, in their use of plant forms and cartouches, Walter Crane.

Dating: 1884 (BM cat). Published by Marcus Ward Ltd, at "half a crown."

Binding: paper covered boards, illustrated with designs from the book. Predominant colors brown and white. Title, illustrator, price and publisher identified on upper cover, in calligraphic s ri₊ ᵗ   ext. w   over: advᵥ .   r 69a and 69b. Backed in brown cloth. Smooth yellow-green endpapers. Edges stained yellow.

   Brit. Lib. personal, U. of Pitts.

*69a. Another issue, part 1 only ("His Grange). Paper wrappers.

*69b. Another issue, part 2 only ("His Book of Littles") Paper wrappers.

70. A POSY [vignette] / of Verse / [vignette] from / HERRICK / *With* / *Designs* / *by* / Charles / Robinson / [vignette] / London, Wells Gardner, Darton & Co.

(2⅞ x 2⅜"): [A]⁸, B-I⁸; pp. [1-14], 15-139, [140], (4 pp. adverts part of sig. I)

Line drawings, many full page, black and white: cupids, boys, and girls in period dress, singing and picking flowers, playing music, or walking in gardens. Floral borders.

Front: "The Parliament of Roses"

Dating: "1903": verso t.p.

1s, 2s; 6d in calf.

Jap. vellum-covered boards. Gold-stamped on upper cover: A POSY / of Verse / from Herrick, in floral border. On spine, in border: A / POSY / of / Verse

   Brit. Lib., personal

71. (revised, enlarged ed. of #70): THE CHILDREN'S POETS / Edited by E. L. Darton / ROBERT HERRICK / Illustrated by Charles Robinson / "But listen to thee, walking in thy chamber / Melting melodious words to lutes of amber." / London / Wells, Gardner, Darton & Co., LTD / [address of press].

(6⅝ x 4½"): pp. [i-iv], v-vii, [viii], 1-109, [110].

Front. ("The Maiden Posies") and five plates, in color on clay paper, tipped in. Most first appeared in black and white in #70 above.

Poems by Herrick on pp. 1-56, followed by those of other Cavalier poets. Pp. 95-100: An essay introducing Herrick.
Dating: 1915 (BM cat)
Price: 1s. In Wells, Gardner, Darton Cat., 1928 & 1936 (2s 3d cloth; is 6d paper-covered boards).
Binding: upper cover: blue and black paper-covered boards, with scrollwork and laurel design. Colored illustration, on clay paper, replica of front., onlaid. In black: THE / CHILDREN'S / POETS / HERRICK. Lower cover: advert for "Children's Bookshelf" series.
  Brit. Lib.

*72. A / Garland of Love / From Herrick & Other Poets / of the 17th Century / [line drawing of boy reading to girl sewing sampler; Restoration costume] / Gathered and Presented with some of / her Drawings by / DAPHNE ALLEN / LONDON / HEADLEY BROS. PUBLISHERS, LTD / Kingsway House. Kingsway, W.C.
Dating: 1917 (E. Cat).
Black and white and watercolor drawings, the latter pasted to tipped-in sheets. Allen was 17 when the book appeared, and had been exhibiting since age 13. Most of the figures are children or cherubic young women.
1s
Binding: clay paper wrappers, upper cover with colored drawing of Cupid with bouquet of roses, reminiscent of keepsake engraving. In center, a floral wreath border, inside which is arranged A GARLAND OF LOVE / *Illustrated* / *by* / DAPHNE ALLEN
  (at Lib. Cong.)

73. *POEMS OF / ROBERT HERRICK* / [rule] / *Selected by Winfield Townley Scott / DRAWINGS BY ELLEN RASKIN* / [vignette: girl's head, crowned with floral wreath] / *Thomas Y. Crowell Company New York.*
(8 x 5⅜"): no sigs; pp. [10], 1-126.
Illus. are line drawings. Two-page spreads introduce *Hesp.* (swan, flowers, stream) and *NN* (flowers, water, setting sun). Vignettes to "His Farewell to Sack," "A Ring Presented to Julia," "An Ode to...Endymion Porter," and "A Thanksgiving to God for his House."
Introd. by W.T. Scott
Dating: copyright date 1967, verso t.p. "First printing."
Price: $2.95; $3.95 Canada. Listed in *Children's Books in Print,* 1968 (with notation as suitable for "grade four and up.")
Binding: yellow cloth. On spine, top to bottom: POEMS OF ROBERT HERRICK CROWELL. Dust jacket: yellow. On front, spine, and back are stylized flowers by Raskin. On front: *POEMS OF / ROBERT HERRICK / Selected by Winfield Townley Scott / DRAWINGS BY ELLEN RASKIN.* On spine: *Scott / POEMS OF ROBERT HERRICK* [vertical] / *Crowell.*
  Mansfield St. Coll., U. of Penna (no DJ), Carnegie Public Library, Pitts.
  Suny Buffalo.

74. ROBERT HERRICK / The Music of a Feast / *Poems for young readers chosen / and introduced / by* / Eleanor Graham / ILLUSTRATED BY / Lynton Lamb / [vignette of boy in 17th-century costume carrying shaft of wheat] / THE BODLEY HEAD / LONDON SYDNEY / TORONTO
(8½ x 5½"): no sig. (gathered in 8's); pp. [1-6], 7-93, [94], [2].
Line drawings, four full-page, for section titles (3 of these appear as vignettes, reduced, *passim*). Fourteen separate vignettes, some repeated. Figures, often children, in period costume, with country landscape background. Two floral

designs.

Dating: verso t.p., 1968.

Price: 18s (on front flap of d.j.)

Red calico-grain cloth. On spine, gold-stamped: The Music of a Feast [vignette] *Robert Herrick* BODLEY HEAD (from top to bottom). Upper and lower cover undecorated. Cream blue endpapers. DJ: white. On front: title (in red), poet's name, and subtitle (in red). Black-and-white reproduction of girl in period costume (on p. 43 in text). On back: reprod. of Marshall portrait bust. Front flap: biographical information about Herrick.

New York Pub. (no d.j.), U. of Pitts. (presentation card to dedicatee tipped in. Ms. Graham remarks that, although she admires the drawings, there is "too much repetition for such a short book.")

IV. *Commercial Editions,* 1921-1980 (But see #88)

75. (shorter, expurgated edition of #11): (within vertical rules at top and bottom of page, made of Fell type ornaments): THE POETICAL WORKS / OF / ROBERT HERRICK / EDITED BY F.W. MOORMAN / WITH A PREFATORY NOTE / BY PERCY SIMPSON / [press device] / HUMPHREY MILFORD / OXFORD UNIVERSITY PRESS / LONDON NEW YORK TORONTO MELBOURNE BOMBAY / 1921 (7¼ x 4⅞"): tipped-in front. + [A]⁴, B-p¹⁶; pp. [i-iii], iv-vii, [viii], [1-5], 6-446, [2].

Series: Oxford Standard Authors See #95 below.

Front: replica of Marshall

Introd. p. vi: "The present reprint...has been prepared, not for the scholar, but the lover of poetry [;] it omits almost entirely the 'Epigrams'...A reprint of Herrick among the Oxford Poets, side by side with the complete text [see #11 above] already issued, gives a welcome opportunity of clearing away those weeds from the flower-garden of the *Hesperides.*"

8s 6d; $1.50 (US Cat. 1928); 9s 6d in thin paper.

Binding Variants: 1) dark blue cloth, blind-stamped rules upper and lower cover, and on spine. Press device gold-stamped upper cover. On spine: HERRICK'S / POETICAL / WORKS / OXFORD

2) red cloth, blind-stamped border, upper and lower covers. "Herrick" in gold-stamped gothic on upper cover. Gold-stamped border and lettering on spine.

NYU (thin paper), Brit. Lib:binding var. 1; U. No. Carolina; var. 2.

*75a. (Second impression): 1936

75b. (Third impression): 1947.

NYU, Penn St. (rebound)

75c. (Fourth impression): 1951. No Front. Pagination identical, but sigs. differ: [A]⁴, B-F⁸. Blue d.j., with passage from John Masefield on front flap. Verso t.p.: "...reprinted in 1936 1947 and 1951."

Hunter Coll. (rebound), personal

75d. (Fifth impression): 1957. [A]⁶, B-2F⁸; pp. [i-v], vi-ix, [x], 2, [1-5], 6-446, [2]. d.j. as in 75c. Price: 12s 6d, $2.75.

Carnegie Free Library, Pitts.

*76. *Selections* (from Herrick). London: J. Cape, 1922. 1s.

*77. *Christmas. Poem.* London: Simon, 1922.

*78. *Poems* (of Herrick). London: John Long, 1923. "The Carlton Classics." 2s. 136 pp.

79. (in triple border): ROBERT / HERRICK / SELECTED & EDITED BY / HENRY NEWBOLT / [press device] / THOMAS NELSON / & SONS LTD / LONDON & EDINBURGH
(6⅛ x 4¼"): 6, 1-15¹⁶; [i-iv], v-xii, [1-2], 3-478, [2].
Front: woodcut showing left-facing profile which emphasizes curly hair and moustache. Secular period costume. Signed "GP." Slightly similar to woodcut portraits on t.p. of #2 above.
Dating: BM, E. Cat: "Sept. '23." 1s. 6d; 60¢. Both Eng. and US Cat. report a "deluxe ed." (3s 6d; $3.50), called "Winchester Classics" in 1938 *Ref. Cat. Introd.*, pp. vii-xii, by J.C. Squire.
Binding variants: 1): blue cloth. Blind-stamped border, upper and lower covers. Gold-stamped on spine: POEMS / OF / HERRICK [small floral ornament]. 2): green calico-grain cloth. Blind-stamped, upper cover: laurel wreath, in which is gothic "h." Title and press stamped on spine. Top edge stained gray. 3): brown leatherette. Title, floral device, publisher gold-stamped on spine. Top edge gilt.
personal (blue cloth, brown leatherette); Harvard (accession date 3/28/24, rebound).

79a. Another issue, t.p. variant: outer and inner borders, and press device, in blue, as are R (1.1), H (1.2) H (1.4), T and N (1.6), S and L (1.7), L and E (1.8). Outer and inner borders of front. port. also in blue. Leaves measure 6¼ x 3⅞". Red cloth.

U. Pitt. (E. Nesbitt's copy)

*79b. (2nd impression): 1929. In CBI and Nelson catalog, 1929.
Note: Any of the binding variants, or the title page variant, noted above might be used in the second impression. Other binding variants also probably exist. Nelson's adverts show d.j.

80. LITTLE BLUE BOOK NO. 701 / Edited by E. Haldeman-Julius / Poems of / Robert Herrick / Edited, with an Introduction, by / Floyd Dell / HALDEMAN-JULIUS COMPANY / GIRARD, KANSAS
(5 x 3¼"): no sigs.: pp. [1-4], 5-64.
Booklet contains 85 poems.
Price: 5 cents
Dating: 1924 (copyright verso t.p.). The Little Blue Books numbered in the low 700's were for the most part published in 1924. In 1927 this title was withdrawn (low sales) and replaced by another title numbered 701. See R. Johnson and G.T. Tanselle, "The Haldeman-Julius 'Little Blue Books' as a Bibliographical Problem," *PBSA* 64 (1980), pp. 51-57. "Poetry in general is hard to sell, even for five cents": E. Haldeman-Julius, *The First Hundred Million* (1928; rpt. N.Y.: Arno, 1974), p. 94.
Binding: blue paper wrappers. Wording same as first 6 lines on t.p.

Univ. of Penna.

*81. *Robert Herrick Selected Poems* (London: Noel Douglas, 1927). The Ormond Poets, #6. Edited by G.D.H. and M.I. Cole.
5¾ x 4¼", 64 pp. 1s. Jap. vellum covered boards with floral design; 2s decorated cloth. In *Ref. Cat.*, 1932, 1940.

82. (in triple border of thick and thin rules): Selected Poems / from Hesperides / ROBERT HERRICK / The Gold Medal Library / London NEW YORK Calcutta.
(5 x 3¼"): pp. [1-5], 6-96 (no sigs).

Dating: NYPL accession date 1930.
Binding: red textured paper-covered boards with black cloth quarter-binding. On upper cover, gold-stamped: "Selected Poems." Edges stained red.
New York Pub.

83. (in triple border, 2nd of which is composed of type ornaments): THE AUGUSTAN BOOKS OF / POETRY / [rule] / ROBERT / HERRICK / [rule] / LONDON: ERNEST BENN LTD. / BOUVERIE HOUSE, FLEET STREET
(8¼ x 5 7/16"): no sigs; [i-iii], iv, 5-30.
Dating: 1932 (CBI, E. Cat). 6d
Paper wrappers. (title on front wrapper).
Brit. Lib.

84. (revised edition of no. 46): *The Poems of* / ROBERT HERRICK / [vignette: globe, Four Winds, "The World's Classics" in scrollwork] / *London* / OXFORD UNIVERSITY PRESS / HUMPHREY MILFORD
[A]⁴, B-Q¹⁶, R⁴; pp. [8], [1-5], 6-486, [2].
"In 'The World's Classics' [Herrick's poems] were first published in 1902...in 1933 they were reset from the edition by F.W. Moorman" (see no. 11 above). Unexpurgated.
2s; 80¢; 50¢ in Canada
Dark blue cloth, blind-stamped borders with horizontal and vertical lines intersecting half-inch from all four corners of boards. Blind stamped device of O.U.P. on center of upper cover. Gold-stamped on spine: POEMS / OF / ROBERT / HERRICK / [star] / [3 sets of double rules] / OXFORD
Univ. of Penn, Suny Buffalo (rebound)

*84a. (second impression of revised edition).
Dating: verso t.p. of 1960 ed gives the date as 1951.

84b. (third impression of revised edition): *The Poems of* / ROBERT HERRICK / LONDON / OXFORD UNIVERSITY PRESS
"In 1933...reset...and reprinted in 1951 and 1960."
Dark blue cloth.
Still in print, 1968.
U. of Penna.

*85. *Poems* [of Herrick] London: Hudson, 1936).
In Ref. Cat. of Current Lit., 1936, '38, '40.
A 136-page selection. 7d.

86. (in triple border): ROBERT HERRICK / *Hesperides & Noble Numbers* / A Selection / [circular vignette: man and woman in boat, embracing] / 1938 / Chatto and Windus / LONDON
(7⅛ x 4½"): [A]⁸, B-C⁸; pp. [1-4], 5-45, [46], [2].
"The Zodiac Books" #10 . 1s. Dist. in US by Transatlantic Arts, 1940 (CBI): 30¢.
Blue paper-covered boards, decorated with small sunburst designs outlined in white. In elliptical white space on upper cover, surrounded by series of white and black circles: *Zodiac Books* / [star] / Hesperides & Noble Numbers / [star] / ROBERT HERRICK / *Chatto & Windus.* Author and title on spine (top to bottom). DJ: design identical to boards.
NYU (Wash. Sq), U. So Ill, Carb, Texas HRC.

87. SOME / POEMS / OF / ROBERT HERRICK / [ornament] / THE POET OF THE

MONTH / *New Directions* / *Norfolk: Connecticut* (11.1 and 2 in red)
no sigs, one 16-leaf gathering, no pagination.
Dating 1942 (so stated on black flap of dust jacket). $1.00 in bds.
Colophon: "...designed by Algot Ringstrom, set in Linotype Granjon and printed by
The Marchbanks Press New York City."
Paper-covered boards. Title in red and black on upper cover, identical to title page's first 6
lines, with rule above *The Poet of the Month.* Dust jacket for hardcover (same design and
color as cover) has list of series for 1942 on back flap, and blurb on front flap: "We all read
some Herrick in school and are familiar with his often-quoted lines. How many of us have
read Herrick for pleasure in the past few months, though all of us would find it a real
pleasure to read his best poems two or three times a year?"
   U. of Penna., personal, Texas HRC

87a. (another issue): Light green paper wrappers, 50¢
   U. of Pa.

88. (in double border): THE LOVE POEMS / OF / ROBERT HERRICK / *Selected, with
an introduction, by* / LOUIS UNTERMEYER / *Editions for the Armed Services, Inc.* / A
NON-PROFIT ORGANIZATION ESTABLISHED BY THE COUNCIL ON BOOKS
IN WARTIME, NEW YORK [lower left, below border: "1056"]

(3⅞ x 5⅝" [oblong]): no sigs.; pp. [1-2], 3-95, [96]. verso t.p.: "THIS EDITION IS
COPYRIGHT, 1946, BY LOUIS UNTERMEYER." Not for sale; distribution to U.S.
servicemen. A "made" book, specially compiled for the series; Untermeyer edited most
such selections. *See Editions for the Armed Services: A History* (NY: E.A.S.: n.d.), pp. 76,
111. Format is suitable for carrying in a military uniform.
paper wrappers, stapled. Upper cover: blue, white, and black lettering and ½" red border
(with yellow lettering) on bottom edge only. 1056 / The *LOVE POEMS* of *Robert* /
Herrick / *Edited by* LOUIS UNTERMEYER / Overseas edition for the Armed Forces ...
U.S. Government property. *Not for Sale*...[in yellow oval]: ARMED / SERVICES / ED. /
[in red border at bottom, in yellow lettering]: SELECTED POEMS. On left half of cover is
picture of closed book in d.j., which bears title and name of editor of present volume,
designed as described above. Lower cover, in red and white border decorated with stars:
approximately 200-word blurb on "the charm of Herrick," with exerpt from introduction.
   U. No. Carolina,

89. THE / *Love Poems* / *of* / ROBERT HERRICK / *and* JOHN DONNE / *Edited with
an Introduction by* / LOUIS UNTERMEYER / [French rule] / RUTGERS
UNIVERSITY PRESS / NEW BRUNSWICK, N.J. [1.2 in calligraphic lettering]
(8 x 4⅞"): no sig; pp. [2], [i-iv], v-xv, [xvi], [1-2], 3-251, [252], [2].
Dating: verso t.p.: copyright date 1948. $3.50; reduced to $1.75 (CBI '49-52). 2.25 in
Toronto (Smithers).
Poems by Herrick on pp. 13-155. Divided into 18 sections, most of which bear names of
Herrick's mistresses.
Red cloth boards, backed in black cloth with title, arranged as on t.p., goldstamped on
spine.
   Penn St. U. of Pitts., U. So. Carolina (rebound) Texas HRC

90. (in triple border, outer composed of type ornaments): *Poems by* / *Robert Herrick* /
selected / *and introduced by* / *Jack Lindsay* / [press device] / *LONDON* / *The Grey Walls
Press*
(7⅜ x 4¾"): no sigs.; pp. [1-4], 5-64.

Verso t.p.: "First published 1948 in the Crown Classics series..." 3s 6d.

Paper covered boards with design, in green, of men sowing and raking the earth, and drawing of rushes, flowers, birdsnest, butterfly. Series title and publisher identified in green. In red: SELECTED / POEMS OF / ROBERT / HERRICK / EDITED BY / JACK LINDSAY. Title and press on spine, running from top to bottom. Dust jacket has identical design.

personal, Texas HRC

91. THE POETICAL WORKS OF / *Robert Herrick [swash R and k]* / EDITED BY / L.C. MARTIN / [press device: open book, 3 crowns in shield] / OXFORD / AT THE CLARENDON PRESS / 1956

(8⅝ x 5¾"): tipped-in front. + [a]⁸, b⁸, c⁴, [B]⁸, C-Rr⁸, Ss⁴; pp. [i-iv], v-xl, [1-4], 5-631, [632]. Oxford English Texts series. 63s; $10.10. See #11 above.

Front: replica of Marshall

Binding: dark blue cloth. Upper and lower cover: blind-stamped border, with device of press on upper cover. On spine, gold stamped: HERRICK'S / POETICAL / WORKS / EDITED BY / L.C. MARTIN / OXFORD. Bordered top and bottom by fancy rule. dust jacket: front cover: 3 sets of Fell type ornaments, in red, with title, editor, and press identified between them. Front flap: exerpt from preface. Lower flap: list of Oxford English Texts. On spine: title and editor, set between 2 sets of Fell ornaments in light green. Lower edge untrimmed.

Brooklyn Public, Texas HRC

91a. (second impression): No date on t.p. Verso t.p.: "reprinted lithographically...from corrected sheets of the first edition 1963."

Binding: dark blue cloth. Dust jacket: light blue paper, title, editor and press in dark blue upper cover and spine. Excerpt from preface on front flap, list of Oxford English Texts on lower cover.

Columbia; U. of Penna; personal (d.j.).

92. ROBERT HERRICK / POEMS FROM *Hesperides* AND / *Noble Numbers* / SELECTED AND INTRODUCED BY / JOHN HAYWARD / [rule] / PENGUIN BOOKS

(6 ¾ x 3¾): [A]⁸, B-G¹⁶, H⁸; pp. [1-7], 8-220, [4].

Dating: verso t.p.: "First published 1961"

3s 6d; The Penguin Poets

Paperback: on spine and both covers: A Morris-like chintz floral pattern (reddish-brown background, blue flowers, black stems). In 5 x 2⅞" white panel on upper cover: *Robert / Herrick* / [star] / *Selected Poems* / EDITED AND INTRODUCED BY / JOHN HAYWARD / [press device] / THE PENGUIN / POETS / 3/6

Harvard, Texas HRC, Suny Buffalo.

92a. (Another issue): imprint variant: PENGUIN BOOKS / BALTIMORE MARYLAND (on cover: "95¢")

Penn State

93. *The Laurel Poetry Series* / *General Editor, Richard Wilbur* / [in square border]: *Herrick* / *Selected, with an introduction* / *and notes, by William Jay Smith*

(6⅜ x 3⅜"): no sigs; pp. [1-12], 13-160.

Verso t.p.: "First printing: August, 1962." 35¢

Paperback: upper cover states author, series, editor, and has profile of Herrick as Restoration rake: prominent nose, thick hair falling over ears and brow, reaching down to lace collar. Slight smile, cold-eyed determination. Artist: Richard Powers, whose suite of portraits of English poets is used for this series. Lower cover: paragraph about Herrick by John Masefield, list of poets in series with the editors.

personal

93a. "Second printing, July, 1969." (personal)

94. THE / COMPLETE POETRY / OF / ROBERT HERRICK / *Edited with an Introduction and Notes / by /* J. MAX PATRICK / [press device: dolphin, anchor, I and D worked into design] / ANCHOR BOOKS / *Doubleday & Company, Inc. / Garden City, New York, 1963.*
(7⅛ x 4⅛"): no sigs.; pp. [i-vii], viii-xvi, [2], [1-5], 6-579, [580], [2].
"The Anchor Seventeenth Century Series"; $1.95
Paperback. Upper cover: title, author, editor in compartment after 17th-century woodcut title-page design. Green background.
The only complete works of Herrick edited by an American scholar. Explanatory footnotes below each poem; the editor states that they are necessary for most 20th-century readers, who are not part of the "ever diminishing group of educated men who have enjoyed training in the Greek and Latin classics." (p. [vii]).
Portrait: A replica of Marshall was to be placed "in the middle of this edition" (p. 7) but was left out. See #94a and b below.

U. No. Carolina, Cornell (paper wrapper preserved)

94a. (2nd impression, NYU Press subedition): *The Stuart Editions* / The Complete Poetry / of / ROBERT HERRICK / EDITED / WITH AN INTRODUCTION AND NOTES / BY / J. MAX PATRICK / [press device] / New York University Press / 1963
(9 x 6"): tipped-in front (bust of Charles II) and replica of Marshall engraving (facing p. 268) + pp. [i-ix], x-xvi, [4], [1-5], 6-579, [580].
$7.50 (9.25 in Canada).
Bound in black cloth, with arabesque design on lower fifth of upper cover, goldstamped. Series, title, editor and press gold-stamped on spine. Blue dust jacket, with arabesque design repeated on upper cover and spine (white on black background), as is series, title, editor and press. Front and back flap summarizes the edition. Lower cover of d.j. lists Stuart Editions.

NYU, Wash Sq.,personal

94b. (3rd impression, revised, Norton Library subedition): THE / COMPLETE POETRY / OF / ROBERT HERRICK / *Edited with an Introduction, Notes, / and a new Foreword / by /* J. MAX PATRICK / [press device] / The Norton Library / W.W. NORTON & COMPANY INC. / NEW YORK
(7¾ x 5"): [2], [i-v], vi-xvi, [2], [1-5], 6-579, [580], [4].
Front: replica of Marshall (left out of 1st impression).
Bibliography (pp. [xv]-xvi) updated, foreword (pp. [v]-vi) added.
Dating: verso t.p.: FIRST PUBLISHED IN THE NORTON LIBRARY 1968 BY ARRANGEMENT / WITH DOUBLEDAY & COMPANY
"The Norton Library Seventeenth-Century Series"; $2.95 In print through 1980.
Paperback: orange, with title and editor in elliptical white space with illustration of 17th-century London waterfront below (upper cover). Excerpt from introduction and statement regarding purpose of the series, lower cover.

U. of Pa (rebound), personal

95. (shortened subed. of #91): THE POEMS OF / ROBERT HERRICK / EDITED BY /

L.C. MARTIN / [press device] / LONDON / OXFORD UNIVERSITY PRESS / NEW
YORK TORONTO / 1965
(8½ x 5⅜"): tipped-in front. + [A]⁸, B-Hh⁸; pp. [i-v], vi-ix, [x], [2], [1-4], 5-478, [6].
Oxford Standard Authors. 30s; $7.00. No. 91 above seems to be a parent edition of this,
lithographic plates being prepared from it for pp. [1]-403, although the footnotes are not
as they are in the 1956 Oxford English Texts ed.
Bound in blue cloth; blind-stamped press device center of upper cover. Goldstamped on
spine: THE / POEMS / OF / ROBERT / HERRICK / OXFORD. Dust jacket in pink,
with THE POEMS OF ROBERT HERRICK in white on upper cover. Below that, in
floral wreath, is profile of Herrick, reminiscent of Schiavonetti (see #1 above). Identified
on front flap as by Charles V. White.
    Carnegie Public Lib., Pittsburgh, Mid-Manhattan Br. NYPL; Penn St. and U. of
Penna (no d.j.)

*95a. (Second impression): 1971. In print through 1978.

96. ROBERT HERRICK / HESPERIDES / 1648 / [woodcut] / THE SCOLAR PRESS
LIMITED / MENSTON, ENGLAND / 1969
8 x 5½". "Reproduced. . . from the British Library copy in the British Museum, shelf-mark
E. 1090." (Leaf 3r of preliminary gathering). Pagination as in that copy, with introductory
note. Preliminary gathering of 8 leaves; first leaf serves as front pastedown and third leaf a
cancel.

85s. "Scolar Press Facsimiles, General Series." Red cloth, on spine: HERRICK [dot]
HESPERIDES 1648 [press device]: top to bottom, gold-stamped.
    U. No. Carolina, Cornell.
*96a. Paper wrappers, 30s.
96b. (second impression): A Scholar Press Facsimile / HESPERIDES / Robert Herrick /
1648.
Light brown cloth, with HERRICK / Hesperides / 1648 / SCOLAR on spine, gold-
stamped. Yellow d.j., with facsimile of part of 1648 t.p. on front; list of facsimile on back
cover and flap. Verso t.p.: "Reprinted 1973"
    personal.

97. ROBERT HERRICK / [rule] / SELECTED POEMS / [rule] / edited with an
introduction / by David Jesson-Dibley / [press device] / FYFIELD BOOKS / Carcanet
New Press
(7 x 4¾"): no sigs; pp. [1-4], 5-90, [4].
Dating: copyright date, verso t.p., 1980. "First published in 1980." One pound 95; 2
pounds 50 ($7.50) in 1984.
Paper wrappers. Upper cover: landscape of hills with shallow river. Lower cover
summarizes Herrick's life and appeal, and lists other "Fyfield Books." Typeface and
illustration in brown on light green background.
    personal

*98. Robert Herrick. Kettering, Northants.: J.L. Carr, 1980.
An envelope sized selection, 30p. "Perfect for cold bedrooms—only one hand and wrist
need suffer exposure"
No longer in print, 1983.

Index

Abbey, Edwin 17, 43, 55-71, 80, 90, 106, 117, 186-87
Aesthetic Movement 23-27, 82-91
Aldin, Cecil 71-72
Aldrich, T.B. 52, 162
Allen, Daphne 165-67
Allingham, Wm. 14, 186
Alma-Tadema, Laurence 52, 57, 62, 106, 156, 157
Avery, Gillian 167

Bell, Robert Anning 93-95
Benjamin, Walter 5, 115, 126
Bowdlerization 11-15, 147
Brock, C.E. 59, 75-77

Cable, James Branch 189-90
Caslon Revival 40, 117
Castle, Florence 77, 109-10
Censorship 11-15, 51, 58-59, 136-38, 146-47
Childhood, impressions of 162-70
Chute, Marchette 176
Collins' Clear-Type Press 46
Coveney, Peter 162
Crane, Walter 83, 96

Daniel, C.H.O. 116-19
Darton, E.L. 164, 165
Davies, W.H. 144
De la Mare, Walter 3, 143, 144, 146, 152, 164, 172, 175, 176, 177, 181, 190
Dean Prior (Devon) 10, 23, 43, 52, 82, 92, 172, 176-77, 186-91
Dell, Floyd 172
Dent, J.M. 6, 16, 49, 93
"Dignity and repose" 35, 52, 90, 92, 134, 163
Dilks, T. Bruce 17, 176
Dobson, Austin 25-26, 43, 55-57, 186
Drake, Nathan 9-11, 15

Easton, Emily 181
Ellis, Lionel 106, 140-41, 187-89, 190
Ellis, Sarah Stickney 21, 42

Farjeon, Eleanor 162, 165

Feminine social roles 21, 35, 42, 59, 91, 106-07, 133, 167
Field, Barron 10, 11, 23
Flint, W. R. 106, 155-59, 175, 183-86, 190
Forbes, Elizabeth S. 76-77, 113
Fraser, Lovat 146, 148-49, 152

Georgian poetry 26, 143-44
Golden Treasury, The 51, 52, 85
Gosse, Edmund 9, 25-27, 61, 91, 92, 93, 105, 176, 181
Grigson, Geoffrey 165, 178
Grosart, A.B. 12, 17, 23, 38, 51
Gross, John 20, 24

Hamilton, Walter 87
Hartrick, A.S. 113, 179
"Hellenism" 87-90, 91-96, 106-07
Henley, W.E. 93, 98-100, 162
Herrick, Robert
—and the decadents 82-83, 93
—and 19th cen. book design 35, 36-52, 56-57, 72-77, 107-09, 113-14, 119-23
—and private presses 113-30, 134-43, 148-59
—as Cavalier gentleman 10-11, 16-17, 23, 24, 148-52, 178, 179-86
—biographical details 15-17, 21-23, 92-93, 138-40, 149-50, 164-65, 171-72, 175-91
—editions, 19th and 20th centuries (see also Appendix)
   —"Bibelots, The" (Herrick's Women, Love, and Flowers) 43
   "British Poets, The" 40
   —"Canterbury Poets, The" 49, 51, 52
   —"Caxton Poets, The" 99-101, 113, 178-79
   —"Century Classics, The" 51, 52
   —"Chapbooks, The" 52, 127
   —"Children's Poets, The" 23, 168
   — Christmas, From the Noble Numbers 116
   —Chrysomela 12, 23, 51, 85

—*Country Garland of Ten Songs, A* 43, 96, 107-08
—Cresset Press 149-52
—"Crowell Poets, The" 165, 170-71
—*Delighted Earth* 134-43, 187-88
—"Early English Poets, The" 38, 40, 85
—"Everyman's Library" 6, 49-50, 114
—*Favorite Poems of Herrick* 50-51, 73-74
—*Flower Poems* 43, 77
—*Garland of Love, A* 165-67
—"Golden Poets, The" 43, 76, 114, 179
—*Herrick His Flowers* 116-19
—*Herrick's Content* 164
—"Hesperides Series, The" 152-54
—"Laurel Wreath Series, The" 43, 75
—"Library of Old Authors" 38, 40
—"Lovers' Library, The" 108-09, 114
—"Lyric Poets, The" 27
—Maitland, ed. 8, 10, 12, 14, 37
—"Morley's Universal Library" 51, 114
—"Muses' Library, The" 6, 12, 38, 40
—*Music of a Feast, The* 165, 171-72
—*One Hundred And Eleven Poems* 155-159, 183-85
—Pickering's *Hesperides* (1846) 38, 40
—Pickering's "Wreath" Ed. (1825) 40
—*Poems Selected...*(Elston) 127-30
—*Poems Selected...* (Kelmscott) 119-27
—*Posy Of Verse From Herrick* 168
—"Red Letter Library" 51
—*Select Poems* (ed. Nott) 9, 11
—*Selections...*(Harpers) 55-72, 186
—expurgation of poems 11-15
—illustrations of poems (see also portraits, individual illustrators)
    —art nouveau 87-90, 93-96, 101-05, 107-09, 128-30
    —erotic emphases 105, 106-07, 133-43, 146-48
    —in children's books 93, 162-73
    —in 1920s 138-43, 146-54
    —in 1950s 155-59
    —in Victorian periodicals 71-72
    —in representational mode 55-80
—19th cen. "rediscovery" 9-11, 15-23
—poems
    "Anthea's Retraction" 171
    "Apparition of His Mistress" 156
    "Argument of his Book" 158
    "Bag of the Bee, The" 101-03, 167

"Bell Man, The" 59, 68-70
"Ceremonies for Christmas" 168
"Corinna's going A-Maying" 59-61, 141
"Country Life, A" 178-79
"Country Life, The" 74, 96
"Delight in Disorder" 63
"Divination by a Daffodil" 89-90
"Gather ye Rosebuds" 77, 95, 99
"Grace for a Child, A" 171, 172
"Here a Little Child I Stand" 171
"His Cavalier" 100
"His Grange, or Private Wealth" 164, 179
"His Poetry His Pillar" 67
"Hock Cart, The" 140, 179
"How Heartsease Came First" 68, 109
"Hymn to the Muses, An" 189
"Lovers How They Come and Part" 139
"Mad Maid's Song" 72
"Mr. Robert Herrick His Farewell Unto Poetry" 137
"New Year's Gift...,A" 74
"Night-Piece to Julia, The" 63-65, 70, 76, 96-98, 167-168, 172
"Oberon's Palace" 100-01
"Primrose, The" 77
"Ring Presented to Julia, A" 71
"Rock of Rubies, The" 72
"Star Song, The" 154
"Thanksgiving to God for His House, A" 164
"To Be Merry" 59-61
"To Blossoms" 167
"To Daffadils" 109-10, 172
"To his Muse" 186
"To Meadows" 93-95
"To Phyllis" 100-01
"To the Virgins, To Make Much of Time" 76, 77, 93, 106
"To the Willow Tree" 74
"To Violets" 168
"Upon a Child That Died" 168
"Upon the Loss of His Mistresses" 184-85
"Upon Mistress Susanna Southwell..." 63, 96
"Upon Love" 100-01
"Upon Sappho" 63, 71-72
"What Kind of Mistress He Would Have" 157-58
"When He Would Have His Verses

Read" 187
"Wounded Cupid, The" 76, 103-05, 167-68
"Writing" 184
—portraits 15-17, 58, 150-52, 171-72, 175-91
Hewlitt, Maurice 183
Horne, Herbert 52

Innocence vs. experience 63
"Isca" 103-05

Jenkyns, Richard 57-58, 87
Jerome, Jerome K. 9, 99

Keepsakes (Albums) 42-43, 74-75
Kipling, Rudyard 98

Lamb, Lynton 169-72
Lang, Andrew 25, 26, 61, 163, 172
Lawrence, D. H. 136, 145
Le Gallienne, Richard 83
Light, Kate 101
Lindsay, Jack 107, 124, 134-45, 183, 187-88
Lindsay, Norman 134, 139-40
Literary periodicals 9, 25, 33, 137
London Aphrodite 137-38

Macauley, Rose 175, 177, 179, 181, 185-86
Marshall, H. E. 164, 179
Masefield, John 52
"Masquerading tendency" 57-58
Meynell, Francis 144-45
Middle class, rise of 9, 14-15, 20
Milford, Humphrey 152-53
Moore, John 176
Moorman, F. W. 176, 177
Morris, William 113, 117, 119-28
Muir, Edwin 164

Nichol, Bessie 74-75
Nott, John 9, 11

O'Kane, Helen 127-30

Palgrave, Francis 12, 21, 23, 43, 51, 52, 176
Parnassians ("Roundeliers") 25, 43
Parsons, Albert 117
Perry-Keene, C. J. 177
Phinn, C. C. 93
Powys, Lleweylln 133, 158-59, 183

Publishing, 19th century 32-36
'bibelot 36, 43-46
—cheap series 46-52
—children's books 162-73
—Daniel Press 116-19
—drawing room gift books 40-46
—editions for the gentleman's library 36-40
—Everyman's Library 49-52
—Elston Press 127-30
—Harper and Bros. 56, 72-73, 113, 122
—Kelmscott Press 114, 115, 119-28, 136, 152
—Osgood and Co. 46, 50-51, 73-74
Publishing, 20th cen.
—Commercial publishers 155
—Cresset Press 149-52
—Franfrolico Press 134-43
—Golden Cockerel Press 144, 145, 155-59 183-86
—Nonesuch Press 136, 145, 155

Raskin, Ellen 169-70
Reid, Forrest 62, 162
Reid, Stephen 71
Repplier, Agnes 9, 185
Rhys, Ernest 16, 52, 83
Richards, Grant 12
Ricketts, Charles 73, 82, 83, 93, 101, 108, 128, 152
Robinson, Charles 96, 168
Rogers, Bruce 124, 152-54
Rossetti, D. G. 68, 69, 84, 141
Rutherston, Albert 148-52, 175, 181
Ryland, Henry 89, 90, 95-96, 105-106

Saintsbury, George 16
Sauber, Robert 72
Savage, Reginald 99-101, 113, 175
Scott, Walter (pub.) 49-51
Sitwell, Edith 176-77
Skelton, John (ils) 164, 179
Southey, Robert 12-14, 34
Squire, John C. 134, 144
Swinburne, A. C. 12, 91, 92, 175

"Tableaux vivants" 58
Taylor, J.R. 93, 114, 148
Thorpe, James 71
Trade bindings 43, 51, 56, 85

Van Doren, Mark 175-76, 183
Veblen, Thorstein 35, 114, 115
"Victorian escapism" 11, 17-21, 61-65, 116
    127, 162-163

Warren, Austin 183

Wolfe, Humbert 145-46, 149-50, 181, 183
Woodroffe, Paul 96-98, 105-09
Woolf, Virginia 145

"Young England" 19-23